CONSTRUCTING AUTHORITIES

[handwritten note:] I THINK THE 2 THINGS most opposed to good counsel are haste + passion; haste usually goes hand + hand w/ folly; passion w/ coarseness + narrowness of mind. Thucydides —

This collection of essays brings together the central lines of thought in Onora O'Neill's work on Kant's philosophy, developed over many years. Challenging the claim that Kant's attempt to provide a critique of reason fails because it collapses into a dogmatic argument from authority, O'Neill shows why Kant held that we must construct, rather than assume, the authority of reason, and how this can be done by ensuring that anything we offer as reasons can be followed by others, including others with whom we disagree. She argues that this constructivist view of reasoning is the clue to Kant's claims about knowledge, ethics and politics, as well as to his distinctive accounts of autonomy, the social contract, cosmopolitan justice and scriptural interpretation. Her essays are a distinctive and illuminating commentary on Kant's fundamental philosophical strategy and its implications, and will be a vital resource for scholars of Kant, ethics and philosophy of law.

ONORA O'NEILL, Baroness O'Neill of Bengarve, is a former Principal of Newnham College Cambridge, sits as a cross-bench peer in the House of Lords and is Emeritus Honorary Professor of Philosophy at the University of Cambridge. She has published widely on Kant's philosophy and her most recent publications include *Acting on Principle*, 2nd edn (Cambridge, 2013).

[handwritten note:] "One always leaves the way open for the establishment / others." —Niccolo Machiavelli —

D1606033

CONSTRUCTING AUTHORITIES

Reason, Politics and Interpretation in Kant's Philosophy

ONORA O'NEILL

p29 — maxims — that reasons have a role to play in XN, etc. They have *suppositional* still and evident, what does this mean?

→ which are formed by maxims or bfs

you did not hold any bfs, other than what you stated in ——, in treaty that she had this Hx of ——, in treaty pl ——

"COWARDICE ASKS the QUESTION: IS IT SAFE?
EXPEDIENCY " " " : IS it POLITIC?
But CONSCIENCE " " " : " " right?
Nd there comes A time when one must take a
POSITION that is neither safe, nor politic,
b/c one's CONSCIENCE tells ONE: "It is right."
— MARTIN LUTHER KING —

CAMBRIDGE UNIVERSITY PRESS

CAMBRIDGE
UNIVERSITY PRESS

University Printing House, Cambridge CB2 8BS, United Kingdom

Cambridge University Press is part of the University of Cambridge.

It furthers the University's mission by disseminating knowledge in the pursuit of
education, learning and research at the highest international levels of excellence.

www.cambridge.org
Information on this title: www.cambridge.org/9781107538252

© Onora O'Neill 2015

First published 2015

Printed in the United States of America by Sheridan Books, Inc.

A catalogue record for this publication is available from the British Library

Library of Congress Cataloguing in Publication data
O'Neill, Onora, 1941–
Constructing authorities : reason, politics, and interpretation in
Kant's philosophy / Onora O'Neill.
pages   cm
Includes bibliographical references and index.
ISBN 978-1-107-11631-3
1. Kant, Immanuel, 1724–1804.   I. Title.
B2798.O59 2015
193 – dc23   2015021705

ISBN 978-1-107-11631-3 Hardback
ISBN 978-1-107-53825-2 Paperback

Contents

Contents

Acknowledgements

I am deeply grateful to my teachers, my colleagues in philosophy and my students across many years, who have not merely tolerated but encouraged and deepened my fascination with Kant's arguments, and to Cambridge University Press for their sustained commitment to making Kant's philosophy so much more widely available than it used to be.

"Confidence comes NOT from ALWAYS being right but from NOT FEARING to be WRONG."
— Peter McIntyre —

Introduction[1]

Authority and vindication

Arguments from authority have a bad reputation among philosophers. Appeals to common sense or public opinion, or to the claims of state or church, or to other supposed authorities, are widely seen as inconclusive and question-begging. Philosophers hope to break free from these authorities and to appeal to reason. But there is an uncomfortable sting in the tail of this bold rejection of authority, since little will be gained unless we can say something convincing about the authority of reasoning itself.

But can this be done? Nobody has tried more vigorously than Immanuel Kant to show that and why reasoning is authoritative. Yet his ambition may seem doomed. Surely any attempt to vindicate standards or principles of reason must fail, because nothing can count as a vindication or justification, unless it is itself reasoned. Yet if it is reasoned, it will presuppose and so cannot vindicate principles or standards of reason. But if it is not reasoned, it will fail to vindicate principles or standards of reason. It seems that any attempt to show that or why reasoning has authority leaves us in an uncomfortable place.

There are well-known ways of seeking to avoid, or at least to postpone, this discomfort. We might claim that reason is a God-given inner light that is, as Descartes had put the matter, 'complete and entire in each one of us', or perhaps embrace a naturalistic version of the same thought. However, many will not see such approaches as vindicating reason, or showing why it has authority. Alternatively we might give up, and conclude that what passes for reasoning is inconclusive, and in the end provides only jumped-up arguments from authority, that claim a bogus status.

But if principles or standards of reason cannot be vindicated, and if they lack authority, much may fall apart. Attempts to give reasons for truth claims or moral judgements, for claims about the justice or fairness of

---

[1] For the key to references to Kant's works see p. 8 below.

political or other institutional arrangements, or for interpretations of texts or situations, may all prove inadequate or inconclusive. So it seems that despite misgivings about the prospects of any critique or vindication of reason, it is worth paying close attention to Kant's attempts to resolve these problems, by following his account of the ways in which the authority of reason can be constructed.

'The most difficult task'

I first began to explore these recalcitrant questions in the 1980s, and this collection contains papers written across many years about Kant's account of reason, about some of its contemporary successors, and about his closely related discussions of autonomy, of politics and of interpretation. Although I had previously worked on some of Kant's central texts, and in particular on his accounts of action and of ethics, I was struck afresh by the fact that he begins the *Critique of Pure Reason* by asking how reason can 'take on anew the most difficult of all its tasks, namely, that of self knowledge, and . . . secure its rightful claims' (*CPR* A xi). Like many others, I had repeatedly read these words, yet had shoved the questions they raise aside, thinking that there was plenty to explore and investigate without addressing them. Gradually, however, I began to appreciate that Kant's philosophy was deeply systematic, and that his attempt to vindicate principles and standards of reason lay at its core. His philosophy no doubt contained errors, false starts, and a range of claims and arguments that he subsequently discarded or revised, or that were mistaken. But an attempt to vindicate reason, and so to show what reasoning is and how and why it has authority, was evidently central to his philosophy. Yet how could this be done?

It took me a long time to work towards a coherent view of Kant's approach to the critique and vindication of reasoning: light dawned *very* gradually over the whole! I came to see that his focus in numerous passages on the critique and vindication of reason, and on the nature and limits of its authority, relies on two linked thoughts. The first thought is that reasoning is fundamentally practical: it aims to provide *standards* or *norms* that thought, action and communication can (but often fail to) meet. The second thought is that norms of reasoning must be followable by others: they must be norms that can be used by a *plurality* of agents. These two thoughts, Kant argued, set certain minimal constraints on anything that can count as reasoning. They make it possible to justify minimal principles or norms of reason by showing that they are standards that must be met if we are to offer or receive, accept or reject, revise or reconsider one another's proposals for acting, for truth claims, or for attempts to communicate.

Kant's approach to the requirements of reasoning draws on an account of what we may call (by analogy with Hume's account of the *circumstances of justice*) the *circumstances of reasoning*. Kant sees those circumstances as arising when a plurality of potential reasoners finds that their communication and interaction are not antecedently coordinated (for example, by instinct, divine plan, pre-established harmony or other sorts of authority). Uncoordinated agents who may disagree with one another can at least *offer* one another reasons for believing their claims or following their proposals for action. But they can do this only if they put forward considerations that they take it others *could follow in thought*, so understand, or *could adopt for action*. In the event – indeed very frequently – those to whom reasons are offered cannot or do not actually follow them, or adopt them. So the basic thought is simply that we do not even *offer* reasons for belief unless we aim to be intelligible to them, and do not even *offer* reasons for action unless we make proposals that they could take up. Norms of reasoning, as Kant sees them, articulate necessary conditions for the possibility of sharing knowledge, of recommending or coordinating action, and of communicating content among a plurality of agents whose agreement is *not* presupposed. This approach provides a minimal starting point for an account of the authority of reason, but does not settle questions about the reach and power of reasoning. Can this spare and modal account of the authority of reason offer enough? Can it provide a discipline or orientation for knowledge, for action or for interpretation?

Kant's constructivism

Kant repeatedly likens the task of reasoning to the task of constructing a building using only the limited materials that are available, and relying on an initially uncoordinated 'workforce', who may not even agree about what they are trying to build. Kant takes it that the standards and norms of human reasoning must be built or constructed from the meagre resources and capacities that are actually available to human beings, which he describes in some passages as 'just enough for the most pressing needs for the beginnings of existence' (*IUH* 8:19–20).

These modest starting points cannot, he thinks, sustain or revive classical philosophical ambitions to build vast metaphysical structures on reason alone:

> although we had in mind to build a tower that would reach the heavens, yet the stock of materials was only enough for a dwelling house, just roomy

> enough for our task on the plain of experience and just high enough for us to look across the plain . . . we have to plan our building with the supplies we have been given and also to suit our needs. (*CPR* A 707 / B 735, trans. OO'N)

The anti-metaphysical implications of Kant's position have found wide acceptance. His criticism of 'our dogmatically enthusiastic lust for knowledge' and his barbed comment that it 'could not be satisfied except through magical powers in which I am not an expert' (*CPR* A xiii) have been echoed by many philosophers. Many consequently applaud his refusal to try to reoccupy 'the battlefield of these endless controversies . . . called metaphysics' (*ibid.*). But their applause for Kant's rejection of certain classical metaphysical ambitions often reflects a generalised enthusiasm for empiricist positions, rather than a considered view of the principles or standards for reasoning that he put forward, or any endorsement of his approach to vindicating them.

As Kant depicts it, we reason only if we act, think or communicate in ways that (we judge) make it possible for others to understand, to accept or to reject our claims or proposals. If we merely assert, or assume, or appeal to 'authorities' that others do not (sometimes even cannot) follow, we fail to offer them reasons. Reasoning is therefore a matter of using our limited capacities and resources to construct and vindicate claims and standards, institutions and practices, *without* depending on claims and standards that have only the backing of happenstantial 'authorities' – such as church or state, 'common sense' or personal preference – that some accept but others reject.

Kant's repeated use of metaphors of *construction* and *collaboration* in his discussions of reasoning make it natural to speak of his approach and method as *constructivist*, and of his aim as the *construction* of reason's authority, and thereby of a basis for offering others reasons for truth claims and moral claims, reasons for favouring some rather than other interpretations of texts and situations, and reasons for pursuing some rather than other practical and political aims.

This line of thought lies behind the quite meagre substantive claims that Kant makes about reasoning. If we are to reason in ways that others can follow, we must in the first place ensure that our reasoning is followable by others: it must exhibit patterns that others can in principle discern and follow and so be *lawlike*. Some uses of reason – which Kant spoke of as 'fully public' or 'autonomous' – are not merely lawlike in form, but appeal only to assumptions that all others can follow: they aim to provide reasons to all and any others, and are fundamental to offering reasons both for truth claims and for moral standards that are intended to have universal scope. Other uses of reason – which Kant calls variously 'conditional', 'private' or 'heteronomous' – are also lawlike in form, but depend on further claims and assumptions that may be accepted by some, but rejected by or inaccessible to others. Such conditional reasoning may variously appeal to established 'authorities' such as the edicts of church and state, received views, or personal preferences, or to what are seen as the facts of a given situation, but without offering any vindication of those appeals.

Of course, a great deal of reasoning is not and need not be 'public' in the demanding sense that Kant defines as *fully* public uses of reason. It can quite properly be conditional on numerous assumptions for which no explicit or complete reasons are given. This is obvious in the case of technical and prudential reasoning, where specific aims and constraints not merely may but must be assumed, but is also true of a great deal of everyday practical reasoning, including ethical reasoning that relies on received social, cultural or political assumptions. *Conditional* or *heteronomous* reasoning can convince those who accept the assumptions on which it is conducted: but it may not reach, let alone convince, others. Kant contrasts such reasoning, with reasoning that is *not* conditional on contingently shared assumptions, so is fit to reach 'the world at large', which he counts as *fully* public reasoning. Without the possibility of some fully public reasoning, all reasoning will have restricted scope: even if it is lawlike in form, it will lack universal reach.

Contemporary constructivisms

Many of the terms Kant used in discussing the vindication of reason and connected themes have acquired new life in recent decades. Contemporary discussions of individuals and their rights constantly invoke conceptions of *autonomy*; contemporary discussions of justice and democracy often make claims about *public reason*. Many contemporary philosophers, in particular political philosophers, follow Kant in proposing *constructive* arguments, and in seeking to build philosophical and political conclusions on parsimonious (but not too parsimonious!) assumptions. However, as I see it, the lines of thought explored by contemporary constructivists differ in various ways from those that Kant proposed. For the most part they propose less exacting – and in my view less exciting – views of autonomy, and of public reason, than those Kant thought important. For example, most discussions of autonomy in recent decades have been resolutely individualistic, and are variably, and in some cases very tenuously, connected to accounts of reason.

The renewed discussion of public reason – including the influential discussions by Rawls and Habermas – focus on discourse and agreement among *actual* publics with their specific inclusions and exclusions, rather than on the necessary conditions for the possibility of discussion or communication among an unrestricted audience. These discussions of conceptions of public reason are closely linked to discussions of democracy, in particular of participatory or deliberative democracy, but do not attempt any wider vindication of reason.

Equally, many contemporary discussions of interpretation say almost nothing about the role of reason in interpretation, which is often simply contrasted with reasoning. Contemporary constructivists writing on politics also often say little about the justification of their framing assumptions about the circumstances of justice, such as existing boundaries or existing categories of social or political life, and offer little by way of justification for these fundamental claims. In my view, the Kantian ancestor of contemporary constructivisms seeks to do more with less. So one of the aims of this collection of essays is to articulate and explore some of the differences between Kant's constructivism and the influential quasi-Kantian constructivisms developed in the late twentieth century.

Reason, autonomy, politics and interpretation

There are many cross-cutting connections between the papers, and they could have been arranged in various ways. I have put them into four groups that reflect their central themes.

The papers in the first group deal with conceptions of reason and with attempts to support them by constructivist methods and approaches. Some of them concentrate on Kant's development of these ideas; others contrast his approach with those taken by leading contemporary constructivists, and in particular with the forms of constructivism that John Rawls developed at various times in arguing for his conception of justice.

The papers in the second group deal mainly with conceptions of autonomy. They focus on some of the deep differences between Kant's view of autonomy and contemporary accounts of autonomy. Kant proposed an account of *principled autonomy* that is closely linked to his account of reason. Most contemporary writing on autonomy focuses on various conceptions of *individual autonomy* that assume (at most) limited accounts of reason, and says nothing about the vindication of reason.

The papers in the third group deal mainly with the interesting connections and analogies that Kant drew between reasoning and politics. His

ASSUMPTIONS HAVE to be CONSTITUTED R CONSTRUCTED RATHER THAN ASSUMED.

writing on political themes – under which he groups not only questions about justice in and beyond states, but questions about history, hope and human destiny – always focuses on action. As Kant sees it, deep connections between reasoning and politics arise because both are activities in which a plurality of participants needs to engage with one another's thought and action, yet find that the very terms of coordination and interaction are disputed. Both in reasoning and in political life, coordination and shared assumptions have to be constituted or constructed rather than assumed.

The papers in the last section deal with connections between reason and interpretation, including the interpretation of sacred texts. Many writers of the European Enlightenment hoped that deism would provide a reasoned foundation for the core of Christian belief. Kant devoted many pages of the *Critique of Pure Reason* to undermining the forms of rational theology on which deists drew, and proposed a wholly different way of approaching sacred texts and traditions, that remained 'within the limits of reason'. He argued that since we are committed to the possibility both of knowledge and of action, we must see the natural world as open to change by our action, so have reason to hope that we can shape the future for the better. On Kant's account, a reasoned orientation to the future is possible only if we are committed to hope that human action can insert the moral intention into the world, hence only on a certain view of human destinies. Commitments to theoretical and practical reason and to the ways in which they can shape knowledge and action are coherent only if linked to reasoned hope for a future in which they can be coordinated.

On the surface this approach may seem remote from religious traditions and their interpretations of their sacred texts. Traditional religions typically rely on supposedly authoritative interpreters, whose reading of sacred texts (at best) relies on 'private' reasoning. He contrasts such approaches to interpretation with that of reasoned interpretation. Reasoned interpretation will not be literal, and may even seem forced, but in taking the demands of morality as the key to interpretation they can offer interpretations that lie 'within the limits of reason', rather than deferring to supposed 'authorities'.

This collection is one of three to be published by Cambridge University Press that brings together papers that I have written on a range of themes over many years. The papers in the other two volumes, *Justice across Boundaries: Whose Obligations?* and *From Principles to Practice: Normativity and Judgement in Ethics and Politics*, draw less, and much less explicitly, on Kant's philosophy. My hope is that the papers in the three volumes form a coherent whole.

Bibliographical note on quotations from and citations of Kant's work

Quotations from Kant's writings mainly cite the texts of the Cambridge edition of the works of Immanuel Kant, which were published by Cambridge University Press beginning in 1996. Abbreviated titles are given parenthetically in footnotes and citations, as indicated in Part 1 of this bibliographical note. Page references cite the standard volume numbers and pagination of the Prussian Academy edition of the works of Immanuel Kant, which is included in the margins of these and most other editions and translations.

Where a chapter was first published before the relevant texts appeared in the Cambridge editions, quotations cite older translations. These are listed in Part 2 of this Bibliographical Note. In cases where the Prussian Academy pagination is not included in the older translation, the relevant page number is cited.

Where I have offered my own translations of a passage, this is indicated parenthetically.

Part 1: Cambridge edition of the works of Immanuel Kant

I. Kant, 1781, *Critique of Pure Reason* [*CPR*], trans. and ed. Paul Guyer and Allen W. Wood (Cambridge University Press, 1996)

I. Kant, 1784, *An Answer to the Question: What Is Enlightenment?* [*WE*], trans. Mary J. Gregor, in *Practical Philosophy* (Cambridge University Press, 1996)

I. Kant, 1784, *Idea for a Universal History with a Cosmopolitan Aim* [*IUH*], trans. Allen W. Wood, in Immanuel Kant, *Anthropology, History and Education* (Cambridge University Press, 2007)

I. Kant, 1785, *Groundwork of the Metaphysics of Morals* [*G*], trans. Mary J. Gregor, in *Practical Philosophy* (Cambridge University Press, 1996)

I. Kant, 1786, *Conjectural Beginning of Human History* [*CB*], trans. Allen W. Wood, in *Anthropology, History and Education* (Cambridge University Press, 2007)

I. Kant, 1786, *What Does It Mean to Orient Oneself in Thinking?* [*WOT*], trans. Allen W. Wood and George di Giovanni, in *Religion and Rational Theology* (Cambridge University Press, 1996)

I. Kant, 1788, *Critique of Practical Reason* [*CPrR*], trans. Mary J. Gregor, in *Practical Philosophy* (Cambridge University Press, 1996)

I. Kant, 1790, *Critique of the Power of Judgement* [*CJ*], trans. Paul Guyer and Eric Matthews (Cambridge University Press, 2000)

I. Kant, 1793, *On the Common Saying: That may be correct in theory, but it is of no use in practice* [*TP*], trans. Mary J. Gregor, in *Practical Philosophy* (Cambridge University Press, 1996)

I. Kant, 1793, *Religion within the Boundaries of Mere Reason* [*R*], trans. George di Giovanni, in Allen W. Wood and George di Giovanni (eds.), *Religion and Rational Theology* (Cambridge University Press, 1996)

I. Kant, 1795, *Toward Perpetual Peace* [*PP*], trans. Mary J. Gregor, in *Practical Philosophy* (Cambridge University Press, 1996)

I. Kant, 1797, *The Metaphysics of Morals* [*MM*], trans. Mary J. Gregor, in *Practical Philosophy* (Cambridge University Press, 1996)

I. Kant, 1798, *The Conflict of the Faculties* [*CF*], trans. Mary J. Gregor and Robert Anchor, in Allen W. Wood and George di Giovanni (eds.), *Religion and Rational Theology* (Cambridge University Press, 1996)

I. Kant, 1800, *Jäsche Logic* [*JL*] (not in the Prussian Academy edition), in J. Michael Young (trans. and ed.), *Lectures on Logic* (Cambridge University Press, 1992), 521–64

Part 2: Older translations of Kant's writings

I. Kant, 1781, *Critique of Pure Reason* [*CPR*], trans. Norman Kemp Smith (London: Macmillan, 1933)

I. Kant, 1784, *What Is Enlightenment?* [*WE*], trans. H.B. Nisbet, in Hans Reiss (ed.), *Kant: Political Writings*, 2nd edn (Cambridge University Press, 1991), 54–60

I. Kant, 1784, *Idea for a Universal History with a Cosmopolitan Aim* [*IUH*], trans. H.B. Nisbet, in Hans Reiss (ed.), *Kant: Political Writings*, 2nd edn (Cambridge University Press, 1991), 41–53

I. Kant, 1785, *Groundwork of the Metaphysic of Morals* [*G*], in *The Moral Law*, trans. H.J. Paton, London: Hutchinson, 1953)

I. Kant, 1786, *Conjectures on the Beginning of Human History* [*CB*], trans. H.B. Nisbet, in Hans Reiss (ed.), *Kant: Political Writings*, 2nd edn (Cambridge University Press, 1991), 221–34

I. Kant, 1786, *What Does It Mean to Orient Oneself in Thinking?* [*WOT*], trans. H.B. Nisbet, in Hans Reiss (ed.), *Kant: Political Writings*, 2nd edn (Cambridge University Press, 1991), 237–49

I. Kant, 1788, *Critique of Practical Reason* [*CPrR*], trans. Lewis White Beck, in *Kant's Critique of Practical Reason and Other Writings in Moral Philosophy* (University of Chicago Press, 1949)

I. Kant, 1790, *Critique of Judgement* [*CJ*], trans. James Creed Meredith (Oxford: Clarendon Press, 1978); includes Academy pagination

I. Kant, 1793, *Religion within the Limits of Reason Alone* [*R*], trans. Theodore M. Greene (New York: Harper and Row, 1960)

I. Kant, 1793, *On the Common Saying: That may be correct in theory but it is of no use in practice* (known as *Theory and Practice*) [*TP*], trans. H.B. Nisbet, in Hans Reiss (ed.), *Kant: Political Writings*, 2nd edn (Cambridge University Press, 1991), 61–92

I. Kant, 1795, *Perpetual Peace: A Philosophical Sketch* [*PP*], trans. H.B. Nisbet, in Hans Reiss (ed.), *Kant: Political Writings*, 2nd edn (Cambridge University Press, 1991), 93–130

I. Kant, 1798, *The Conflict of the Faculties* [*CF*], trans. Mary Gregor (New York: Abaris Books, 1979)

PART I

Authority in reasoning

CHAPTER I

Vindicating reason[1]

Critique of reason

Whatever else a critique of reason attempts, it must surely criticise reason. Further, if it is not to point towards nihilism, a critique of reason cannot have only a negative or destructive outcome, but must vindicate at least some standards or principles as authorities on which thinking and doing may rely, and by which they may (in part) be judged. Critics of 'the Enlightenment project' from Pascal to Horkheimer to contemporary communitarians and postmodernists detect its Achilles' heel in arrant failure to vindicate the supposed standards of reason that are so confidently used to criticise, attack and destroy other authorities, including church, state and tradition. If the authority of reason is bogus, why should such reasoned criticism have any weight?

Suspicions about reason can be put innumerable ways. However, one battery of criticisms is particularly threatening, because it targets the very possibility of devising anything that could count as a vindication of reason. This line of attack is sometimes formulated as a trilemma. Any supposed vindication of the principles of reason would have to establish the authority of certain fundamental constraints on thinking or acting. However, this could only be done one of three ways. A supposed vindication could appeal to the presumed principles of reason that it aims to vindicate – but would then be circular, so fail as vindication. Alternatively it might be based on other starting points: but then the supposed principles of reason would lack reasoned vindication, so could not themselves bequeath unblemished pedigrees. Finally, as a poor third option, a vindication of reason might suggest

---

[1] 'Vindicating reason' in P. Guyer (ed.), *The Cambridge Companion to Kant* (Cambridge University Press, 1992), 280–308. Citations from Kant's work refer to translations listed in Part 2 of the Bibliographical Note, or where indicated are my own. References are to the Prussian Academy pagination, and in addition to page numbers of any cited translation that lacks the Academy pagination.

that reasoning issues in uncompletable regress, so that prospects of vindicating any claim, including claims to identify principles of reason, never terminate: To reason is only to keep the door open to further questioning. In each case the desired vindication eludes. These unpromising thoughts lend some appeal to Pascalian faith, to Humean naturalism or even to postures of postmodernity as responses to the challenge of scepticism about reason.

If the *Critique of Pure Reason* is to live up to its title and its reputation it must deal with scepticism with regard to reason. The whole magnificent and intricate critical structure will have little point if it draws on an unvindicated or unvindicable conception of reason. Yet it is far from clear where or how Kant handles these topics. I shall try here to trace some of his moves, drawing in particular on passages in the earlier sections of the *Transcendental Doctrine of Method*, but also on widely scattered passages in the prefaces, the *Transcendental Dialectic* and various shorter writings. I shall try to show that Kant addresses this fundamental topic persistently and with great subtlety, and that he offers an account of what it is to vindicate reason quite different from the foundationalist account that critics of 'the Enlightenment project' target, and usually attribute to Kant. Whether his account is wholly satisfactory is a large and complicated question, on which I offer sparse comments.

Reason and logic

It is helpful to begin by asking what sort of thing we expect a vindication of reason to vindicate. One account, with impeccable Cartesian and rationalist ancestry, sees principles of reason as formal principles of logic and method. These principles are to be algorithms for the formation and transformation of simple truths, and to provide axioms that wholly (according to rationalists) or partly (according to many others) constrain acceptable thinking and doing. The vindication of these axioms is problematic. Some boldly insist that they have divine warrant, even that God has installed these principles 'whole and complete in each of us';[2] others are discreetly silent.

This is not Kant's view. He insists that principles of reason and of logic are distinct. In the prefaces of the *Critique of Pure Reason* he claims that

[2] René Descartes, *The Discourse on the Method* in *The Philosophical Writings of Descartes*, trans. John Cottingham, Robert Stoothof and Dugald Murdoch (Cambridge University Press, 1985), Vol. I, 112. For discussion of contrasts between Descartes and Kant on these themes, and more generally on the connections between reason and politics in Kant see Reinhard Brandt, 'Freiheit, Gleichheit, Selbstständigkeit bei Kant' in *Die Ideen von 1789 in der deutschen Rezeption*, ed. Forum fur Philosophie, Bad Homburg (Frankfurt am Main: Suhrkamp, 1989), and Onora O'Neill, 'Reason and politics in the Kantian enterprise' in *Constructions of Reason: Explorations of Kant's Practical Philosophy* (Cambridge University Press, 1989).

logic was invented and completed in one stroke by Aristotle, that it has precise boundaries and that its success is consequent upon these limitations (B viii–ix). By contrast the prefaces depict human reasoning as 'a merely random groping' (B xv) that repeatedly falls into contradictions and has yet to find the 'secure path of a science' (B xiii). For Kant logic is abstracted either from the use of the understanding or from that of reason, and its vindication would have to be derived from theirs, rather than conversely. However, the fact that logic is derivative in this way allows us to use its structure as a clue or key to the cognitive structures from which it is derived.[3] No doubt there are many questions to be raised about Kant's treatment of logic, but it is at least clear that this is not the place to look for his vindication of reason.

Reason and understanding

On Cartesian accounts a vindication of reason must be the first of philosophical tasks. Kant does not treat the matter in this way. The *Critique of Pure Reason* begins, in the *Aesthetic* and the *Analytic of the Doctrine of Elements*, with discussion of the 'lower faculties of knowledge', sensibility and understanding. Only in its last and longest section, the *Transcendental Dialectic*, does Kant turn to questions about reason, the 'higher faculty of knowledge'. There he mainly exposes and undermines excessive rationalist claims about the powers of reason. Vindication of reason is still postponed.

The first pages of the Dialectic stress some differences between lower and higher faculties of knowledge and acknowledge that investigating the latter raises difficulties that did not arise in investigating the powers of understanding, because we lack all insight into the supposed real use of reason (*CPR* A 299 / B 355). This may seem unsurprising – would not Leibniz have agreed that *we* lack complete insight? – but Kant insists that *no* real use can be vindicated. The fundamental point of the Copernican turn is that no correspondence of reason to reality be presumed. The use of reason is not assigned any counterpart to the reduced, empirical realism that Kant allows the understanding. The parallel that he draws between understanding and reason is only that both are 'faculties of unity'; but the unity the two achieve contrasts sharply:

---

[3] Passages where general logic is treated as a key for transcendental logic run across *CPR* A 67–83 / B 92–109 and A 303–5 / B 359–61. The methodological point is summarised at the beginning of the Dialectic: 'Following the analogy of concepts of understanding, we may expect that the logical concept will provide the key to the transcendental, and that the table of the functions of the former will at once give us the genealogical tree of the concepts of reason' (*CPR* A 299 / B 356).

> Understanding may be regarded as a faculty which secures the unity of appearances by means of rules, and reason as being the faculty which secures the unity of rules of understanding under principles. Accordingly, reason never applies itself directly to experience or to any object, but to understanding, in order to give to the manifold knowledge of the latter an *a priori* unity by means of concepts, a unity which may be called the unity of reason, and which is quite different in kind from any unity that can be accomplished by the understanding. (*CPR* A 302 / B 359; cf. A 644 / B 672)

In these 'provisional' passages Kant warns his readers that:

> multiplicity of rules and unity of principles is a demand of reason, for the purpose of bringing the understanding into thoroughgoing accordance with itself... But such a principle... is merely a subjective law for the orderly management of the possessions of our understanding... [so that] The unity of reason is therefore not the unity of a possible experience, but is essentially different from such unity. (*CPR* A 305–7 / B 362–3)

Kant evidently rejects the rationalist claim that the principles of reason can provide a unique and integrated answer to all possible questions. In the *Transcendental Dialectic* the central objection to rational psychology, rational cosmology and rational theology is that the rationalist tradition treats each domain as an object of theoretical inquiry, where necessary truths about soul, world and God are to be reached by intuition or analysis, and where there is no essential difference between the unity achieved by rules and by principles.

A main objective of the *Transcendental Dialectic* is to show how any view of principles of reason as divinely inscribed axioms or rules of thought, that correspond to reality, leads to contradictions – to paralogisms, antinomies and impossibilities. Kant rejects the *pièces de résistance* of the whole metaphysical tradition. He deems human reason quite simply incompetent for these illusory tasks. While the Copernican turn was put forward in the preface 'only as an hypothesis' (*CPR* B xxii n.), the arguments of the *Transcendental Dialectic* support the hypothesis that reason does not conform to the real, by inflicting heavy damage on metaphysical systems that assume such correspondence.

Ideas of Reason and striving for unity

In the introductions of the *Transcendental Dialectic* we also find suggestions that, as in the case of understanding, logic offers a clue to the structure of the faculty of knowledge from which it is supposedly abstracted. However, in this case the clue is given not by the traditional logic of terms but by syllogistic. This is not because syllogistic is 'more abstract' than the logic of terms, but because it links distinct propositions into larger units: it achieves a different sort of unity, and potentially a very extensive, even systematic unity:

> From this [discussion of syllogistic] we see that in inference reason endeavours to reduce the varied and manifold knowledge obtained through the understanding to the smallest number of principles (universal conditions) and thereby to achieve in it the highest possible unity. (*CPR* A 305 / B 361)

However, the attempt to achieve unity of knowledge is not guaranteed by any really existing unity. There is no metaphysical proof that all aspects of our thinking and doing can be integrated into a single, systematic unity. No Principle of Sufficient Reason, no *ens realissimum*, guarantees the principles of reason or the completeness of knowledge. On the contrary, human knowledge is threatened by chaos, while knowledge and action are divided by a 'great gulf' that provides the most profound challenge to the possibility of a complete and systematic philosophy. Complete unity can then be no more than an 'endeavour',[4] whose success is not guaranteed, and that is ultimately shown to be unattainable.

At the end of the introduction of the *Transcendental Dialectic* Kant confronts the suspected limitations of reason by posing a dilemma. He asks:

> Take the principle, that the series of conditions ... extends to the unconditioned. Does it, or does it not, have objective applicability (*objektive Richtigkeit*)? ... Or is there no such objectively valid principle of reason, but only a logical precept (*eine bloß logische Vorschrift*), to advance towards completeness by an ascent to ever higher conditions and so to give to our knowledge the greatest possible unity of reason? (*CPR* A 308–9 / B 365)

Either reason has objective validity, and its principles are not essentially different from the rules of the understanding, as these were understood by rationalists, since their real use is underpinned by the objective unity of experience. Or reason is only a *precept* or *prescription* to seek unity. We know well enough that the upshot of the *Transcendental Dialectic* is to reject the first horn of the dilemma. It follows then that Kant must understand reason as a precept for the task of achieving 'the greatest possible unity'. Striving for this greatest possible unity aspires to overcome or dispel the threatened hiatuses of thought and action – with no guarantee of success.

---

[4] Kant often uses far stronger terms than 'endeavour': Reason undisciplined veers between 'restless striving' and 'passionate desire' (cf. *CPR* A 786 / B 814).

Kant does not presuppose that integrated answers to his three fundamental questions 'What can I know?', 'What may I do?' and 'What may I hope?' must be available; he does not assume even that human knowledge must or can form a complete and systematic whole.

Precepts and Ideas of Reason

Although the *Transcendental Dialectic* is so clearly a sustained polemic against rationalism, and against the rationalist conception of reason as guarantor and mirror of reality, there is a good deal in the text that deflects attention from the active, striving (as opposed to passive, mirroring) character Kant ascribes to reason. When Kant speaks of principles of reason in the *Dialectic* he often uses terms that fit best with a conception of reason as mirroring reality. He speaks not of precepts or maxims of reason – which would indicate at once that he thinks of reason as consisting of practical principles for guiding thinking and doing – but in traditional rationalist, indeed Platonist, terms of *Ideas of Reason*. He defends his appropriation of this misleading Platonic term, not because but *in spite* of its metaphysical resonance. The term suits not because Kant too wants to endorse a classical, theoretical conception of reason, as correspondence of thought to its real archetypes, but because Plato's Ideas are potent symbols of striving for the most encompassing unity. The Platonic Ideas are an image of the unity of the highest principles that guide a quest for the Good and the Beautiful as well as the True. Kant allows himself this borrowing, which parallels his own three fundamental questions, but rejects the entire Platonic account of the metaphysical basis of unity and success in these quests. He firmly rejects all thought that his Ideas of Reason correspond to any real archetypes, and adopts a position that is irreconcilable with any form of the Platonic vision of Ideas as patterns for knowledge and mathematics.[5] In spite of this unequivocal rejection of any real use of the Ideas of Reason, the borrowed terminology is unavoidably associated with the strongest forms of realism, and can mask the quite different Kantian conception of Ideas of Reason, which are conceived as precepts for seeking unity of thought and action, rather than as archetypes that guarantee that unity is to be found.

---

[5] Kant remarks with an odd mixture of animus against and defence of Plato: 'In this I cannot follow him, any more than in his mystical deduction of these ideas, or in the extravagances whereby he, so to speak, hypostatised them – although, as must be allowed, the exalted language, which he employed in this sphere, is quite capable of a milder interpretation', *CPR* A 314 n. / B 371 n.

Unity of reason and plurality of precepts

Granted that the Ideas of Reason are precepts, it is surely puzzling that Kant thinks a plurality of distinct Ideas can create 'the greatest possible unity'. He introduces a wide range of principles of reason under a variety of labels. There are 'Postulates of Reason' and 'Maxims of Reason' as well as 'Ideas of Reason'. All can count as principles of reason, and aim at a single sort of unity, because all are forms or aspects of a single principle, which can be formulated in multiple ways. This explains why Kant speaks both of 'the principle of reason', and of many ideas or principles of reason. He says of the underlying principle:

> The principle of reason is thus properly only a *rule*, prescribing a regress in the series of the conditions of given appearances, and forbidding it to bring the regress to a close by *treating* anything at which it may arrive as absolutely unconditioned... Nor is it a *constitutive* principle of reason... [but] rather a principle of the greatest possible continuation and extension of experience, allowing no empirical limit to hold as absolute. Thus it is a principle of reason which serves as a *rule*, postulating what we ought to do in the regress, but *not anticipating* what is present *in the object as it is in itself, prior* to *all regress.* Accordingly I entitle it a *regulative* principle of reason. (*CPR* A 509 / B 537)

It is not hard to connect various formulations of this principle to one or another of Kant's own basic questions. Answers to 'What can I know?' are guided by Ideas or precepts of scientific inquiry, including

> It is a logical postulate of reason, that through the understanding we follow up and extend as far as possible that connection of a concept with its conditions (*CPR* A 498 / B 526)

and

> *Entia praeter necessitatem non esse multiplicanda.* (*CPR* A 652 / B 680)

Answers to the question 'What ought I do?' are guided by the formulations of the Categorical Imperative, and their more determinate implications (principles of duty, of justice, and so forth). Answers to the question 'What may I hope?' are guided, *inter alia*, by the Postulates of Practical Reason and by maxims of seeking purposiveness, which provide accounts of various possible 'bridges' across the 'great gulf' that would otherwise sunder our grasp of knowable nature and of the demands of morality on freely acting beings. Kant maintains that the contradictions to which the use of reason as a constitutive principle leads can be avoided by this more modest, regulative conception of reason, in its various formulations. If we view principles of reason as precepts for the conduct of thinking, acting and their coherent connection, hence as ways of achieving an active grasp rather than a passive response to the manifold of life, then although we will never regain the heights that rationalist conceptions of reason claimed to conquer, we can unite a wide range of our experience and actions without lapsing into contradiction:

> When they [regulative principles] are treated merely as *maxims*, there is no real conflict, but merely those differences in the interest of reason that give rise to differing modes of thought. In actual fact, reason has only one single interest, and the conflict of its maxims is only a difference in, and a mutual limitation of, the methods whereby this interest endeavours to obtain satisfaction. (*CPR* A 666 / B 694)

Even if we accept Kant's view that the many Ideas of Reason are all aspects of one striving for unity, reason has not been vindicated. What is it that shows that striving for unity is fundamental to reason? What shows that such striving has authority for the regulation of all thought and action? Kant's answers to these questions in the *First Critique* are given partly in prefatory remarks and partly in the concluding *Doctrine of Method*.

Reason in the prefaces: disintegration or self-discipline?

If we go back to the passages in the prefaces in which Kant introduces the theme of reason in the *Critique of Pure Reason*, we can see that from the beginning of the book he represents human reason as a form of striving that *both* leads to contradictions, hence is a source of problems, and yet seeks *unity*, so may be capable of resolving the problems it has generated. The prefaces depict human reason as repeatedly frustrated striving for completion and unity, in a being whose capacities seem inadequate for what it yearns to do, yet also as a capacity to discipline the use of these very powers and so perhaps to resolve its self-inflicted problems. On the one hand Kant's initial diagnosis is that human reason leads to catastrophe, because it

> begins with principles which it has no option save to employ . . . rising with their aid to ever higher, ever more remote, conditions. . . But by this procedure human reason precipitates itself into darkness and contradiction. (*CPR* A vii–viii, cf. B xiv–v)

On the other hand Kant repeatedly gestures towards the thought that this same flawed capacity carries its remedy within it:

> Reason has insight only into that which it produces after a plan of its own, and ... it must not allow itself to be kept, as it were, on nature's leading-strings, but must itself show the way with principles of judgement based upon fixed laws, constraining nature to give answer to questions of reason's own determining. (*CPR* B xiii)

We have perhaps become so used to reading such turns of phrase as mere personification that we do not sufficiently note that throughout the *Critique of Pure Reason* reason is depicted as an *active* capacity that both *generates and may resolve problems. Reflexive structure* is part of the key to understanding Kant's conception of vindicating reason.

Vindicating reason: a reformulation

If such passages are no mere turns of phrase, but Kant's actual picture of reason, and if reason has no real or objective source or archetype, then the question of the vindication of reason has to be posed anew. To vindicate reason could not be to derive its principles from elsewhere or to show their correspondence to real archetypes. It would be to identify whatever fundamental precept can guide thought and action authoritatively for beings in whom neither is steered by any 'alien' reality or by necessity. This does not seem to make the task of vindicating reason any easier. Why should any precept have general authority for such disoriented beings? How could any be vindicated? Why should any have any authority for us?

The question is only complicated by the fact that if reason's principles are precepts for seeking the greatest possible unity, these precepts must apply both to thinking and to doing. Kant often stresses the basic unity of theoretical and practical uses of reason (e.g. *G* 4:391). Yet why should one and the same principle be authoritative for both tasks? Indeed, if the notorious Categorical Imperative is the 'supreme principle of practical reason', as Kant insists, then does not practical reason have its own, distinct 'supreme principle'? Many doubt whether the Categorical Imperative can guide practice; even those who think that it can, and that it is vital for morality, may well doubt whether it could either be or be closely linked to the supreme principle of reason in general. Further, Kant's attempts to vindicate the Categorical Imperative remain in dispute, so do not seem promising models for the vindication of theoretical uses of reason. The task of constructing a critical vindication of reason seems no less demanding than the rejected task of vindicating reason within the framework of rationalist metaphysics.

The *Doctrine of Method*: the building of reason

So far I have aimed to distinguish Kant's account of reason from others, without saying anything positive about his approach to the task of vindication. However, Kant tells us a great deal about the reformulated task. Numerous passages throughout the *Doctrine of Method* leave it beyond doubt that he holds that reason's principles are vindicable, and intends to show how the task must be carried out. These texts begin with an extended and deep comparison between the critical project and a building project:

> If we look upon the sum of all knowledge of pure speculative reason as a building for which we have at least the idea within ourselves, it can be said that in the *Transcendental Doctrine of Elements* we have made an estimate of the materials, and have determined for what sort, height, and strength of building they will suffice. Indeed it turned out that although we had in mind a tower that would reach the heavens, yet the stock of materials was only enough for a dwelling house – just roomy enough for our tasks on the plain of experience and just high enough for us to look across the plain. The bold undertaking had come to nothing for lack of materials, quite apart from the Babel of tongues that unavoidably set workers against one another and scattered them across the earth, each to build separately following his own plan. Our problem is not just to do with materials, but even more to do with the plan. Since we have been warned not to risk everything on a favorite but senseless project, which could perhaps exceed our whole means, yet cannot well refrain from building a secure home, we have to plan our building with the supplies we have been given and at the same time to suit our needs. (*CPR* A 707 / B 735; trans. OO'N)

A few preliminary comments on this passage may be useful. First, Kant is drawing on a long tradition of comparisons between building and philosophy, which goes back to antiquity, and had been extended by the rationalists and above all by Descartes. Second, he is also drawing on the darker story of the building of the tower of Babel, whose builders aspired to a splendid tower that exceeded their own capacities, and who were forced into a life of dispersed nomadism after its collapse. Third, it may seem impertinent that after the 700 difficult pages of the *Doctrine of Elements*, Kant should tell his readers that all that he has offered so far is an 'inventory of the building materials' for constructing the edifice of reason. Yet just this would be appropriate if he holds that a vindication of reason is needed, but that he has not yet provided one.

Reflexivity and the building of reason

The clue to the late placing of the vindication of reason is that Kant regards it as a reflexive task, which has to assemble certain 'materials' before it can begin. This was signalled from the very first pages of the *Critique of Pure Reason*, where human thinking and doing are depicted as undisciplined striving that leads into tangles and contradictions. Kant's critique of rationalism shows that this striving cannot be disciplined by conforming to some given (outside, 'alien') reality. Striving for such conformity would be analogous to the hubris of the builders of Babel: both projects must collapse.

However, the failure of rationalism – of foundationalism – may not seem enough to require a reflexive approach. Might not the fate of the builders of Babel, who failed in their project of building and settlement, provide a more accurate model for human thinking and acting? Once again Kant has signalled from the very beginning of the *Critique of Pure Reason* that this 'postmodern' attitude too is untenable. We are in no position to live without reason. The striving that leads us into tangled thought and action is already reasoning, but unreliable reasoning. The question that we must ask ourselves is not 'Why should any principles count as those of reason?' but, rather, 'Given that we try to reason, how can we mitigate the dangers of the principles on which we unavoidably rely?'

Kant speaks of a critique of reason as a *task* because we are unavoidably committed to thinking and acting, hence unavoidably partially, incipiently reasoning beings, yet with the 'peculiar fate' (*CPR* A vii) that our reasoning constantly falls into difficulty and contradiction. The disasters of metaphysics arise from an unrestricted use of quite common and daily ways of thinking and acting, which we can hardly give up. (For example, the antinomies suggest that contradictions can readily be generated by iterated use of the principle of causality, or those of counting or dividing.) Metaphysical hubris is no more than the further extension of the very principles we rely on. Hence any vindication of human reason will have to identify principles for guiding the ways of thinking and doing that we have to hand, and cannot jettison, and must use these very principles both as 'material' and as source of a 'plan'. Neither foundationalism nor postmodernism is a genuine option for us. In terms of the humble vocabulary of the building trades, our only feasible option is to ask: 'What can be built with the materials and workforce available to us?'

At this point an objection might be that metaphors of building or construction cannot shed light on a reflexive task. Buildings, it might be said, need foundations, hence metaphors of construction are only appropriate if we accept a foundationalist conception of the vindication of reason – for example, that of Descartes. However, this objection overlooks the possibility of constructions without foundations, such as kites or space satellites, whose components are mutually supporting, although no part of the structure forms a foundation for the rest. Moreover, it also fails to note that the components even of structures that do rest on foundations are and must be mutually supporting in many ways. There is nothing amiss in Kant's strategy of using building metaphors while renouncing the thought that we are given an 'absolute' orientation by some external criterion that demarcates 'up' from 'down', and permits us to identify foundations or axioms for thought or action (cf. *WOT*; and 'Orientation in thinking: geographical problems, political solutions', Chapter 9 below). Indeed, in many ways Kant's conception of the building of reason is more prosaic than that of the rationalists whom he criticises. Kant represents attempts to construe practices of reason as a matter of proceeding with the 'materials' and 'workforce' that our daily practice of defective reasoning has made available to us, and rebuilding these in ways that reduce dangers of collapse or paralysis in thought or action. The construction of reason is to be seen as process rather than product, as practices of connection and integration rather than as once and for all discovery or laying of foundations.

In advancing this conception of the task of vindicating reason, Kant shows nothing about the structure of reason. He merely points to a possibility between rationalism and scepticism – between foundationalism and postmodernism. We may be able to build an adequate account of reason out of available materials and capacities. If we can, we will not, of course, have achieved a presuppositionless vindication of reason. But we would perhaps have shown that the strategies of thought on which we have to rely provide the materials and the plan for constructing an account of some principles that have wholly general authority for thinking and acting. Kant outlines this approach in the opening sections of the *Doctrine of Method*.

The *Doctrine of Method*: what does Kant vindicate?

Reason is discussed under four headings in the *Doctrine of Method*: the *Discipline of Reason*, the *Canon of Reason*, the *Architectonic of Reason* and the *History of Reason*. Here I shall restrict myself to the first of these. Kant discusses the discipline of reason between *CPR* A 708 / B 736 and *CPR* A 794 / B 822. He begins with some short but important introductory remarks, which are followed by four sections that include criticism of the philosophical methods of rationalists ('dogmatists') and sceptics. I shall reverse the order and sketch his criticism of supposed alternatives first.

The 'dogmatic', or rationalist, conception of reason is modelled on the supposed method of mathematics. Kant regards this method as totally inappropriate. The rationalists made two crucial mistakes. First, they wrongly thought that mathematics consisted of analytic propositions, which form only a small part of it; second, they imagined that philosophy could ape the mathematical method of basing proofs on definitions and axioms. It was this second error that led them into the project of building a 'tower that should reach the heavens'. A more accurate examination of the available building materials and workforce would have shown them that philosophy has neither definitions nor axioms, so can produce no proofs, and so to the realisation that it is necessary to

> cut away the last anchor of these fantastic hopes, that is, to show that the pursuit of the mathematical method cannot be of the least advantage in this kind of knowledge (*CPR* A 726 / B 754)

and to the conclusion that

> In philosophy the geometrician (*der Meßkünstler*) can by his method build only so many houses of cards. (*CPR* A 727 / B 755)

Mathematics cannot be done *more analytico*, and philosophy cannot be done *more geometrico*. Mathematical method provides no wholly general model for reasoning.

The second section on the discipline of reason rejects the sceptical suspicion that reason is really no more than polemic – that is, war. The goal of polemic is victory. Conversation, argument, and writing are often polemicised, in the sense that various sorts of force and pressure can he brought to bear through them, and that they may aim at victory. However, polemic always has the disadvantage that no wider validity can be ascribed to its results. Coerced 'agreement' or 'understanding' does not outlive the coercion, and does not reach the uncoerced. Polemic can lay no claim to provide a wholly general discipline for thinking or acting. Anybody who seeks an unrestricted audience has to renounce polemic. Kant proposes that a better image of reasoned exchange is that of citizens in free debate:

> Reason must in all its undertakings subject itself to criticism; should it limit freedom of criticism by any prohibitions, it must harm itself, drawing upon itself a damaging suspicion. Nothing is so important through its usefulness, nothing so sacred, that it may be exempted from this searching examination, which knows no respect for persons. Reason depends on this freedom for its

very existence. For reason has no dictatorial authority; its verdict is always simply the agreement of free citizens, of whom each one must be permitted to express, without let or hindrance, his objection or even his veto. (*CPR* A 738–9 / B 766–7)

A debate between citizens can serve as an image for reason, not because it follows given (hence 'alien') rules of procedure or order, or because it relies on common presuppositions, but because both are processes with a plurality of participants, whose coordination is not guaranteed or imposed by a ruler or other powers. (Of course, this is not wholly true of actual debates between citizens, but then we do not expect metaphors to work without any restriction whatsoever.) The negative aspect of Kant's criticism of those who construe reason as polemic is easily followed: thoughts and action that depend on unvindicated authorities will hold only where this authority is accepted, so cannot produce general understanding or agreement or resolve all conflicts of belief and action.

These criticisms of the mathematical and the polemical conceptions of reasoning also support one further, negative conclusion: in the construction of reason it would be no solution to the collapse of rationalism or to the threat of anarchy to appoint some well-organised local 'builder' who would erect a more modest version of the project. This solution, the metaphorical counterpart to forms of relativism or communitarianism, once more subjects thought and action to some arbitrary, if less ambitious, power. Its results could have only arbitrarily restricted significance. However, it remains quite unclear what positive conditions a construction of reason must meet.

The *Doctrine of Method*: Kant's proposals

Kant's positive proposals are outlined succinctly in the short passages that deal explicitly with the discipline of reason (*CPR* A 708–12 / B 736–40). These precede the accounts of the failings of the methods of rationalism and of polemic just summarised. His diagnosis, both in the prefaces and in the introductory remarks at the beginning of the *Doctrine of Method*, stresses the fact that we lack not only the *materials* for the grand projects of rationalism, but more crucially a *plan* for using those that we have.[6] What plan does Kant then propose? And how could any particular plan

---

[6] Cf. 'if the various participants are unable to agree on a common plan of procedure' (*CPR* B vii); 'reason has insight only into that which it produces after a plan of its own' (*CPR* B xiii as well as *CPR* A 707 / B735).

be justified? Even if we now grasp why a vindication of reason must be a reflexive task that begins with available materials and capacities, still there will surely be a plurality of realisable plans. If we can establish only necessary and not sufficient conditions for reasoned thinking and doing, should we not also suspect that there can be no vindication of reason?

At the beginning of this short section Kant asserts that reason needs a 'discipline'. A discipline is

> The compulsion, by which the constant tendency to disobey certain rules is restrained and finally extirpated. (*CPR* A 709 / B 737)

He then notes

> that reason, whose proper duty it is to prescribe a discipline for all other endeavours, should itself stand in need of a discipline may indeed seem strange. (*CPR* A 710 / B 738)

However, the strangeness of reason's discipline is then promptly explained by pointing out that it is a form of *self-discipline*. Here Kant develops the many earlier passages in which the task of critique of reason has been characterised as a reflexive task.[7] This reflexive discipline is needed because the task is peculiar:

> where, as in the case of pure reason, we come upon a whole system of illusions and fallacies, intimately bound together and united under common principles, its own and indeed negative lawgiving (*eine eigene und zwar negative Gesetzgebung*) seems to be required, which, under the title of a *discipline*, erects a system of precautions and self-examination out of the nature of reason and the objects of its pure employment. (*CPR* A 711 / B 739; trans. amended OO'N)[8]

What does Kant mean by reason's 'own and indeed negative law-giving'? Which plan is the plan of reason? Will it be enough to have only 'a system of precautions and self-examination'? Have we been told anything of substance?

There are in fact three substantive points here. First, the discipline of reason is *negative*; second, it is *self-discipline*; third, it is a *law-giving*. That it is *negative* is in any case part of the definition of a discipline and is a corollary of the rejection of 'alien' authorities – of foundationalism.

---

[7] See *CPR* A ix, B xiii, A 747 / B 775, A 750 / B 778 as well as passages cited below.
[8] I have amended Kemp Smith's translation here because it imposes a foundationalist reading. He has it that the 'system of precautions and self-examination' is 'founded on the nature of reason and the objects of its pure employment'. Kant writes that it is erected out of them (*errichtet . . . aus*). He presents the nature of reason and the objects of its pure employment as the *material* for the self-discipline of reason, whereas Kemp Smith's wording makes them the (unvindicable) foundation.

Nothing has been assumed from which positive content could be derived; nor can anything of the sort be assumed without begging the question. That it is *self-discipline* confirms that reasoning is a reflexive task, which works on the available material of our incipient and often disastrous everyday practices of reasoning. That the discipline of reason is *a lawgiving* entails that it is at least lawlike. Lawlikeness presupposes that a plurality of agents, or at least of cases, may fall under reason's principles.

Any lawgiving that is to be both self-imposed and negative – that is, without content – can impose no more than the mere form of law. The discipline of reason can require only that no principle incapable of being a law count as a fundamental principle for governing thought and action. Any fundamental principle with determinate content would implicitly subject thought and action to some or other 'alien' and unvindicated 'authority'. Hence Kant views the fundamental principle of reason as that of governing both thinking and doing by principles that others too can adopt and follow. We recognise here a more general version of the supreme principle of practical reason, whose best-known version runs: *Act only on that principle through which you can at the same time will that it be a universal law (G* 4:421).[9] As in the case of the discussion of practical reason in the *Groundwork*, the fundamental principle of reason in general is without content: it demands simply that thinking as well as acting not violate the form of law.

This conclusion invites not the criticism that Kant's account of reason provides no discipline, but that it does not provide nearly enough. It certainly does not provide sufficient instructions for thinking and doing. This is not inadvertence on Kant's part: he constantly rejects conceptions of reason, such as the Principle of Sufficient Reason, which supposedly give sufficient instructions for all thinking and acting (for example, see *CPR* A 783 / B 811). His insistence that 'reason is no dictator' reiterates the thought that there is no algorithm that fully determines the content of reasoned thought and action. Nor should we 'expect from reason what obviously exceeds its power' (*CPR* A 786 / B 814). Reason offers only necessary conditions for thought and action – in Kant's terminology a 'Canon' for adequate thought and action (*CPR* A 795 / B 823ff.; cf. *G* 4:424). Since the non-speculative theoretical use of reason has only regulative warrant, we can aim at the systematic unity of knowledge, but only in

---

[9] We also recognise a line of argument closely parallel to some by which Kant hopes to vindicate the Categorical Imperative as conformity to law as such, and as unconditional: see e.g. *G* 4:402, 421, 431; see also Thomas E. Hill, Jr., 'Kant's argument for the rationality of moral conduct', *Pacific Philosophical Quarterly* 66 (1985), 3–23.

awareness that the ideal of completeness is not attainable (*CPR* A 568 / B 596): The regulative principles of reason serve only 'to mark out the path toward systematic unity' (*CPR* A 668 / B 696).

In the case of the spurious speculative employment of reason, we have even less than a canon. Here the discipline of reason can be used only as a dialectical 'system of precautions and self-examination' that curbs unwarranted metaphysical speculation. Kant's conception of reason cannot rehabilitate any of the speculative proofs of God's existence, although the idea of a supreme being may still be used to regulate and integrate, indeed may be needed to regulate and integrate, thinking and doing.[10]

It is neither deficiency nor inadvertence that the supreme principle of reason is 'only' *the precept of staying within the confines of some possible plan.* This modest conception of reason, which may be rendered in political metaphors as a matter of lawfulness without a lawgiver,[11] is the one presented in the *Doctrine of Method,* and the one that is adumbrated in Kant's earlier and endorsed in his later discussions of what it may take to discipline 'our adventurous and self-reliant reason' (A 850 / B 878) without kowtowing to rationally groundless authorities.

Selected corroborations of the interpretation

This reading of Kant's approach to the vindication of reason in the *Critique of Pure Reason* can be corroborated by numerous passages in other works. Kant discusses its theoretical import in the essay *What Is Orientation in Thinking?* and its practical import in many works, including *What Is Enlightenment?* The topic is handled in another way in the passages on the *sensus communis* in the *Critique of Judgement.* Here I offer only a few illustrations, beginning with some further reflections on Kant's stress on the importance of a *self-imposed plan* in the introductory paragraph of the *Doctrine of Method.*

The chastened builders of the tower of Babel, who cannot wholly turn their backs on building projects, are not forced to settle in a highly specified new building. Rather they are advised to settle on *some* feasible plan that *all* of them can share. The condition that they must meet if they are to

[10] Here I skip over a vast range of texts, including particularly Book II, ch. III, and the appendix of the *Transcendental Dialectic, CPR* A 642–704 / B 670–732 as well as the *Critique of Practical Reason* and *Religion within the Limits of Reason Alone.* See the chapters in Part IV, below.

[11] Kant uses this phrase in a different context in the *Critique of Judgement* (*CJ* 5:241), where he speaks of 'conformity to law without a law' (*Gesetzmäßigkeit ohne Gesetz*) and links its role in judgements of taste very closely to the better-known formula of 'purposefulness without purpose' (*Zweckmäßigkeit ohne Zweck*).

avoid the fate of 'nomads' – isolation, dispersal, non-communication – is to adopt *some* plan, that neither posits unavailable resources nor is unsharable with others. The advice could be rejected, and even if it is followed much will remain open. Unlike Descartes, Kant does not think that there is a unique edifice of reason, or that it could be created by any solitary builder. On Kant's account we think and act reasonably provided we neither invoke illusory capacities or authorities – that is what it is to take account of our actual resources and starting point – nor base our thinking or acting on nonlawlike, hence unsharable, principles.

These constraints allow that innumerable differing ways of thought and of life may meet the constraints of reason. Nevertheless reason constrains. Kant identifies three recurrent modes of unreason. It is unreasonable to posit capacities, insights and transcendent authorities that we lack: this is the unreason of transcendental realists, including Platonists and some fundamentalist theists. It is unreasonable to assume that thinking and acting can be wholly arbitrary or nonlawlike, as sceptics and postmodernists claim to. It is unreasonable to assume that the fundamental principles of thought and action can appeal only to some local authority, as the acolytes of *Schwärmerei* or communitarianism do. His constant insistence that reason is lawlike yet submits to no 'alien' authority summarises his rejection of these three modes of unreason. To think and act reasonably is to make sure that the basic precepts by which both are disciplined are lawlike, yet do not appeal to spurious authorities.

Second, this reading contributes to an adequate understanding of the well-known 1784 essay *What Is Enlightenment?*[12] This essay has often been condemned as a shallow defence of freedom of opinion, which endorses 'enlightened' despotism. This focus wholly fails to face the central puzzle of the text, which is that Kant equates enlightenment not with reason but with an oddly characterised practice of reasoning publicly. The essay begins by contrasting those who are unenlightened, who submit to others' authority and opinions, and those who are enlightened, in that they speak publicly in their own voice. Kant's conception of a 'public use of reason' is highly unusual: it is one that addresses 'the entire public' (yet may actually reach only 'men of learning'), whereas 'a private use of reason is that which

[12] For a more extended version of this reading of *What Is Enlightenment?* and of parallels with the slightly later *What Is Orientation in Thinking?* see Onora O'Neill, 'The public use of reason' in *Constructions of Reason* and 'Enlightenment as autonomy: Kant's vindication of reason' in Peter Hulme and Ludmila Jordanova (eds.), *The Enlightenment and Its Shadows* (London: Routledge, 1990). For historical background to *What Is Orientation in Thinking?* see Frederick Beiser, *The Fate of Reason: German Philosophy from Kant to Fichte* (Cambridge, MA: Harvard University Press, 1987).

a person may make of it in some particular civil post or office' (*WE* 8:37) – that is, what we would term a position in the *public* service. A 'public' use of reason is not defined by its large audience, and indeed cannot take place in the public service, if relations of command and obedience demand 'private' uses of reason. Kant attaches importance to 'public' uses of reason because they alone are not premised on accepting some rationally ungrounded or 'alien' authority (whether the edicts of Frederick II, political ideologies or religious dogmas). Hence they alone are full uses of reason, and 'private' uses of reason are to be understood as defective, deprived or *privatus*. Hence the essay points *away* from a conception of 'public' reason that is characteristic of public life both under enlightened despotism and in bureaucratised modern states, towards a quite different conception of what fully reasoned communication would be.[13]

No doubt the essay is too vague about the social conditions for fully 'public' reasoning. Kant does little more than gesture to two 'ideal types' of thinking and acting, in which reason is respectively fully and defectively embodied. However, the essay illuminates Kant's reasons for viewing autonomy, that is, the principle of not submitting to groundless authorities, as the core of reason, hence of enlightenment. Autonomy, as Kant understands it, is not mere self-assertion or independence, but rather thinking or acting on principles that defer to no ungrounded 'authority', hence demands principles all can follow. For Kant, autonomy is living by the principles of reason; and reason is nothing but the principle that informs practices of autonomy in thinking and doing. He does not reject the view that the Enlightenment is the movement of reason. Rather he recasts and deepens this conventional view by showing that reason, correctly understood, is the principle of thinking and acting on principles all can freely adopt.[14]

A third text that corroborates this reading is the less well known essay of 1786, *What Is Orientation in Thinking*. Here Kant asks not which principles have authority for action, but which have an unrestricted ('orienting') authority for thinking. He claims that only the principle of autonomy in

---

[13] Kant's approach here and in the passages on the *sensus communis* (discussed subsequently) are a form of discursive grounding of reason. His approach differs from (at least a standard reading of) Habermas's version of this approach in that he does not invoke an *ideal* of transparent communication, in which all discursive claims can be redeemed, but rather points to conditions for *possible* communication, leaving it open how far this will enable settlement of truth claims, moral claims or other claims.

[14] The connection drawn between reason and autonomy in *What Is Enlightenment?* and *What Is Orientation in Thinking?* provides a key to understanding the connections between reason and autonomy that structure Parts 2 and 3 of the *Groundwork*. See also the chapters in Part II below.

thinking can have any general authority; hence autonomy is all there is to reason. To reason just is to think in a lawlike (principled) way, without deference to any alien 'law'. It avoids both 'lawlessness' (i.e. nonlawlikeness) and 'submission' (i.e. to 'alien' authorities), noting that

> if reason will not subject itself to the law which it imposes on itself, it must bow beneath the yoke of laws which someone else imposes upon it; for nothing, not even the greatest absurdity, can continue to operate for very long without any law. (*WOT* 8:145; Reiss 248)

Once again, this essay makes it very clear that Kant does not think reason lives up to rationalist fantasies. Reason is indeed the basis of enlightenment, but enlightenment is no more than autonomy in thinking and in acting – that is, of thought and action that are lawful yet assume no lawgiver. Reason cannot determine everything: it provides a negative discipline for avoiding disoriented thinking, but offers no sufficient instructions for thought or action:

> *To think for oneself* means to look within oneself (i.e., in one's own reason) for the supreme touchstone of truth; and the maxim of thinking for oneself at all times is *enlightenment*. Now this requires less effort than is imagined by those who equate enlightenment with *knowledge*, for enlightenment consists rather in a negative principle in the use of one's cognitive powers; and those who are exceedingly rich in knowledge are often least enlightened in their use of it. To employ one's own reason means simply to ask oneself, whenever one is urged to accept something, whether one finds it possible to transform the reason for accepting it, or the rule that follows from what is accepted, into a universal principle governing the use of one's reason. (*WOT* 8:146–7 n.; Reiss 249 n.)[15]

Finally this minimal account of reason as lawfulness without a lawgiver – as avoiding both anarchy and submission to groundless powers – can be recognised once again in the trio of interconnected maxims that Kant groups together in section 40 of the *Critique of Judgement* (*CJ* 5:293–6) as comprising the *sensus communis*. He introduces the term *sensus communis* not simply in connection with taste, but as of far more general import:

> we assume a common sense as the necessary condition of the universal communicability of our knowledge, which is presupposed in every logic and every principle of knowledge that is not one of scepticism. (*CJ* §21, 5:239)

---

[15] Compare also the very late *Conflict of the Faculties*, where Kant writes 'the capacity to judge according to autonomy, that is freely (but in accord with the principles of thinking in general) is called reason' (*CF* 7:27; trans. OO'N).

At a later stage the three maxims of the *sensus communis* are presented as exemplifying the requirements for preserving lawlikeness without assuming a lawgiver. These are not maxims of common sense in the sense that they refer to accepted views. Rather they are maxims of

> a critical faculty which in its reflective act takes account (*a priori*) of the mode of representation of everyone else, in order, *as it were*, to weigh its judgement with the collective judgement of mankind. (*CJ* §40, 5:293)

These are maxims for a plurality-without-preestablished-harmony, that is, for a plurality of agents who, like the builders of Babel, lack a preinscribed shared plan. The three maxims enjoin such agents to think for themselves, to think from the standpoint of everyone else, and to think consistently (cf. *CJ* §40, 5:294). The first maxim proscribes submission to 'alien' authorities. Taken alone, refusal of submission might, however, lead to anarchy or to isolation. The second maxim prescribes the antidote to anarchy and isolation by requiring that agents think from the standpoint of others – that is, that their thinking be based on principles that are at least possible for others. However, any process of thought or action that is guided by the maxims both of rejecting submission and of sustaining lawlikeness – in other words, rejecting 'lawgivers' while maintaining 'lawlikeness' – will be in constant flux and revision, hence may well generate contradiction and hiatus. Hence the need for the third maxim, which enjoins a process of consistency-restoring review and revision. The third maxim, far from being trivial, is indispensable for any sustained process of thought or action that embodies the other two.

The passages on the *sensus communis* differ in many ways from Kant's discussions in other writings of a single supreme principle of reason. They distinguish different aspects of reason's task more sharply; they make more evident that the Kantian vindication of reason presupposes plurality-without-preestablished-harmony.[16] In these passages political metaphors wholly replace the metaphors of construction that predominate in the opening discussion of the *Doctrine of Method*. The political metaphors offer particularly apt ways of characterising modes of unreason. To reject the first maxim is to submit either to the powers that be or to supposed transcendent realities; it is to fantasise and defer to some 'authoritative'

---

[16] It follows that, despite long traditions of reading Kant as presenting a 'philosophy of the subject', his starting point is rather that of plurality. This raises very large issues about the proper evaluation of Kant's critique of rational psychology and his own account of subjectivity, which must be left aside here. Kant's distinctiveness lies in the fact that his discursive grounding of reason presupposes plurality, and the possibility of community; it does not presuppose 'atomistic' subjects, actual communities or ideal communities.

lawgiver. To reject the second maxim is to assume that the basic principles of thinking and doing need not be followable by others – that they
can be lawless rather than lawlike. To reject the third maxim is to fail
to integrate the demands of rejecting illusory lawgivers and of sustaining
lawlikeness. Taken in conjunction, the three maxims define constraints for
a dynamic process in which the demand for lawfulness without a lawgiver
can be realised among a plurality. Reason is here sketched not as abstract
principle, but as the lawlike guidance of thinking and doing in a dynamic
process that neither submits to outside control nor fails to acknowledge differences of opinion and practice, and which treats resulting contradictions
and tensions as demanding revision.

Confirmations and objections

This interpretation of Kant's vindication of reason construes reason as the
principle of guiding thinking and doing in ways that others too can follow,
granted that no coordination with others is given from 'outside' by any
'alien' authority. Of course, this is only the supreme principle of reason, and
it would have to be elaborated in a vast range of more specific principles,
which could be embodied in varied social and cognitive practices. More
specific principles could be derived from the supreme principle of reason
by showing either that their denials assume some 'alien' authority, or that
they are not lawlike, so cannot be followed by others. Such principles
would have to count as unreasonable; their rejection would constitute the
adoption of subordinate principles of reason. This strategy *may* enable
Kant to show that principles of logic or of duty, or Ideas or Postulates of
Reason, are indeed subsidiary requirements of reason; however, his account
of the vindication of the supreme principle of reason cannot establish which
derivations along these lines will work, and I cannot here go far into the
success of his many attempts to identify subordinate principles of reason.

A few more general issues can, however, be dealt with. First, to what
extent do the objections that have been raised against supposed vindications
of reason hold against Kant's position? Does he invoke arbitrary starting
points? Is his attempt at vindication circular? Is it an unending regress?

First, his starting point. Kant does not begin from supposed axioms of
reason, of logic or of method, but rather from the unsatisfying character of
daily attempts to reason. From a supposed divine perspective, these starting
points might indeed be arbitrary. However, that perspective is unavailable
to us – and nobody who enjoys it has to worry about vindicating reason.
We, however, have no choice but to start from our predicament. For Kant

this starting point serves to pose the problem rather than to provide axioms or foundations for its resolution.

Second, Kant's proposed solution is circular in the sense that he quite deliberately identifies the vindication of reason with a reflexive process, in which the indispensable elements for the *self*-discipline of thought and action are principles that are not 'alien', hence groundless, authorities. To become (more fully) reasonable is to discipline available attempts at reasoning by available modes of reasoning. In keeping with this, Kant holds that reason progresses and has a history.

Third, Kant's proposed vindication of reason is indeed open-ended. A discipline is not a proof but a practice, in this case a practice for regulating thinking and doing. Moreover, because this discipline constrains but does not generate what count as reasoned ways of thought and life, the task of reason cannot be defined in terms of some final product – a completed edifice of reason, comprising a finished system of all truths – but only in terms of a process of subjecting proposed thought and action to the discipline. Reason dictates neither thought nor action; its discipline is construed as process, not as the once and for all discovery of secure foundations.

Kant's vindication of reason may then seem to incur not just one but all three of the catastrophes from which attempts to vindicate reason are said to suffer. However, here appearances mislead. Unvindicated axioms, circular argument or unending regress would each constitute catastrophe for an attempt to provide foundations for reason; but Kant makes no such attempt. His initial hypothesis, the Copernican turn, repudiates foundationalism. In its stead he offers considerations about ways in which processes of thought and action must be disciplined if they are not to count as unreasoned. To appreciate his alternative vision we have to shed foundationalist expectations and try to assess this account of how we might construct principles that are authoritative for all thinking and doing, granted that such authority can neither be conferred nor be imposed.

For anyone who shares Kant's doubts about forms of foundationalism, this programme will have many attractions. However, some will fear that the conception of reason that he vindicates, far from being too ambitious – as its rationalist predecessors so plainly were – is so minimal that it can have no significant role. If the whole huge critical undertaking is only going to get us this far, then might not Kant just as well have conceded quite explicitly that he was undertaking neither critique nor vindication of reason and recognised that he was a sceptic – or indeed the first postmodernist? On this point I offer one historical and one systematic thought.

The historical thought is that Kant could hardly have attacked the tradition that had fused Platonist and Christian origins into rationalist metaphysics simply by rejecting its aspirations. If such strategies were available to Derrida or to Rorty, it was in part because they wrote as post-Kantians, as Nietzsche already did, and attacked only a profoundly damaged metaphysical tradition.

The systematic thought is that only detailed investigation can show whether and how far principles of knowledge or morality or postulates of hope can be derived from the supreme principle of reason. Even if such investigations can establish some subordinate principles of reason, still these constraints will not fully determine knowledge, action or hope. To those who expect reason to determine everything, this may seem a deeply disappointing failure. If Kant is right, such disappointment is itself a symptom of undisciplined metaphysical passions (cf. *CPR* A 786 / B 814). Even if reason is 'only' a 'system of constraints', these may prove a demanding discipline for thought, for action and for hope.

Although this cannot be shown without undertaking the detailed investigations, the point may be illustrated by the case of principles of logic. Rationalists expected logic to offer us algorithms for knowing, rules that offer complete instructions for handling every case that falls under them, and that could in principle be used to generate the system of truth. Indeed, it is because formulae of logic and of mathematics are our paradigm algorithms that we may be led to think that this must be where we should look for indubitable foundations for systematic thought and knowledge. However, when we reflect about the standing of such formulae, it becomes clear that they cannot provide indubitable foundations for actual thinking and doing, unless not only the abstract formulae, but their application to cases, are algorithmic. However, applications of algorithmic formulae are not algorithms. Kant insists on this as firmly as Wittgenstein does. He points out that 'general logic can supply no rules for judgement' (*CPR* A 135 / B 174). If 'general logic' cannot supply rules for judgement, it cannot provide a foundation for thinking, for doing, or for the structure of hope that Kant believes articulates underlying links between the domains of thought and action.

The first question that we must raise about (general) logic is rather whether actual cognitive processes provide the vindication for its abstract formulae, or the other way round. The question cannot be answered by thinking of the vindication of logical or mathematical formulae as internal to a system of formulae. To do so only raises the question of the vindication of the formal system. However, if we think of such formulae or systems of formulae as having wider validity, as authoritative for any process of thought or action, we must either assume that they have the type of vindication foundationalists aspire to, or accept that their vindication derives from that which we can offer for these processes of thought and action. Such a constructivist vindication of formulae of logic would then have to begin by seeing which supposed logical principles could be rejected and which could not, without our thinking and doing precipitating itself into 'darkness and contradiction' and consequent frustrations (*CPR* A vii / B xiv). Such a line of thought might reveal the difference between a Principle of Sufficient Reason, which indeed leads into problems, and a Principle of Noncontradiction, whose rejection leads into problems. Only principles of the latter sort could count as subordinate principles of reason. Only they might point away from the predicament in which 'ever and again we have to retrace our steps, as not leading us in the direction in which we desire to go' (*CPR* B xiv).

The Kantian approach to the vindication of reason is fundamentally a modest affair. It does not disclose any hidden route back to the Principle of Sufficient Reason. The heroic challenges of rationalist demands to ground reason are rejected, as are their difficulties. All that is vindicated is a precept of thinking and doing without relying on any fundamental principle which either presupposes some arbitrary 'authority', or cannot be followed by others. Minimal indeed, but far from empty. Any form of relativism that 'submits' to some arbitrary power (state, church, majority, public opinion, ideology or dictator) as the source of reason is rejected. So is any form of rationalism that 'submits' to supposed divine or other 'necessities'. So is any form of scepticism or postmodernism that equates 'reason' with happenstantially available ways of thought. Within these constraints we may be able to work out how far the Kantian conception of reason guides and constrains what we can know, what we ought to do, and what we may hope.

CHAPTER 2

Kant: rationality as practical reason[1]

Kant is famous for undertaking a critique of reason and for calling two of his most significant works *critiques of reason*.[2] These titles raise suspicions. Does Kant genuinely criticise reason, thereby calling into question the very processes by which any reasoned thought or action – including any criticism of reason – should be conducted? Or does he give these pretentious titles to works that deploy rather than criticise reason? Indeed, could anything really, seriously count either as a *critique* of reason or as a *vindication* of reason? Isn't the very idea that we could *show* that certain ways of thinking or acting are reasoned or reasonable absurd? After all, the demonstration must either build on assumptions that lack reasoned vindication, or be supported by arguments that deploy the very conception of reason supposedly vindicated. So it will be either unreasoned or circular: either way it will fail to vindicate reason. We have grounds for suspecting that no ways of organising thinking or acting have unconditional authority, and that Kant *cannot* have vindicated reason.

Kant's attempt to give an account of practical reason that offers unconditional reasons for action and provides the basis for a reasoned account of human duties is spectacularly ambitious: even if it fails in some ways it is worth the closest attention. Here I aim to give as coherent account of that attempt as I can offer, although I shall say nothing about the connections Kant draws between practical and theoretical reason.[3] Since practical

---

[1] First published as 'Kant: rationality as practical reason' in Alfred J. Mele and Piers Rawling (eds.), *The Oxford Handbook of Rationality* (Oxford University Press, 2004), 93–109. Unlike 'Vindicating reason', above, this chapter concentrates on practical uses of reason.

[2] References to Kant's works use the abbreviations listed in the Bibliographical Note, Part 1, and the page numbers of the Prussian Academy of Sciences edition, which are given in the margins of each translation.

[3] See Susan Neiman, *The Unity of Reason* (Oxford University Press, 1994); Onora O'Neill, *Constructions of Reason: Explorations of Kant's Practical Philosophy* (Cambridge University Press, 1989), and 'Vindicating reason', Chapter 1 above; Paul Guyer, 'Kant's deductions of the principles of right' in Mark Timmons (ed.), *Kant's Metaphysics of Morals: Interpretative Essays* (Oxford University Press, 2002), 23–64.

reasoning aims to shape and select action, I begin with a short account of Kant's views on action.

Practical reasoning and the agent perspective

Agents use practical reasoning to shape or guide their future action. Since practical reason has to bear on action yet to be done, it cannot bear on act *tokens*: there are no relevant, individuable act tokens at the time that practical reasoning takes place. So practical reasoning has to bear on *act types* (including *types of attitude*). It might be used to provide reasons for thinking that certain types of action or attitude are required or forbidden, recommended or inadvisable.

As Kant sees it, types of action are specified by act descriptions, while normative claims are expressed in principles that incorporate act descriptions. Agents may consider, explore, test, adopt or reject practical principles. Kant speaks of the principle an agent adopts as *determining an agent's will*: it fixes – in the sense of *making determinate* rather than of *causing* – some aspects of the action or attitude to which an agent is committed. Kant calls the more significant determinations of an agent's will *maxims* (*G* 4:402 n., 4:421 n.; *CPrR* 5:19), which he sees as the practical analogues of *beliefs*. Individuals may *believe* a theoretical claim or proposition at or for some time; they may make a practical proposition their *maxim* at or for some time. Like beliefs, maxims have propositional structure and content, so are apt for reasoning. Kant's most basic thought about practical reason is that reasoning can bear on action because it is formed or shaped by maxims, which have propositional structure and content.

In classifying only the more general principles that agents adopt as maxims, Kant is true to the etymology of the term. A maxim is the *maxima propositio*, a high- or highest-level proposition determining an agent's will at some time. The maxim an agent adopts will govern and inform other more specific decisions and aspects of his or her action or attitudes. For example, anybody who has adopted a maxim of not deceiving others is likely to express it in refraining from lying, in restraint in gossip, in care about checking facts and many other ways. Maxims can be for the long or the short term. They may be deeply entrenched in an agent's character or in the constitution of a collective agent (*R* 6:89), or adopted in face of a particular situation or for a short period. Kant usually speaks of agents as adopting a range of distinct maxims at a given time, but in a few passages he suggests that we can speak of the *deepest* or *most fundamental* principle of a person's character as a single maxim that governs their adoption of other more specific maxims, and thereby their entire life, often for a prolonged period.[4] However, maxims are always adopted (and discardable,) so something for which agents are responsible and which they might change.

There have been many discussions of the ways by which we may know Kantian maxims.[5] On some readings of Kant, agents are conscious of their maxims and know them by introspection. However, this interpretation is hard to reconcile with Kant's views of the limits of human self-knowledge: he claims that we are not transparent to ourselves, but rather opaque (*G* 4:406–12). Hence the notorious passages in which he points out that we cannot *know* whether there has ever been a *truly* loyal friend, or that we have acted *purely* for the sake of duty (*G* 4:407–8).[6] On other views, maxims are ascribed to agents on the basis of a range of evidence, of which introspective evidence forms at most part. Both introspective and ascriptive views of knowledge of maxims focus on the *retrospective*, usually *third person* task of identifying the maxim(s) on which an act was done. In concentrating on the methods by which we can discover which maxim(s) are held by an agent at some time, they overlook the fact that the main task of practical reasoning is *prospective*. In reasoning about action we consider maxims that could be adopted, viewing them as principles or prescriptions for whose adoption reasons might – or might not – be found. A prospective and prescriptive account of maxims provides the basis not for discovering which maxim(s) an agent actually adopts on a given occasion, but for determining which maxim an agent has reason to adopt. The basic task of practical reasoning is to guide action rather than to adjudicate past acts.

Since Kant takes a prospective and practical approach (to reasoning about action) he can largely avoid the problem of showing how we are to discover agents' maxims, or work out the 'relevant' description for any act. When we try to assess action retrospectively, we have to work out which of many descriptions and principles satisfied by a given act is relevant for assessment. If assessment is undertaken for some specific purpose, such as financial audit or legal judgement, conformity or lack of conformity to relevant descriptions can be judged. And if the main aim of moral assessment were to judge agents' maxims retrospectively, we would apparently need a general way of finding out what maxims they have

4 See the discussion of making either the moral law or self-love one's most fundamental maxim and so determining one's basic disposition, *R* 6:22ff.
5 Barbara Herman, *The Practice of Moral Judgement* (Cambridge, MA: Harvard University Press, 2002); O'Neill, *Constructions of Reason;* Jens Timmermann, 'Kant's puzzling ethic of maxims', *Harvard Philosophy Review* 8, no. 1 (2000), 39–52.
6 See Marcia Baron, *Kantian Ethics Almost without Apology* (Ithaca, NY: Cornell University Press, 1995).

'really' adopted. Kant says a good deal about retrospective judgement of action in his discussions of reflective judgement,[7] but unlike some leading writers on moral perception, appraisal or judgement,[8] he assigns priority to prospective, practical reasoning rather than to a retrospective, spectator perspective on action or ethics.

The potential maxims on which agents may bring practical reasoning to bear may be of many sorts. They do not have to be morally admirable: for example, Kant discusses a group of hard-bitten 'sophistical' maxims of political expediency.[9] A neutral view of the moral status of maxims is appropriate: if practical reasoning is to show why we should adopt some rather than other principles as maxims, setting prior limits on which principles are to be adopted as maxims would beg questions. Nor does Kant propose a method for ensuring that agents assemble all possible maxims for consideration. Agents may well fail to consider some principles that they have reason to adopt as maxims. However, Kant takes it that agents are not likely to be systematically blind to the central principles of duty, which are repeatedly relevant to decisions and action.

Hypothetical Imperatives

Some commentators have imagined that since Kant holds that practical reasoning can set unconditional requirements (so is a *Categorical Imperative*), he must deny that practical reasoning sets conditional requirements. Such a position would, of course, be absurd. Reasoning cannot guide action – cannot be *practical* – without taking a view of the connections between types of action and types of effect, between means and ends, between action and world.

Kant's account of instrumental reasoning is adjusted to his view that reasoning bears (in the first instance) on potential determinations of the will or maxims, and thence on action. He speaks of the fundamental principle of instrumental reasoning as the *Principle of Hypothetical Imperatives*, and formulates it as an abstract principle for rational willing. Hypothetical Imperatives 'represent the practical necessity of a possible action as a means to achieving something else that one wills (or that is at least possible for one

---

[7] In reflective judging 'only the particular is given, for which the universal is to be found' (*CJ* 5:180).

[8] David Wiggins, 'Deliberation and practical reason' in his *Needs, Values, Truth: Essays in the Philosophy of Values* (Oxford: Blackwell, 1987), 215–37; John McDowell, 'Deliberation and moral development' in Stephen Engstrom and J. Whiting (eds.), *Aristotle, Kant and the Stoics* (Cambridge University Press, 1996), 19–35.

[9] They include 'Fac et Excusa'; 'Si fecisti, nega' and 'Divide et impera' (*PP* 8:374–5).

to will)' (*G* 4:414; also *G* 4:414–19; *CPrR* 5:19–20).[10] This principle requires commitment to the maxim 'Whosoever wills the end also wills (insofar as reason has decisive influence on these actions) the indispensable necessary means to it that are within his power' (*G* 4:417).

Kant argues that those hypothetical imperatives that supposedly guide the pursuit of happiness do not, strictly speaking, set *requirements* for action. Happiness is an indeterminate ideal – an 'ideal of the imagination' (*G* 4:418) – so means-end reasoning directed at the pursuit of happiness yields at most approximate, *pragmatic imperatives* or *counsels of prudence*. These commend ways of living that generally conduce to happiness, such as 'frugality, courtesy, reserve, and so forth' (*G* 4:418). Other hypothetical imperatives are grounded in technical and causal requirements. They set genuine requirements, but only for those pursuing specific ends. Kant speaks of them as *technical imperatives* or *rules of skill*. Rules of skill are morally neutral: knowing the effects of poisons is as useful to poisoners as it is to physicians (*G* 4:415).

Kant's account of means-ends reasoning is clearly less ambitious than those favoured in many contemporary accounts of rational choice. He does not assume that we can list 'options' exhaustively, that we have complete or even very extensive knowledge of causal connections or probabilities, or that there is a metric for ranking or aggregating the value of ends. His account of instrumental reasoning does not provide enough structure for much in the way of judgements of efficiency, and says little about the distinction between willing necessary and sufficient means. On the other hand, he also does not place the entire burden of practical reasoning on means-ends reasoning.

Categorical Imperatives: universal law

In every area of life, instrumental reasoning is undertaken in pursuit of agents' chosen ends: these choices orient and require determinate means-ends reasoning. However, on Kant's account, specifically moral reasoning needs more than a combination of chosen ends and means-ends rationality. Those who hope to get by on this basis will defend some form of 'heteronomy in ethics'.[11] They choose to make some intrinsically arbitrary ends the basis of their ethical reasoning. Their choices may

---

[10] See also Thomas E. Hill, Jr., *Dignity and Practical Reason* (Ithaca, NY: Cornell University Press, 1992), chs. 1 and 7; Allen Wood, *Kant's Ethical Thought* (Cambridge University Press, 1999).

[11] See the discussion on heteronomy and autonomy in ethics at *G* 4:440–4 and that of public and private uses of reason in *WE* 8:35–42, and the chapters in Part II below.

variously endorse or defer to self-interest, religious dogma, established ideology, community 'values' or some version of self-development. Even those who propose an account of human flourishing or happiness as the foundation and context for moral reasoning do not escape this arbitrariness, given that they lack an adequately determinate account of human happiness or flourishing. Kant's claims about the arbitrariness of heteronomous ethics are not hard to appreciate. Yet the thought that there could be any way of avoiding heteronomy in ethics looks quite implausible. How can there be *any* unconditional requirements on action? What reason have we to think that there is anything that could count as the rejection of heteronomy in ethics – as *autonomy in ethics*?

Kant's answers to these questions can be found mainly in the *Critique of Practical Reason* and the *Groundwork of the Metaphysics of Morals*, although significant additional analyses and comments occur throughout his later writings on ethics, politics, religion and history. His thoughts are often difficult to follow, in part because he offers several seemingly distinct (yet supposedly equivalent) formulations of the supreme principle of practical reasoning, the Categorical Imperative. I shall begin with some comments on the well-known *Formula of Universal Law* (FUL), the formulation most closely linked to Kant's attempted vindication of practical reason. Finally, I will comment on some of the other formulations and on Kant's claims about their equivalence.

FUL proposes a doubly modal requirement as the basis for moral reasoning. Its best-known version runs: *Act only in accordance with that maxim through which you can at the same time will that it become a universal law* (*G* 4:421). Many commentators – not least among them John Stuart Mill – have claimed that this is too little. Despite his protestations, Kant must in the end go beyond the modal demand set out in FUL if his conception of practical reason is to guide action. Surely almost any maxim that *can* be adopted by an individual agent *can* also be adopted by all agents? The only maxims that cannot be adopted by all are, it may seem, those that are intrinsically incoherent, so cannot really be adopted by individuals either (e.g. a maxim of being a popular recluse). Even maxims that refer to positional goods (e.g. a maxim of becoming richer than everyone else) could be *adopted* by all, although failure to achieve the maxim's aim would be guaranteed for all but the most successful agent. It seems that a requirement to act only on maxims that can be willed as universal laws cuts little ice.

Such criticisms oversimplify Kant's account of FUL. Kant views FUL as demanding that an agent be *able to will* the maxim he or she proposes to adopt 'as a universal law'. Willing is not merely a matter of *thinking* or of *wishing* some practical proposition; it is matter of making a certain proposition one's maxim, of adopting it as a determination of one's will, and this means engaging with the demands of the *Principle of Hypothetical Imperatives* (G 4:394). Willing a maxim 'as a universal law', although only a hypothetical test (I cannot *literally* will for others), requires agents to consider whether everyone *could make the proposed maxim the determination of his or her will*, so must engage (hypothetically!) with the demands of the Principle of Hypothetical Imperatives.

When I will a maxim 'as a universal law' I do not (even hypothetically!) will that *everyone act on the maxim* at some moment, or at all moments. Very many practical principles, including principles of great and of trivial moral significance, cannot be acted on by everybody at any one time and place. If everyone tries to help a drowning child or to swim across a river simultaneously, overcrowding and mutual obstruction would guarantee that some cannot act. Kant's question is whether *everyone could will a maxim*. There is nothing incoherent in everyone *willing* to rescue a drowning child or to swim across a river, or even a particular river – but not everyone can act simultaneously on either principle in a given location. (Anyone who wills a child's rescue will remain on the shore if wading in would obstruct the rescue.)

At this juncture it may seem that the demand that agents act only on maxims that they can will as universal laws fails to guide action for quite a different reason. Its problem is not that it is 'too specific', that it rules out each determinate act as impermissible on the grounds that nothing can be done by everyone at a given time and place. Its problem is that it is 'too general', since it requires only that agents can *adopt* maxims that could be adopted by all, so perhaps rules out nothing. Surely, if *anyone* can adopt a practical principle, then *everyone* can adopt it.

Kant thinks that this is not the case. Some principles can readily be adopted by a given agent or a minority of agents, *but only on the assumption that they are not adopted by all others*. For example, adopting a maxim of promising falsely commits an agent to supporting means to promising falsely, hence to maintaining enough public trust for promises to gain acceptance. But willing false promising 'as a universal law' (*per impossibile*) commits an agent to willing the consequences of universal false promising, which include the destruction of trust, hence is incompatible with willing any reliable means to false promising – for oneself or for others. That is why Kant thinks that we *cannot* will false promising, coercion and many other types of action that victimise others 'as universal laws'. He points out that we do not even pretend to do this:

std of care it to ensure effects/pain in the past are causing the conflicts/ Now. That they have the same cause – What was causing the conflict/ Our the past

If we now attend to ourselves whenever we transgress a duty we find that we do not in fact will that our maxim should become a universal law – since this is impossible for us – but rather that its opposite should remain a law universally: we only take the liberty of making an exception to it for ourselves or even just for this once. (*G* 4:424)

But why is rejecting maxims that cannot be willed 'as universal laws' a formula for identifying *duties*? Even if we accept that FUL appears to show that some maxims of false promising cannot be 'willed as universal laws' – cannot be universalised – is this more than a curiosity? Why should we think that FUL picks out principles of action that we ought not to adopt? And even if it does, why should we think that it is a version of the 'supreme principle of morality'? And why, above all, should we think that this curious formula is the fundamental principle of practical reason? Further, why should we think that the other formulations of the Categorical Imperative, which Kant claims are equivalent to FUL, are also versions of the supreme principle of morality and of the fundamental principle of practical reason?

Universal law as a principle of practical reason

Before turning to the other formulations of the Categorical Imperative I shall consider why Kant sees FUL as (one version of) the supreme principle of practical reason. Kant's claims about practical reason can seem bombastic: phrases such as 'the supreme principle of practical reason' arouse suspicion. Yet Kant is very cautious about what reason, including the practical use of reason, can provide.

This caution about the authority of reason is expressed in vivid terms in the prefaces and introduction of the *Critique of Pure Reason*. As Kant sees it, we do not even know where or how to begin the 'tasks of reason'. Reason is not *given* to us; it is not 'whole and complete in each of us', as Descartes supposed.[12] We constantly find ourselves using ways of thinking and acting that we speak of as reasoned; but we also find that daily reasoning goes horribly wrong. Particularly when we seek to extend our reasoning beyond experience, and aspire to reach metaphysical conclusions, we constantly find that *EXTEND OUR THINKING BEYOND EXPERIENCE*

[12] René Descartes, 1637, 'Discourse on the method of rightly Conducting One's Reason and Seeking the Truth in the Sciences' in John Cottingham, Robert Stoothof and Dugald Murdoch (trans.), *Philosophical Writings of Descartes*, Vol. I (Cambridge University Press, 1985).

> We have to retrace our path countless times, because... [reason] does not lead where we want to go, and it is so far from reaching unanimity in the assertions of its adherents that it is rather a battlefield... Still more, how little cause have we to place trust in our reason if in one of the most important parts of our desire for knowledge it does not merely forsake us but even entices us with delusions and in the end betrays us! (*CPR* B xv; see also A viii; B xiv)

As is well known, Kant's central proposal for bringing the weary battles of metaphysics to an end is to insist that human reason cannot give us a route to knowledge that reaches beyond possible experience and the presuppositions of experience.

He insists that we must be wary of what we take to be the powers of human reason, and put them too to the test. Reason itself must be judged and scrutinised:

> Reason should take on anew the most difficult of all its tasks, namely that of self-knowledge, and institute a court of justice by which reason may secure its rightful claims, while dismissing all its groundless pretensions... this court is none other that the *critique of pure reason* itself. (*CPR* A xii)

Yet the idea of vindicating reason by appeal to a 'court' or 'tribunal' can seem absurd. What procedures of judging could have the status to determine what does and what does not qualify and count as reasoning? Since there is no more general or fundamental claim to authority in organising thinking and acting than an appeal to reason, how can reason itself be judged? How can any 'tribunal of reason' have standing to judge the competence and limits of reason? And how, if reason cannot be judged, can appeals to reason gain any authority? Perhaps the daring and demanding thought that reason lacks credentials leads to the conclusion with which postmodernists flirt: perhaps what passes for reason among us has no authority at all.

Kant's move at this point[13] has seemingly become more familiar during the last thirty years through the work of John Rawls, Jürgen Habermas, Thomas Scanlon and others. He proposes a *justification* or *vindication* of reason, rather than a *proof* or *foundation* for reason. Justification differs from proof in that it is directed to some audience: and unconditional justification must be directed to audiences without assuming that they meet any specific conditions, so must be accessible to all agents. Procedures that can serve to reach a limited audience who share a particular conception of the world (perhaps embodied in shared beliefs or prejudices, in shared community or

---

[13] Kant makes the same move in his account of freedom, for which he offers a *vindication* or *defence* rather than a proof. See *G* 4:445–63.

citizenship) can at best have restricted authority.[14] At most they can provide a basis for parochial, conditional reasoning. By contrast, unconditional reasons must be fit to reach 'the world' (*WE* 8:38; in other translations 'the world at large'), rather than a restricted audience with whom an agent happens to share much. Reasoning that can reach only a restricted audience is incomplete or conditional: Kant calls it *private* or *heteronomous* reasoning. Reasoning that can reach the world at large is unconditional: Kant calls it *public* or *autonomous* reasoning. The fundamental move on which Kant's vindication of reason depends is the requirement that it be *fit for universal use*, rather than adapted to some restricted audience. By contrast, appeals to any local, restricted consensus or agreement would provide only parochial, limited and conditional reasons for action.

Those who aspire to offer reasons to unrestricted audiences, so assume no prior conditions that secure agreement, face a hard task. Their attempts at reasoning will fail unless they ensure that their proposals are accessible to an unrestricted audience.[15] Those who propose *reasons to accept certain beliefs* to 'the world at large' must ensure that all others can in principle *follow* the moves that they make in presenting their thoughts: they must aim for intelligibility, without overtly or covertly assuming prior agreement. Those who propose *reasons for acting* to 'the world at large' must aim not only for intelligibility: they must propose principles of action that others not merely can follow in thought, but could adopt as principles of action. I do not offer reasons for action to all if I propose principles of action that I know some others *cannot* adopt. Another way of putting this requirement is to say that those who seek to offer practical reasons to an unrestricted audience must *Act only in accordance with that maxim through which [they] can at the same time will that it become a universal law* (*G* 4:421). FUL states (a version of) the supreme principle of practical reason because it states the condition for anything to count as a reason for action for an audience about whom we make no special, restrictive assumptions. It is therefore a requirement for giving unconditional reasons for action, a Categorical Imperative for the adoption of maxims. The underlying reason why Kant thinks that practical reasoning has to propose maxims that are fit to be

[14] Kant would therefore be unconvinced by John Rawls's conception of the reasonable as a form of public reason shared by fellow citizens within a bounded democratic society. He would think it inadequate as vindication of reason because it presupposes and does not justify bounded territories, citizenship and democracy. See 'Autonomy and public reason in Kant, Habermas and Rawls', Chapter 8 below.

[15] Accessibility is not the same as motivational sufficiency. For discussion of the motivational claims of Kant's view of practical reason see Christine Korsgaard, *Creating the Kingdom of Ends* (Cambridge University Press, 1996, esp. ch. 11).

universal laws is *that no other maxims can coherently be offered as reasons to all.* At most they could be coherently be offered as reasons to a restricted range of agents who accept *some further, rationally ungrounded assumption or attitude.*

Universal law and moral duties

If practical reason amounts to a demand to act only on principles that have the form of law, that can be principles for all, it offers only an *indirect* and *incomplete* standard for morality. I shall consider the implications of offering an *indirect* standard of morality in this section, and those of offering an *incomplete* standard, below (pp. 50–1).

FUL provides only an *indirect* standard for guiding action since it identifies principles that ought to be rejected, rather than principles that ought to be adopted, or that it would be good to adopt. However, knowing that some principles ought to be rejected can guide action. If I know that a principle of revenge cannot be universalised, I have reason to reject a maxim of revenge. If I know that a principle of coercing others cannot be universalised, I have reason to reject a maxim of coercion.

Such reasons are, however, less than conclusive. It is sometimes impossible, hence not obligatory, to refrain wholly from types of action whose maxims we have reason to reject. For example, Kant as is well known, doubts whether human society can exist without some coercion: he is neither a pacifist nor an anarchist. Rather he argues that the very principle of rejecting coercion cannot be respected without using some coercion. A just political system not merely *may* but *must* coerce to limit coercion, and more generally hinder freedom in order to limit hindrances to freedom (*MM* 6:230–3).[16] In acting on a maxim of rejecting coercion we have to deploy certain very specific forms of coercion. In identifying principles that we cannot universalise, so have reason to reject, Kant does not commit himself to principles of duty that are blind to circumstances and realities, or deny the possibility of conflicts between the various claims of (one or more) moral principles.

FUL can be used to identify further principles of action that cannot be willed as universal laws. Principles of doing violence, of victimising, or of

---

[16] See also Herman, *The Practice of Moral Judgement*; Leslie Mulholland, *Kant's System of Rights* (New York: Columbia University Press, 1990); Katrin Flikschuh, *Kant and Modern Political Philosophy* (Cambridge University Press, 2000); Guyer, 'Kant's deductions of the principles of right' in Mark Timmons (ed.), *Kant's Metaphysics of Morals: Interpretative Essays* (Oxford University Press, 2002).

undermining others' capacities to act in other ways, cannot coherently be willed as universal laws because their universal adoption (*per impossibile*) would predictably undercut the possibility of adopting those very principles for at least some others.[17] Those who adopt such principles in effect view themselves as enjoying exceptional moral status: they may know that their maxims cannot serve as principles for all, but see this as irrelevant because they do not view all others as their moral equals. On Kant's view, reasons for rejecting principles of action that cannot be universalised enable us to identify the fundamental principles of duty.

Kant divides basic duties into two classes, identified respectively by what he terms the *contradiction in conception* and *contradiction in the will* applications of FUL:

> We must *be able to will* that a maxim of our action becomes a universal law: this is the canon of moral appraisal of action in general. Some actions are so constituted that their maxims cannot even be *thought* without contradiction as a universal law of nature . . . In the case of others that inner impossibility is indeed not to be found, but it is still impossible to *will* that their maxim be raised to the universality of a law of nature because such a will would contradict itself. (*G* 4:424)

The *contradiction in thought* (or *in conception*) test identifies maxims of *strict (narrow, perfect) duty*, including duties of justice. It picks out maxims of action that cannot coherently be thought of as principles for all. The contradiction in the will test identifies maxims of *wide (imperfect) duty*, including duties of virtue. It picks out maxims that can coherently be *thought of* as principles for all, but cannot be *willed as* principles for all in a world of interacting agents. For example, Kant thinks that *taken in isolation* a maxim of mutual indifference or a maxim of neglecting to develop any skills or talents could consistently be universalised: they pass the *contradiction in conception* test. But nobody can consistently will that these principles be universally adopted in any world of interacting agents whose members must (by the fact that they are instrumentally rational) will to receive others' help and to rely on others' skills if and when their own are insufficient: they fail the contradiction in the will test.

The contradiction in the will test can be looked at in more than one way. On a minimal reading it is a matter of prudence. No reasonable agent who acknowledges *her own* finitude and vulnerability, and consequent inability to achieve all her ends unaided, can coherently will to be part of a

---

[17] See Herman, *The Practice of Moral Judgement*; Baron, *Kantian Ethics Almost without Apology*; O'Neill, *Constructions of Reason*.

world of agents who are indifferent to others' needs or who systematically neglect to develop human skills: in doing so she would flout the demands of instrumental rationality. On a wider reading, no reasonable agent who acknowledges *others'* finitude and vulnerability, so knows that nobody can achieve all their ends without help, can will universal indifference to human needs or to the development of human skills. Willing universal mutual indifference amounts to willing a world in which agency and capacities fail for some or many, so undermining action. For similar reasons, no rational agent can consistently will universal failure to develop skills. Willing universal failure to develop skills amounts to willing a world in which some or many find their capacities to act at risk. Kant, of course, acknowledges that some *individuals* may get away with large amounts of indifference to others, and with failure to develop skills: free riders often get away with it. He denies, plausibly enough, that we can will either sort of free riding as a universal law for a world of interacting agents.

Universal principles and judging cases

Arguments from FUL to these broad principles of duty also offer a very *incomplete* standard for morality. The perennial allegation that Kantian practical reason is *too abstract* or *too formalistic* sees this incompleteness as a serious defect. The charge of *formalism* is that Kant identifies only very general principles of duty, whereas we need to know just what to do in particular circumstances. Kant himself pointed this out:

> A physician, a judge or a ruler may have at command many excellent pathological, legal or political rules, even to the degree that he may become a profound teacher of them, and yet, none the less, may easily stumble in their application. For, although admirable in understanding, he may be wanting in natural power of judgement. He may comprehend the universal *in abstracto* and yet not be able to distinguish whether a case *in concreto* comes under it. (*CPR* A 134 / B 173)

Discussions of judgement, including practical judgement, are ubiquitous in Kant's writings. He never assumes agents can move from principles of duty, or from other principles of action, to selecting a highly specific act in particular circumstances without any process of judgement. He is as firm as any devotee of Aristotelian *phronesis* in maintaining that principles of action are not algorithms, and do not entail their own applications. There has been a good deal of discussion of the details of Kant's views on practical, including ethical, judgement. His discussions of these topics are numerous, complex and perhaps most abundant in the *Metaphysics of*

Morals, which addresses many aspects of practical judgement, including deliberation, casuistry and conflicts of obligation.

A second version of the charge that Kant's ethics is seriously incomplete objects that it is possible to devise artfully tailored maxims that can be willed as universal laws, but are morally obnoxious.[18] For example, instead of testing a general maxim of revenge or false promising, as Kant does, we might test maxims permitting persons of specific sorts or status to exact revenge or to promise falsely, knowing that deception or revenge by narrowly specified categories of agents could be willed as universal laws without contradiction. Such proposals for undercutting the implications of Kant's ethics overlook two difficulties. First, they are based on according some people exceptional moral status, denied to others, so reject Kant's fundamental view that human beings are moral equals. Second, those who advance it fail to note that basic principles of duty do not fall away when we consider a more closely specified line of action. The general duty to reject revenge does not fall away just because a proposed act of revenge falls under more specific descriptions and principles; a general duty of fidelity does not evaporate because an agent is tempted by a scam that is open to few.

Universal laws and ends in themselves

Perhaps the most mysterious feature of the Categorical Imperative is that Kant formulates it in several distinct ways that look quite different, but which he claims are equivalent. It is common to group the various formulations under four or five headings. Here I shall discuss the well-known *Formula of the End in Itself* (FEI) and *Formula of Autonomy* (FA), but say nothing specifically about the *Formula of the Law of Nature* (FLN) and the *Formula of the Kingdom of Ends* (FKE). There are two reasons, considerations of space apart. Most immediately, I bracket FLN because it is in many respects similar to FUL, and FKE because it is readily understood if sense can be made of FEI. Secondly, and more importantly, FEI and FA are the origins of the resonant contemporary moral ideals of *respect for persons* and of *autonomy*. Yet it is far from clear that either FEI or FA is equivalent to FUL, or that either is a version of the supreme principle of morality, rather than one moral principle among others. Still less is it obvious why either should count as a version of the supreme principle of practical reason.

FEI is formulated in the *Groundwork of the Metaphysics of Morals* in the words *So act that you use humanity, whether in your own person or in the person of any other, always at the same time as an end, never merely as a means*

---

[18] See Herman, *The Practice of Moral Judgement*; Wood, *Kant's Ethical Thought*, ch. 7.

(*G* 4:429). Kant himself views FEI as the most intuitive version of the Categorical Imperative; many recent accounts of Kantian ethics go further and dismiss FUL in order to concentrate on FEI's demands for respect for persons.[19] Certainly, FEI does not look equivalent to, or even like, FUL. Yet if no equivalent reading can be found, Kant's ethical theory will fall apart: the deepest arguments used to justify the Categorical Imperative are directed mostly at *FUL*, so can provide grounds for *FEI* only if it can be read as equivalent to *FUL*.[20]

The fundamental difference between FUL and FEI is that FUL constrains what agents should (may, may not) do, whereas FEI constrains how agents should (may, may not) be treated. The two formulae consider requirements on action respectively from the agent's and the recipient's point of view. FEI, however, is more explicit than FUL about those on the receiving end of action. It requires right treatment *of humanity*,[21] whereas FUL requires action on maxims that can be principles *for all*. If FUL and FEI are to be read as equivalent, it is essential to read them using a common account of the scope of ethical concern. For example, it is common to read FUL as requiring action on maxims that can be principles *for all human agents*, so using the same view of the scope of ethical concern as is explicit in FEI. Alternatively, both FUL and FEI could be read as setting requirements on action by (and treatment of) rational natures, human or other.[22]

Even when FUL and FEI are read using a common view of the scope of ethical concern, their equivalence is not obvious. Why should acting on principles that can be principles for all amount to treating others as ends and not as mere means? The issue can best be approached by considering first what is meant by 'treating others as mere means'. Kant distinguishes interaction with others that respects and preserves their capacities as agents, in which persons permissibly use one another as *a means*, from action that uses unwilling others as *a mere means*. We use others as mere means when we treat them not as agents, but as things or tools, as something to be 'used by this or that will at its discretion' (*G* 4:428). Those who adopt such maxims do not always damage others' agency (they may lack opportunity

[19] See *G* 4:436; Hill, *Dignity and Practical Reason*; Wood, *Kant's Ethical Thought*.
[20] See O'Neill, *Constructions of Reason*, ch. 7.
[21] Kant discusses the claims of *humanity*, of *rational nature* and of *sentient nature* in many passages, especially in *G* 4:448 onwards and in *MM*. For discussion of his humanism, and of charges of speciesism levelled against him, see Allen W. Wood and Onora O'Neill, symposium on 'Kant on Duties Regarding Nonrational Nature', *Proceedings of the Aristotelian Society* Supp. Vol. 72 (1998), 189–228.
[22] Hill, *Dignity and Practical Reason*, ch. 2.

or power) but the *standard* results of such action damage agency. We cannot will any of numerous maxims of victimising as universal laws: in doing so we would will results that would undercut the means for like action for some or for many. Those who treat others as *mere means* act on maxims that they *cannot* will as universal laws. This argument does not establish the equivalence of the FUL and FEI, but only that the first part of FEI – *do not use [others] merely as means* – follows from FUL. Strict duties can be derived either by applying the *contradiction in conception* test aspect of FUL, or by adhering to the part of FEI that prohibits treating others as mere means.

The second part of FEI enjoins treating others as 'ends in themselves', and corresponds to the contradiction in the will test application of FUL, by which maxims are tested not for inner coherence, but for fitness as laws for a possible world of agents. In treating others as ends in themselves, we treat them as persons, as beings who have objective worth: this requires more than refraining from treating them merely as means. We treat others as ends by acting in ways in which a world of agents can be sustained: by acting on maxims that can form part of a system of maxims that can be willed without contradiction, that harmonise with the necessary conditions for sustaining a world of agents (*G* 4:430–1).

Provided that FUL and FEI are read using a common view of the scope of ethical concern, the difference between them is in the end a matter of perspective. FUL is a test for *ways of acting* that could be adopted by all agents in a world of agents; FEI is a test for *ways of being treated* that could be accepted by all agents within some world of agents. Within a world of agents, the perspectives of agency and recipience consider the same set of possible actions from different points of view. Both formulate procedures for rejecting maxims whose universal adoption would undermine at least some others' possibilities of like action.

Universal laws and autonomy

In many ways the Formula of Autonomy (FA) is closer to FUL than it is to FEI. In the *Groundwork* Kant writes 'The principle of autonomy is . . . to choose only in such a way that the maxims of your choice are also included as a universal law in the same volition' (*G* 4:439).[23] The puzzle is not so much that Kant sees FA as a version of the Categorical Imperative – it is,

---

[23] See Wood, *Kant's Ethical Thought*, 163–4 for a listing of versions of FA and an argument that FA is quite distant from FUL.

after all, quite close to FUL[24] – but rather to understand why he speaks of it as the formula or principle of autonomy. How can he view autonomy as basic to morality, or claim that 'Morality is thus the relation of actions to the autonomy of the will'? (G 4:439)[25]

This puzzle can be resolved by distinguishing Kant's conception of autonomy adequately from contemporary conceptions. Most current discussions of autonomy see it as a property of individual agents, which they may have to a greater or lesser degree, and may express in some domains of life more than in others. Contemporary conceptions of autonomy generally equate it with forms of personal independence or self-expression, or with acting on certain distinctive, supposedly 'autonomous', preferences.[26] Such conceptions of individual autonomy are widely discussed, and their ethical merits widely disputed. These discussions are irrelevant to understanding Kantian autonomy. Kant never writes of autonomous *selves* or *persons* or *individuals*. He predicates autonomy *of reason, of ethics, of principles, of willing.*[27] Although contemporary advocates of individual autonomy often claim Kantian ancestry for their ideas, the claim is bogus, made plausible only by distorting Kant's conception of autonomy in major ways.

For Kant the idea of autonomy captures the two central aspects of his account of practical reason and of ethics: that duty is a matter of acting on principles or laws, and that those principles or laws should not be derived from arbitrary starting points. Principles are autonomous on Kant's view not because they express some particularly striking or independent personal decision or attitude, but because they are *not derived from elsewhere.* 'Self-legislation', as Kant writes of it, does not mean that each self or each agent chooses or 'legislates' moral principles for all (coherent only where there is some extraneous, hence unreasoned, source of coordination). He understands self-legislation as *the law giving of reason* rather than as *the law giving of individuals.* He remarks that

> it is requisite to reason's lawgiving that it should need to presuppose only *itself*, because a rule is objectively and universally valid only when it holds without the contingent, subjective conditions that distinguish one rational being from another (*CPrR* 5:20)

and states that autonomy requires a

> *lawgiving of its own* on the part of pure and, as such, practical reason [which] is freedom in the *positive* sense. (*CPrR* 5:33)

---

[24] See *ibid.* ch. 5.

[25] Even more strikingly he equates it with practical reason: 'the power to judge autonomously – that is, freely (according to principles of thought in general) – is called reason' (*CF* 7:27).

[26] See chapters in Part II below. [27] See Hill, *Dignity and Practical Reason*, ch. 4.

For Kant the element *self* in the term *self-legislation* indicates a *reflexive* claim that lawgiving, and hence principles and maxims, not be derived 'from elsewhere', that is from sundry arbitrary assumptions or conditions. Kantian autonomy is a matter not of self-expression by individual selves who 'legislate', but of agents choosing maxims – 'laws' – that are non-derivative, so nonconditional.

This conception of autonomy as willing that does not appeal to arbitrary (bogus, or at best conditional) 'authorities' is the basis of Kant's contrast between *autonomous ethics* and positions that advocate forms of *heteronomous ethics*. The proponents of heteronomy in ethics derive supposed moral principles from 'authorities' such as church or state, ideology or market forces, public opinion or personal preference, individual choice or majority vote.[28] The practical reasoning deployed in heteronomous ethics is therefore essentially instrumental or conditional: it is simply a matter of choosing action that implements the standards of the supposed 'authority' effectively and efficiently.

As Kant sees it:

> If the will seeks the law that is to determine it anywhere else than in the fitness of its maxims for its own giving of universal law – consequently if, in going beyond itself, it seeks this law in a property of any of its objects – heteronomy always results. (*G* 4:441)

If we are to offer reasons for action that are relevant to *all* others, we must begin by ensuring that we offer reasons they *can* offer and consider, accept or refuse. We cannot do this by relativising our reasons for action to any 'authority' that some – or many – may have no reason to accept, and may in fact reject. Rather than trying to build personal independence or other conceptions of individual autonomy into ethics, Kant argues that we should ensure that what we propose to others is based on principles that are *fit* to be laws, hence on principles that they at least *could* adopt. This seemingly slender modal requirement demands that we reject all forms of heteronomous ethics in favour of acting on principles that are fit to be universal laws, hence also that we not treat others as mere means or as less than ends. Kant sums up these views on reason and morality in the striking claim that 'the moral law expresses nothing other than the *autonomy* of pure practical reason' (*CPrR* Theorem IV, 5:33).

[28] See note 5 above.

CHAPTER 3

Kant's conception of public reason[1]

The idea that public reason provides the basis for justifying normative claims, including fundamental ethical and political claims, has acquired new resonance in recent decades. Yet it is not obvious whether or how the fact that a process of reasoning is public can contribute to fundamental justification. Indeed, since conceptions of reason, of the public and of the boundaries between public and private are various and strongly contested, any claim that public reason justifies is multiply ambiguous. Moreover, some popular conceptions of public reason are quite ill-suited to any justification of fundamental norms. I offer three contemporary examples.

First, reasoning might be thought of as public simply because it is actually done in public or by the public, for example in a context of political debate or of discussion in the media. Publicity in this sense may be crucial for any proposal to have democratic legitimation, variously conceived; but it cannot supply fundamental justifications. Democracies presuppose bounded territories and distinctions between citizens and non-citizens, and more broadly between members and non-members (aliens, resident and other); democratic process presupposes at least a rudimentary range of institutions such as the rule of law and at least minimal personal and civil rights. All of these demarcations and institutions would themselves have to be justified before democratic legitimation could be seen as providing or contributing to any fundamental form of normative justification. Similar points are true of those more widely conceived forms of public reasoning or debate which are structured by powerful formative institutions – publishers, the media, telecommunications providers, educational institutions, to name but a few – whose nature and influences would once again themselves have to be justified before the processes of public debate they structure

[1] First published as 'Kant's conception of public reason' in Volker Gerhardt, Rolf-Peter Horstmann and Ralph Schumacher (eds.), *Kant und die Berliner Aufklärung* (Akten des IX. Internationalen Kant-Kongresses), Vol. I (Berlin: Walter de Gruyter, 2001), 35–47.

could be seen as providing or contributing to any fundamental form of normative justification.

A second view of public reason locates its justificatory power not in democratic process, narrowly or widely conceived, but in the shared, publicly accepted categories and norms of communities. In communitarian writing we find a version of the thought that the fundamental categories and norms (of a community, of a tradition) are constitutive of identities, so cannot coherently be questioned (they are *nicht hintergehbar*), so by default achieve what must pass for the most fundamental sort of justification that can be mustered. Normative justification cannot but be internal to communities, since there is no way of engaging with the categories and norms that outsiders deploy. Such conceptions of justification may seem appealing among the like-minded, at least when they have no wish to query their like-mindedness, but are patently inadequate for an account of normative justification in a globalising world in which there is constant interaction among those who are not like-minded. Far from revealing a secure grasp of social reality, communitarian and other relativist conceptions of normative justification take nostalgic flight from the world in which we now live.

A third conception of public reason was put forward by John Rawls, particularly in *Political Liberalism*. The distinctive feature of his approach is that it takes seriously the thought that normative and cultural pluralism rather than homogeneous community is the natural outcome of free reasoning.[2] However, this conception of public reason too offers no fundamental justifications.

As Rawls sees it, no appeal to shared values will work in a world in which people with diverse categories and norms find themselves interacting: communitarian justification must fail. Nevertheless we can appeal to a certain conception of reasonable *persons*, who (in Rawls's view) are committed to a form of reciprocity: they 'are willing to propose principles and standards of co-operation and to abide by them willingly, given the assurance that others will likewise do so'.[3] Given that the facts of pluralism preclude the possibility of identifying such principles with comprehensive ethical norms, Rawls argues that reasonable persons 'are ready to work out the framework for the public social world',[4] and must construct rather than discover principles of justice by public reasoning among those who

---

[2] He writes that 'pluralism is not seen as a disaster but rather as the natural outcome of human reason under enduring free institutions'. John Rawls, *Political Liberalism* (New York: Columbia University Press, 1993), xxiv; see also 47, 55.
[3] *Ibid.* 49.   [4] *Ibid.* 53.

are fellow citizens. Public reason as Rawls construes it is 'citizens' reasoning in the public forum about constitutional essentials and basic questions of justice'.[5]

Evidently this conception of public reason as reciprocity among members of the public relies on many of the background assumptions on which conceptions of democratic legitimation depend. For Rawls, public reason has its context in a 'bounded society', which he views as 'a more or less complete and self sufficient scheme of co-operation . . . existing in perpetuity',[6] whose citizens enter by birth and leave by death, and whose politics are democratic. Various considerations suggest that this essentially *civic* conception of public reason cannot justify fundamental norms. In the first place, the conception presupposes, so cannot justify, many fundamental social arrangements, such as boundaries, democracy and citizenship. Secondly, it is left unclear whether reasonable action, as Rawls understands it, is intrinsically public: on the one hand he holds that 'the reasonable . . . addresses the public world of others';[7] on the other hand he notes that 'Not all reasons are public reasons, as there are the non-public reasons of churches and universities and of many other associations in society.'[8] Presumably the idea is that reciprocity among a wide but nevertheless restricted range of reasoners (co-religionists, scholars) constitutes reasoning appropriate for the relevant limited domain, but that only reasoning among *all* fellow citizens, that abstracts from the differences between them, constitutes fully public reason and can achieve the public justification of political norms at which political liberalism aims. Thirdly, the identification of reasonableness with commitment to reciprocity is itself open to questions, some of which Rawls leaves unanswered. For example, in *Political Liberalism* he shifts between a *motivational* and a *modal* conception of the reasonable: the motivational conception stresses the *willingness* of reasonable persons to seek and live by fair terms of cooperation, the modal conception stresses their *capacity* to do so. A conception of the reasonable might centre on one, but hardly on both of these views.[9]

---

[5] *Ibid.* 10 and see also 'Public reason, then, is public in three ways: as the reason of citizens as such, it is the reason of the public; its subject is the good of the public and matters of fundamental justice; and its nature and content is public, being given by the ideals and principles expressed by society's conception of political justice, and conducted open to view', 213. See also 'Constructivism in Rawls and Kant' and 'Changing constructions', below.

[6] *Ibid.* 18.   [7] *Ibid.* 53.

[8] *Ibid.* 213. See also the discussion of Kant's conception of private reason, below.

[9] For further detail see Onora O'Neill, 'Political liberalism and public reason: a critical notice of John Rawls's *Political Liberalism*', *Philosophical Review* 106 (1997), 411–28.

Scope and authority: 'private' reason and polemic

The limitations of these three conceptions of public reason do not show that every conception of public reason is irrelevant to fundamental justification; indeed they may provide clues for the construction of a more convincing conception of reason. One important clue can be found in the way in which the failure of each conception arises from its attempt to draw on other powers, institutions or practices and to enlist their authority on behalf of reason. In each case it is the appeal to claims that lack reasoned vindication that undermines the possibility of fundamental normative justification. Just as the novice cyclist who clutches at passing objects and leans on their stability to improve his balance thereby fails to balance at all, so a would-be reasoner who leans on some socially or civilly constituted power or authority which lacks reasoned vindication offers only conditional reasons.

Kant made this negative point with crystal clarity when he drew a famous, and in my view still too little appreciated, distinction between public and private uses of reason. He characterises uses of reason that appeal to rationally ungrounded assumptions, such as the civilly constituted authority of church or state, not as *public* but as *private*. In *What Is Enlightenment?* he speaks of the official reasoning of military officers, of pastors of the established church and of civil servants as *private*: these functionaries hold and derive their authority from their civil or public office, and their communications when acting officially are not (fully) reasoned because they assume the authority and the edicts of that civil power. Kant states quite explicitly that 'the private use of reason is that which one may make of it in a certain *civil* post or office with which he is entrusted' (*WE* 8:37). By the same token he would classify the sorts of reasoning achieved in processes of democratic legitimation, as well as those advocated by communitarians and by late Rawlsians, as private, or at least as not fully public, in each case because they appeal to the authority of civilly and socially constituted institutions and practices. He contrasts such 'private' uses of reason with 'the public use of one's reason . . . which someone makes of it *as a scholar* before the entire public of the *world of readers*' (*WE* 8:38), a scholar 'who by his writings speaks to the public in the strict sense, that is, the world' (*WE* 8:38).

Kant frequently uses a variety of idioms to convey the basic insight that fundamental reasons, and with them the authority of reason, cannot derive from or be subordinate to any other power or authority. For example in passages in the *Doctrine of Method* of the *First Critique* he makes the same point by insisting that reasoning must be *uncoerced*. There he writes:

> If you grasp at means other than uncoerced reason, if you cry high treason, if you call together the public . . . as if they were to put out a fire, then you make yourself ridiculous . . . it is quite absurd to expect enlightenment from reason and yet to prescribe to it in advance on which side it must come out. (*CPR* A 746–7 / B 774–5)

The Conflict of the Faculties reiterates this negative point: 'reason is by its nature free and admits of no command to hold something as true' (*CF* 7:20), and elaborates its implications for the tasks of the university.[10] Giving up the 'argument' from supposed authority is no easy matter. In fact the 'higher' faculties of theology, law and medicine live by arguments from authority: they derive their authority from the state which institutes, regulates and restricts them, and assigns them the task of professional education and practice. Like the state officials of *What Is Enlightenment?*, these faculties speak with a voice of duly constituted authority, namely that of civilly constituted and regulated professions. Like the speech of those officials, the teaching of these faculties is in Kant's sense of the term a private use of reason. In these passages Kant depicts the 'higher' faculties not as wholly abandoning reason, but as aiming for a conditional sort of reasoning, that will reach only those who accept a common authority. The audience is (at most) 'the people as a civil community' (*CF* 7:34).

By contrast, Kant claims, the 'lower' faculty of philosophy[11] has no commitment to professional education or practice, and is not or should not be regulated by the state because its discipline is that of reason:

> It is absolutely essential that the learned community at the university also contain a faculty that is independent of the government's command with regard to its teachings; one that, having no commands to give, is free to evaluate everything, and concerns itself with the interests of the sciences, that is, with truth: one in which reason is authorised to speak out publicly. (*CF* 7:19–20)[12]

The teaching of the 'lower' faculty is therefore 'directed to a different kind of public – a learned community devoted to the sciences' (*CF* 7:34). This

---

[10] E.g. 'when it is a question of the truth of a certain teaching to be expounded in public the teacher cannot appeal to a supreme command or the pupil pretend that he believed it by order' (*CF* 7:27).

[11] Kant conceives of the 'philosophy' faculty as covering a wide range of humane studies; he divides it into departments concerned with *historical cognition* (history, geography, philology, humanities) and departments concerned with *rational cognition* (pure mathematics, pure philosophy, metaphysics of nature and of morals). See *CF* 7:28.

[12] He asserts specifically that 'the government reserves the right itself to *sanction* the teachings of the higher faculties, but those of the lower faculties it leaves up to the scholars' reason' (*CF* 7:19) and 'The lower faculty . . . occupies itself with teachings which are not adopted as directives by order of a superior' (*CF* 7:27).

theme is continued with considerable detail in the appendix to Part I of *The Conflict of the Faculties*,[13] whose theme is the conflict between one of the 'higher' faculties, that of theology, and the 'lower' faculty. Here Kant revels in pointing out what their appeal to ecclesiastical authority costs the 'biblical theologians' of the 'higher' faculty, and points out that their task can be only to teach ecclesiastical faith dogmatically to an audience of the faithful. By contrast, he asserts, the 'philosophical theologians' of the 'lower' faculty, who rely on reason to interpret the world and texts, even the texts of Holy Scripture, can communicate not merely with restricted audiences, but with the world at large.

In these and many other passages Kant sets out a dilemma. If we appeal to any civilly or socially constituted powers or authorities, let alone to mere brute force, we limit our own attempts to reason, and achieve at best communication of restricted scope and authority. Like the novice cyclist who loses the very balance he seeks in clinging to stable objects, reasoners lose the very authority they aspire to in making such appeals.

But have they any alternative? Neither the passages in the *Conflict of the Faculties* nor those in *What Is Enlightenment?* get beyond the negative point. They do not show whether or how the aspirations and responsibilities of the 'lower' faculty can be achieved. An account of the proper procedure of the lower faculty and of its authority is still needed. By itself, insistence that reason cannot be derived from powers or authorities of other sorts takes us only a limited distance. It leaves us in need of some positive account of the means by which some but not other uses of cognitive capacities, which are not derived from spurious sources, are to be counted as reasoned. Surely reasoned thought and action demand more than the rejection of or resistance to spurious sources of reasons.

Scope and authority: the 'lawless' use of reason

An obvious response to the limitations of democratic, communitarian and civic conceptions of public reason, and of the many other private uses of reason to which Kant draws attention, is to insist that serious reasoning should not be beholden to any civilly constituted authority, indeed to any contingent power or authority for which no justification is provided, and that this independence is the condition of reaching audiences of wider scope.

---

[13] See *CF* 7:36ff.; many of Kant's claims in this appendix have parallels in *Religion within the Boundaries of Mere Reason*.

However, this response is easier to formulate than to understand. Kant's favoured image of public reason is the reasoning of scholars, the reasoning of the Faculty of Philosophy communicating with the world at large. It has evident limitations. Perhaps in the eighteenth-century world of international correspondence and communication among the learned this example was as good an image as Kant could find for reasoning that is not beholden to the edicts and assumptions of bounded states and institutions, practices and roles, and their coercive powers. But he certainly knew that the realities of scholarly life seldom lived up to this ideal. The burden of argument in *What Is Enlightenment?*, and of passages in many other texts, is the vulnerability of such communication; his aim is to show that states, even despotic states, have an interest in allowing scholars 'The least harmful of anything that could even be called freedom: namely, freedom to make *public use* of one's reason in all matters' (*WE* 8:36). In Kant's view, states and governments that refuse to accord their citizens this 'most innocuous freedom' act to their own detriment. This argument is not wholly convincing, since the interests of rulers, and especially of despots, even when they claim to be 'enlightened', may well be threatened by the ferment of unrestricted intellectual inquiry.

However, the deeper question is not whether governments, including despotic governments, have a genuine interest in permitting free inquiry, but whether we can say anything about the requirements of reasoned communication other than asserting the negative point that it should not, indeed cannot, defer to the edicts and assumptions of civil or other powers or authorities. Is reasoning merely a matter of freedom from restrictions, of unfettered and unstructured words, of a market place, a bazaar, a babble – of utterances? Is there perhaps nothing beyond a postmodernist play of (quasi) signifiers?

Other texts make it clear that Kant does not think of freedom from interference as the sole requirement of reason, or specifically of public reason. Although the emphasis in *What Is Enlightenment?* is very much on the need for public uses of reason to be free from restraint or control by the civil powers, the text is far more than a banal and timid contribution to the literature on free speech. Indeed, by contemporary standards, Kant limits the domain of free speech severely – so severely that his image of 'public' reason as modelled on scholarly communication may be read as suggesting only that rulers should allow those whose communication has little impact on civic life to say what they wish! But the text does not advocate a merely permissive view of the proper use of human cognitive capacities.

Even in *What Is Enlightenment?*, where the freedom rulers accord their subjects is a central concern, Kant is far from viewing public reason as mere absence of constraint. He depicts those who make free public use of their reason not as abandoning all intellectual discipline, but as judging carefully, as seeking intellectual maturity and autonomy, as pursuing 'the calling of each individual to think for himself' (*WE* 8:36). Although wise rulers will leave subjects free to make public use of reason, Kant does not for a moment assume that uncoerced reason must amount to unconstrained babble.

The distinction Kant draws between acceptable and unacceptable uses of freedom to reason is more deeply explored in *What Does It Mean to Orient Oneself in Thinking?*, published the year after *What Is Enlightenment?* The earlier essay focuses on reasons why rulers should accord freedom to speak and to communicate to their subjects, the later on the proper use of this freedom, and the reasons why mere absence of constraint is not enough for reasoned thinking. Kant contends in *What Does It Mean to Orient Oneself in Thinking?* that nothing could deserve to be called reason if it was wholly without structure and discipline. He pointedly asks the critics of reason 'have you thought about . . . where your attacks on reason will lead?' (*WOT* 8:144), and contends that if they assume that reason is no more than freedom in thinking they will find that the very freedom they prize stands in the way of communicating with others: we cannot communicate our thoughts or offer one another reasons for action without imposing a certain structure or discipline on our thought and speech.

Kant's initial move is to argue that freedom of thought cannot be separated from freedom to communicate. Thought, speech and writing all presuppose possible audiences, hence pluralities of potential thinkers, speakers and communicators:

> freedom to think is opposed **first** of all to civil compulsion. Of course it is said that the freedom to speak or write could be taken from us by a superior power, but the freedom to think cannot be. Yet how much and how correctly would we think if we did not think as it were in community with others to whom we communicate our thoughts, and who communicate theirs with us! Thus one can very well say that this external power which wrenches away people's freedom publicly to communicate their thoughts also takes from them the freedom to think – that single gem remaining to us in the midst of all the burdens of civil life. (*WOT* 8:144)

The option of solitary thinking is not open, in Kant's view. Even a private use of reason assumes some plurality. But if the background authorities and institutions that private uses of reason accept and depend upon are unvindicated, we must ask whether serious, public reasoning must be wholly unconstrained or 'lawless'. Kant's answer is an emphatic 'no'.

He uses a fierce and sometimes sarcastic rhetoric[14] to characterise those who purvey the illusion that reasoning could be without all structure or discipline, or imagine that such absence of structure and discipline could be liberating. He had clear targets in mind, including sundry purveyors of religious enthusiasm, superstition and exaggerated views of the powers of genius. Today his targets might include sundry postmodernists, sceptics and deconstructionists. All of these opponents of reason blindly fail to see where unstructured liberation by itself will lead:

> if reason will not subject itself to the laws it gives itself, it has to bow under the yoke of laws given by another; for without law, nothing – not even nonsense – can play its game for long. Thus the unavoidable consequence of *declared* lawlessness in thinking (of a liberation from the limitations of reason) is that the freedom to think will ultimately be forfeited and – because it is not misfortune but arrogance which is to blame for it – . . . will be *trifled away*. (*WOT* 8:145)

The illusions of 'lawless' thinking end not merely in confusion but in disaster:

> First genius is very pleased with its bold flight, since it has cast off the thread by which reason used to steer it. Soon it enchants others with its triumphant pronouncements and great expectations and now seems to have set itself on a throne which was so badly graced by slow and ponderous reason. Then its maxim is that reason's superior lawgiving is invalid – we common human beings call this **enthusiasm**, while those favoured by beneficent nature call it illumination. Since reason alone can command validly for everyone, a confusion of language must soon arise among them; each one now follows his own inspiration. (*WOT* 8:145)[15]

Such anarchic, 'lawless' thinking yields mere babble and is defenceless in the face of the claims of dogma, rabble rousing and superstition.

Scope and authority: autonomy and public reason

If 'lawless' thinking ends not in freedom of thought and communication, but in gibberish and isolation, even in superstition and cognitive disorientation, and vulnerability to tyrants and demagogues, then any activity in

---

[14] A reasoned rebuttal of the deniers of reason would hardly be possible – as those who have tried to engage reasonably with postmodernists have often discovered.
[15] See also *CPR* A 707 / B 735.

human life that can count as reasoned must be structured. In particular it must have enough structure for us to distinguish thoughts and proposals that provide good reasons from those that provide only poor reasons, so enabling us to decide which we ought to accept and which we ought to reject. Reasoning, whether theoretical or practical, must have some normative force.

How can this authority and normative force be found or constructed, if they cannot be borrowed from elsewhere? When thinking and acting are structured only by the borrowed categories and norms of particular civil or social institutions and practices, they can achieve only limited, conditional authority and normative force. As Kant sees it, such categories and norms can ground no more than partial, 'private' uses of reason, which can reach and be followed only by those others who grasp and accept the same categories and norms. So if anything is to count as *more* than 'private' reason, in Kant's sense of the term, if there is to be anything that is to count as *fully public reason*, then the structures and disciplines which constitute it cannot be derived from existing institutions and practices. But what provides the internal discipline or structure of fully public reasoning? Kant's answer is straightforward:

> Freedom in thinking signifies the subjection of reason to no laws expect those which it gives itself; and its opposite is the maxim of a **lawless use** of reason (in order, as genius supposes, to see further than one can under the limitations of laws). (*WOT* 8:145)

Public uses of reason must have *lawlike* rather than *lawless* structure, but since they are not to derive their lawlikeness from any external sources, this lawlikeness will have to be *self-legislated*. Since the terms *self-legislation* and autonomy (in Kant's usage) have the same meaning, it follows a commitment to public reason and to autonomy are one and the same. Kant is quite explicit:

> The power to judge autonomously – that is, freely (according to principles of thought in general) – is called **reason**. (*CF* 7:27)

This identification of reason with autonomy is initially startling, because contemporary interpretations of autonomy sees it largely as a matter of independence rather than of reason. Kant never equates autonomy with independence; unlike most recent 'Kantian' writers he views autonomy or *self-legislation* as emphasising not a *self* that does the legislating, but rather legislation that is not done by others, that is not derivative.[16] Nonderivative

---

[16] See the chapters in Part II below.

'legislation' cannot require us to adopt the actual laws or rules of some institution or authority; it can be only a matter of requiring that any principle we use to structure thought or action be *lawlike* and have universal scope This is what it is to conform to 'the principles of thought in general'.

At the end of *What Does It Mean to Orient Oneself in Thinking?* Kant elaborates this interpretation of reason as autonomy by identifying reasoned thinking with the practice of adopting principles of thinking and acting that have the form of law, which can be adopted by all.

> the maxim of always thinking for oneself is **enlightenment**. Now there is less to this than people imagine when they place enlightenment in the acquisition of *information*; for it is rather a negative principle in the use of one's faculty of cognition... To make use of one's own reason means no more than to ask oneself, whenever one is supposed to assume something, whether one could find it feasible to make the ground or the rule on which one assumes it into a universal principle for the use of reason. (*WOT* 8:146n)

In this passage Kant again states quite clearly that autonomy or thinking for oneself, as he conceives it, is never a matter of mere or 'lawless' freedom in thinking or doing: we think, judge and act autonomously only if we structure our freedom by adhering to and adopting principles that could be universally followed or adopted, which must therefore combine the formal structure of a law, that is to say the formal structure of a universal principle, with universal scope.

Kant's conception of autonomy builds on the notions of *plurality* and *law*. We think and act autonomously only if and to the extent that we think and act on principles which could be principles for all, rather than principles that are fit only for limited audiences as defined by some civil or other authority or ideology. The form of independence that counts for Kantian autonomy is not the independence of the individual 'legislator', but the independence of the principles 'legislated' from whatever desires, decisions, powers or conventions may be current among one or another group or audience.

Reasoning, whether theoretical or practical, is only a matter of structuring thought and action in ways that others *could* follow. In one respect this conception of public reason as autonomy parallels various contemporary conceptions of public reason (as well as Kant's own conception of private reason): all conceptions of reason are thought of as requiring that thought and action be conducted on principles that others can follow or adopt. The single, but crucial, difference between recent conceptions of public reason (and Kant's conception of 'private' reason) and Kant's conception of reason as autonomy is that the former all address *bounded pluralities*, defined by civic or social institutions, practices and ideologies, whereas for Kant public reason requires thinking and acting that address an *unrestricted plurality*: the world at large.

If these considerations are convincing, Kant has connected the authority and the scope of reason, indeed he has vindicated a specific conception of public reason by requiring that it be serviceable across the widest scope. Reasoning is a matter of using patterns of thought or adopting principles of action that others too can follow or adopt. If we aspire to reach only local and like-minded audiences there will be shared assumptions enough from which to reason. But the result will be no more than a private use of reason, that is comprehensible and convincing only among the like-minded. If we seek to reach beyond restricted circles where there are shared authorities or shared assumptions that can carry the burden of reason-giving, we have to supply a structure that the members of a wider, potentially diverse and unspecified, plurality can follow, by adopting and following principles of thought and action that an unrestricted audience can follow. Kant notes that there is less to this than people imagine: but what there is may still surprise us by its combination of normative authority and extensive scope in guiding thought and action.

Some surprises of reason

I finish with a few comments on ways in which, as I see it, Kant's account of reason may still surprise us. A bare list might include the following points. This is an account of reason that is neither individualistic nor anchored to a philosophy of consciousness; it is an account of reason that is equally relevant to thinking and to acting; it is an account of reason that is closely linked to Kant's view of autonomy and almost without connection to contemporary views of autonomy.

First, by approaching the nature and authority of reason in this way Kant has taken a straightforward view of the need for anything that is to count as reasoning to provide reasons *to others*. He conceives of reasoning as directed to an audience. Private uses of reason are directed to restricted audiences, public uses of reason are directed to unrestricted audiences. It would, however, be misleading to label Kant's conception of reason 'dialogical', because he does not (unlike a number of contemporaries) think that it is the product of real-time, actual dialogue. Kant's arguments are about the necessary conditions for anything to count as a reason, and his most basic thought might be put quite crudely as the thought that we do not give others reasons unless we present them with a pattern of thought which can be followed, and that we do not give them unconditional reasons unless we give them patterns of thought which they can follow without assuming some arbitrary starting point.

CHAPTER 4

Constructivism in Rawls and Kant[1]

The ambitions of constructivisms in ethics

John Rawls's writing across the last three decades of his life advances the best-known form of Kantian constructivism. During this period his understanding of the terms *constructive* and *Kantian* changed in various ways. I shall try to trace some of these changes in this chapter and to contrast Rawls's views with the form of 'Kantian constructivism' which (I argue) can plausibly be attributed to Kant himself.

The metaphor of construction has had a wide use in twentieth-century theoretical and philosophical writing. On a minimal understanding, it is no more than the thought that certain entities are complex, because they are composed out of other more elementary entities. This thought may seem quite neutral about the sorts of things that are elementary and the sorts of things that may be composed out of them. In this very general sense, logical atomism, the procedure of the *Tractatus* and Carnap's *Aufbau* programme, in which complex statements are constructed from elementary statements, are all forms of constructivism. So too are many anti-realist views of science, theory and society, which speak, for example, of the social construction of reality (of meaning, of science) or the construction of social identity or the construction of modern France out of more elementary components, such as beliefs, attitudes or interactions.

However, this minimalist understanding of constructivism as ontologically neutral misleads. By and large, the term *constructive* is favoured by anti-realists.[2] Realist positions argue that certain facts or properties are

---

[1] An earlier version of this chapter appeared under the title 'Kantian constructivisms' in Julian Nida-Rümelin (ed.), *Rationality, Realism, Revision: Proceedings of the 3rd International Conference of the Society for Analytical Philosophy* (Berlin: De Gruyter, 1999).

[2] For discussion of links between anti-realism and ethical constructivism see David O. Brink, *Moral Realism and the Foundations of Ethics* (Cambridge University Press, 1989); Ronald Milo, 'Contractarian constructivism', *Journal of Philosophy* 122 (1995), 181–204; Larry Krasnoff, 'How Kantian is constructivism?', *Kant-studien* 90, no. 4 (1999), 85–409.

features of the world, so need not be based on or constructed out of other elements. Of course, realists too may think that there are simple and complex facts and properties; but they will not be generally inclined to think of the latter as constructions, because this would suggest that they are constructed by some agent or agency, a thought which realists reject. However, there is plenty of confusion in the use of the terms *constructive*, *constructivist, constructionist* and their cognates, in particular because some anti-realist writing on science and society speaks of facts as constructed, so appropriating one of the central terms of realist thought for their own purposes.[3]

Ethical constructivists share the anti-realism of many other constructivist claims and positions. Unlike moral realists, they doubt or deny that there are distinctively moral facts or properties, whether natural or non-natural, that can be discovered or intuited and will provide foundations for ethics. John Rawls put the point succinctly in 1989 in 'Themes in Kant's moral philosophy', where he denied that ethical

> first principles, as statements about good reasons, are regarded as true or false in virtue of a moral order of values that is prior to and independent of our conceptions of person and society, and of the public and social role of moral doctrines.[4]

If there were an independent moral order of values, and it could be known, moral realism could be established and constructive approaches to ethics would be redundant.

Anti-realism comes in many forms in ethical and political theory, and much of it is not constructivist. Constructivisms are distinctive among anti-realist ethical positions, not only in claiming that ethical principles or claims may be seen as the constructions of human agents, but also in two further respects. They also claim that ethical reasoning is practical: it can establish practical prescriptions or recommendations, which can be used to guide action, and it can justify those prescriptions or recommendations. Objectivity in ethics is not illusory. Constructivists reject not only those positions that give up on the entire project of justification (e.g. emotivism

---

[3] The appropriation is etymologically sound: facts are originally *facta* – done or made by agents rather than given to them, as *data* are. Nevertheless the appropriation confuses in that the realist understanding of facts as given, there, or (as we say) brute, hence not constructed, is now long established. Moreover, social constructionists sometimes slide between the plausible thought that concepts may be (socially) constructed, and the controversial thought that truths whose assertion deploys those concepts are also constructed. Realists too can view concepts as socially constructed.

[4] John Rawls, 'Themes in Kant's moral philosophy' (TKMP) in Eckart Förster (ed.), *Kant's Transcendental Deductions* (Stanford University Press, 1989), 95; also in John Rawls, *Collected Papers*, ed. Samuel Freeman (Cambridge, MA: Harvard University Press, 1999), 497–528.

or scepticism), but also positions such as relativism, communitarianism and social constructionism applied to ethical beliefs, which deploy severely restricted conceptions of justification.

Constructivist approaches to ethics are therefore distinctive and ambitious. They hold that, although realist underpinnings are unobtainable, (some) objective, action-guiding ethical prescriptions can be justified. The challenge is to see whether and how this combination of ambitions can be sustained.

The evolution of Rawls's constructivism

Throughout Rawls's earlier work he advocated a particular constructive procedure, the Original Position (OP), as the way to justify principles of justice. However, as his work developed he changed his views of the range of ethical positions that can be constructed, of the justification of OP, and of the audiences who can be given reasons to accept OP. Broadly speaking, he took an increasingly refined and restricted view of all three.

In his earlier work, and in particular in *A Theory of Justice*,[5] Rawls hoped that it might prove possible to justify not only principles of justice, but other ethical principles; he saw OP as justified because the principles of justice it endorses are in reflective equilibrium with 'our' considered judgements; he views this approach as providing reasons for action for a loosely specified 'us', hence for anybody. In his later work he qualifies all three claims. In *Political Liberalism*[6] Rawls concluded that constructive methods can be used to identify principles of justice, but not other principles of morality; that the procedures for constructing them – still OP – are justified not by reflective equilibrium but by a distinctive conception of public reason, shared by (and possibly only by) fellow citizens in a liberal democratic polity, and that these fellow citizens thereby constitute the sole and rather restricted audience for constructive reasoning about justice.

Although his views changed in these ways, Rawls at all times maintained not only the view the principles of justice can be constructed, but a broadly Kantian view both of substantive normative claims and of their justification. His Kantianism amounts to far more than acceptance of a liberal account of justice, or rejection of consequentialist ethics. As the title of one of his major works indicates, what he sought was always a specifically

---

[5] John Rawls, *A Theory of Justice* (Cambridge, MA: Harvard University Press, 1971). Page references to this work will be given parenthetically using the abbreviation *TJ*.

[6] John Rawls, *Political Liberalism* (New York: Columbia University Press, 1993). Page references to this work will be given parenthetically using the abbreviation *PL*.

Kantian form of constructivism.[7] A closer look at the stages through which his Kantian constructivism – perhaps Kantian constructivisms – developed is instructive.

In *A Theory of Justice* Rawls spoke not of constructivism, but more broadly of a procedure for agents to identify principles of justice which provided 'constructive criteria', that is to say procedures for settling moral questions (*TJ* 34, 39–40, 49, 52). Here the emphasis is on the practicality of a theory that provides constructive criteria or procedures. Rawls contrasted his position with forms of 'intuitionism', which he characterised as impractical because they provide only a plurality of unranked principles, hence no constructive procedure for resolving moral problems. This initial broad conception of ethical construction classified both Utilitarianism and Rawls's own more Kantian views as constructive: both are contrasted with procedures in ethics that offer no constructive criteria, so are not, or not reliably, practical. Many non-Kantian writers, for example David Gauthier, rightly saw their own work as (aiming at) constructive criteria in this rather minimal sense, despite the fact that their approach was in no way Kantian.[8] Not all constructivists are Kantian constructivists.

By contrast, Rawls always saw his own work as Kantian as well as constructive. Although in *A Theory of Justice* he described his specific form of constructivism not as *Kantian*, but as *Contractarian*, he claimed there that his work was to carry 'to a higher level of abstraction the familiar theory of the social contract as found in Locke, Rousseau and Kant' (*TJ* 11). The level of abstraction is presumably higher because OP is a constructive procedure which conceives of the parties who construct principles of justice under particularly abstract descriptions, namely as lacking all knowledge of their own distinguishing social features.[9]

However, the fundamental strategy of justification of *A Theory of Justice* appealed not to individual preferences, nor even to a notional hypothetical

---

[7] However, it was only midway in his work that Rawls began to use the explicit phrase 'Kantian constructivism'.

[8] In *Morals by Agreement* (Oxford: Clarendon Press, 1986), 4, David Gauthier attributes a closely similar conception of constructive ethics to Rawls, citing a passage from *TJ* 42, where Rawls claims that the theory of justice is 'a part, perhaps the most significant part, of the theory of rational choice'. However, in *PL* Rawls explicitly rejects his earlier formulation, 52–3, stating that he no longer holds that the reasonable can be derived from the rational, and that his theory of justice is not constructed out of agreement based on individual preferences, 82ff. The gap between Kantian and non-Kantian forms of constructivism is wide.

[9] Strictly speaking Rawls's strategy depends not just on abstract but on idealised conceptions of persons, motivation and societies, which creates various problems. See Onora O'Neill 'Constructivisms in ethics' in *Constructions of Reason: Explorations of Kant's Practical Philosophy* (Cambridge University Press, 1989), 206–18, and 'The method of *A Theory of Justice*' in *John Rawls: Eine Theorie der Gerechtigkeit*, ed. Otfried Höffe (Berlin: Akademie Verlag, 1998), 27–43.

agreement or social contract, nor even to the constructive procedure of OP, which is a derivative notion, but to the quite different conception of reflective equilibrium. OP is used to construct principles of justice, but is itself to be justified: it is characterised in various works as a 'procedure', a 'thought experiment', a 'device of representation' and a 'model conception',[10] and always seen as requiring deeper justification. The justification by reference to reflective equilibrium between the principles of justice OP generates and 'our considered judgements' is a coherentist justification;[11] it introduces a certain conception of the reasonable (as opposed to the merely, instrumentally rational), a conception which Rawls reworked and developed in the account of public reason in his later writings.

In his 1980 *Kantian Constructivism in Moral Theory* Rawls gave the term 'constructivism' a more prominent use. He 'specifies a particular conception of the person as an element in a reasonable procedure of construction' (*KC* 516): 'agents of construction' are seen as 'free and equal moral persons' who think of themselves as 'citizens living a complete life in an on-going society' (*KC* 517), which constitutes a closed and bounded system (*KC* 536), and draw on 'the public culture of a democratic society' (*KC* 518) to argue for principles of justice. Stripped to its essentials, Rawls here maintains that

> Kantian constructivism holds that moral objectivity is to be understood in terms of a suitably constructed social point of view that all can accept. Apart from the procedure of constructing the principles of justice, there are no moral facts. (*KC* 519)

In *Kantian Constructivism* Rawls saw Kant's work as closely cognate, and deplored the failure of earlier writers to see that Kant offered a constructive rather than a minimally formalist approach to ethics.[12] However, here and elsewhere, Rawls recognised that his constructivism is Kantian, but

---

[10] See in particular 'Kantian constructivism in moral theory' (*KC* in further references), *Journal of Philosophy* 77 (1980), 515–72 which labels the Original Position a model conception (520) and 'Justice as fairness: political not metaphysical' (*JFPM* in further references), *Philosophy and Public Affairs* 14 (1985), 223–51 which views it as a device of representation (236ff.) (Rawls had introduced the latter term in *KC* 533). Both terms serve to deflect misreadings, which treat the Original Position as Rawls's fundamental justificatory strategy – a reading that Rawls would regard as non-Kantian.

[11] In appealing to 'our considered judgements' Rawls does not smuggle in reliance on some special way of knowing (he criticises rational intuitionists for doing this). He simply takes it that we have pre-theoretical moral beliefs and sentiments. See James Griffin, *Value Judgement: Improving our Ethical Beliefs* (Oxford University Press, 1996), ch. 1, for a clear discussion of appeals to intuition by those who are not intuitionists.

[12] According to Rawls, Sidgwick and Bradley both mistakenly read Kant's ethics as minimal formalism, while G.E. Moore and W.D. Ross overlook interesting Kantian possibilities because their rational intuitionism, which Kant would have viewed as (perfectionist) heteronomy, claimed knowledge of independent moral truths (*KC* 555–9, *TKMP* 95ff.).

that it is not Kant's. The main difference in method, as he sees it in *Kantian Constructivism*, is that his position assigns 'primacy to the social', and specifically that it is designed for citizens, indeed fellow citizens, whereas Kant's 'account of the Categorical Imperative applies to the personal maxims of sincere and conscientious persons in everyday life' (*KC* 552):[13] the OP procedure is not the more individualist Categorical Imperative procedure.

Rawls sees this difference in method as explaining why he and Kant reach different ranges of substantive ethical claims. While Kant hoped to provide a quite general method for addressing ethical issues, including questions of justice, Rawls came to the conclusion that his Kantian constructivism could build an account only of justice: we can construct a reasoned account of the right, but not of the good (*KC* 534); of justice, but not of virtue:

> Justice as fairness, as a constructivist view, holds that not all the moral questions we are prompted to ask in everyday life have answers. (*KC* 563)

This emphasis on the limits of his constructivism became even more prominent in Rawls's later writings, where he insists that, since we cannot give a reasoned account of the good, we are bound to be neutral as between competing 'conceptions of the good', unless they conflict with justice. Constructivism does not provide a comprehensive moral theory. Nor do constructive arguments reach all possible audiences: they are based on the shared culture of fellow citizens, so provide reasons for action only for those whose most basic commitments they presuppose.

The limits of Rawls's later constructivism are most clearly etched in his 1993 *Political Liberalism*, whose aim is specifically to 'bring out the bases of the principles of right and justice in practical reason' (*PL xxx*). The conception of practical reason or reasonableness, which Rawls advances in this work, is specifically a conception of public reason.

> Persons are reasonable when . . . they are ready to propose principles and standards as fair terms of co-operation and to abide by them willingly, given the assurance that others will likewise do so. (*PL* 49)

The others who may share a commitment to 'govern their conduct by a principle from which they and others can reason in common' (*PL* 49n.) are once again envisaged as fellow citizens, and moreover specifically as fellow citizens of a democratic society:

---

[13] The difference Rawls notes is explicitly based on contrasting his position with Kant's *Groundwork* rather than with Kant's work on justice. There is much more to be said on the respects in which Kant's position is and is not fundamentally individualist.

public reason is characteristic of a democratic people: it is the reason of
its citizens, of those sharing the status of equal citizenship. [It is] public in
three ways: as the reason of citizens as such, it is the reason of the public; its
subject is the good of the public and matters of fundamental justice; and its
nature and content is public. *(PL* 213)

Fellow citizens are thought of as sharing a bounded and closed society with
some common basic political institutions, which are now presupposed
rather than justified in Rawls's theory of justice.

In effect Rawls's work after 1985 assigned primacy not merely to the social,
but very specifically to the political.[14] He emphasised that his conception of
reasonableness differed from that accepted by communitarians, for whom
shared social norms may count as reasons. Since he takes pluralism seriously,
he does not assume that social norms will be shared by all fellow citizens,
or can provide reasons for action for all. Nevertheless he sees justification
as reaching only fellow citizens with whom we antecedently agree on *some*
matters:

> justification is addressed to others who disagree with us, and therefore it
> must always proceed from some consensus, from premises we and others
> publicly recognise as true. *(JFPM* 229)

The form of constructivism that Rawls reached by the time he wrote *Political Liberalism* was deeply political in its focus on justice to the exclusion
of other ethical issues, in its fundamental justification of the proposed
procedures for identifying principles of justice, and in its insistence that
justification is internal to a 'bounded society' (remarkably like a state)
rather than universal or cosmopolitan. In many ways its resonance is more
Rousseauian than Kantian.

Kantian constructivisms and practical reason

The deepest questions that can be raised about each version of Rawls's constructivism are about the conceptions of reasonableness invoked. Constructive procedures for establishing principles of justice cannot build ethical
conclusions from nothing: they aim to build them by justifiable procedures
which agents of construction can follow. We may quite reasonably ask why
we should take 'reflective equilibrium with our considered judgements'
or 'a suitably constructed social point of view that all can accept' or 'the

---

[14] Rawls comments in *JFPM* that he would have done better to title his 1976 Dewey lectures not
'Kantian constructivism in moral theory' but 'Kantian constructivism in political philosophy',
224.

public reason of citizens in a democratic society' as (partly) constitutive of reasonableness. There are other possibilities, including the form of Kantian constructivism that Kant himself proposed.

Although much of Rawls's work is quite un-Kantian,[15] his characterisation of his method for establishing principles of justice and of his conclusions as both Kantian and constructivist makes good sense. Yet, as he notes, many commentators have not thought that Kant's method of establishing ethical principles is constructive at all. Some have thought that Kant, despite his disavowals, peddles one more form of rational intuitionism and is a covert moral realist; others that he offers only a minimal formalism. If those who see moral realism in Kant were right, he and Rawls would share little. If those who see minimal formalism in Kant are right, Rawls's Kantianism would amount to their shared anti-realism, their common aspiration to non-relativist justification in ethics and their shared liberal views about justice, but would not extend to a common ambition to construct a range of ethical conclusions.

Nevertheless, there are good reasons for agreeing with Rawls that Kant's method in ethics is constructive. A background consideration is that Kant combines anti-realism with claims to identify objective moral principles: a constructive approach fits well into his wider philosophy. More specifically, there are many junctures at which Kant appeals explicitly to constructive procedures, including his accounts of the justification of theoretical reason and of mathematical reasoning.[16] Finally, and most significantly, there are reasons to think that Kant's conception of ethical justification is more radically constructive than the one that Rawls proposes.

Kant's method in ethics clearly resembles Rawls's method in several negative respects. He proposes a procedure for justifying ethically important principles of action by appeal to a conception of practical reasoning that does not build on supposed moral facts or actual individual preferences. The procedure(s) envisaged – stated in the various formulations of the Categorical Imperative – are thought of as procedures agents can use to identify ethically acceptable basic principles of action, hence as practical, and as providing a justification for those procedures. Kant's famous arguments against heteronomy in ethics reject 'procedures' of ethical reasoning that invoke either the (illusory) independent values of moral realism to sustain some form of perfectionism or the (unvindicated) value of mere preferences

---

[15] For example, his conception of practical reason, his separation of the justification of principles of justice from the justification of other moral principles, his anti-cosmopolitanism.

[16] For constructivist claims about the vindication of reason and mathematics see in particular the earlier part of the *Doctrine of Method* in the *Critique of Pure Reason*.

to sustain ethical subjectivism, utilitarianism or preference-based forms of contractarianism.

These negative points are easily established. The best-known version of Kant's procedure of construction, the Categorical Imperative, is the Formula of Universal Law,[17] which enjoins agents to 'act only on that maxim through which you can at the same time will that it should become a universal law': agents should reject principles of action which they take it cannot be adopted by all.[18] There is no reference here, or in Kant's underlying theory of action, to any given moral reality or to desires or preferences.

Still, negative points are not enough to show that Kant too takes a constructive approach to ethics. Kant can be read as an ethical constructivist only by showing that (despite rejecting rational intuitionism) he proposes a method agents can use to identify specific principles with practical implications, and that he justifies this method.

For present purposes I shall take it that the Categorical Imperative identifies procedure(s) that have practical implications: that they can identify at least some ethical principles, including principles of justice.[19] The more demanding question is whether they can themselves be justified without reintroducing some form of moral realism by the back door. Kant evidently takes it that constructive procedures for ethics are not arbitrary, and that they constitute the weightier aspect of practical reason, or reasonableness. Just as Rawls insists that the rational and the reasonable are both relevant to justifying principles of justice, but that they are distinct, so Kant insists that the principles of the Hypothetical and Categorical Imperatives are

---

[17] See Immanuel Kant, *G* 421. I do not mean to suggest that one rather another formulation of the Categorical Imperative is favoured by a constructive reading of Kant. The entire picture offered in this chapter could be developed using any of the formulations as illustrative. For a constructivist approach to the Formula of the End in Itself see Thomas E. Hill, Jr., 'Kantian constructivism in ethics', *Ethics* 99 (1989), 752–70, also in his *Dignity and Practical Reason* (Ithaca, NY: Cornell University Press, 1992), 226–50.

[18] What this tells us is rather less than some of Kant's critics assume and uncritical admirers hope: Kant is concerned with principles that cannot be adopted by all. If his procedure had been to rule out principles that cannot be acted on by all (successfully, at a given time), the critics who have perennially pointed out how implausible such an ethics would be would have a highly damaging criticism of Kant.

[19] For discussion of the practicality of the Categorical Imperative see Onora O'Neill, *Constructions of Reason*, Part II (Cambridge University Press, 1989) and *Acting on Principle*, 2nd edn (Cambridge University Press, 2013); Thomas E. Hill, Jr., *Dignity and Practical Reason* (Ithaca, NY: Cornell University Press, 1992); Barbara Herman, *The Practice of Moral Judgement* (Cambridge, MA: Harvard University Press, 1993); Marcia Baron, *Kantian Ethics Almost without Apology* (Ithaca, NY: Cornell University Press, 1995); Christine Korsgaard, *Creating the Kingdom of Ends* (Cambridge University Press, 1996); Allen Wood, *Kant's Ethical Thought* (Cambridge University Press, 1999).

both relevant to justifying ethical principles and that they are mutually irreducible.

Yet it is not easy to see why Kant thinks these procedures constitute requirements of practical reason or reasonableness. He and Rawls may end up with parallel difficulties, both proposing a procedure for identifying specific practical principles, but failing to show convincingly that this procedure is grounded in or expresses (some conception of) reasonableness. Their positions may be constructive in the limited sense that they propose procedures for guiding action, but not in the fuller sense of justifying those procedures. If so, neither Rawls nor Kant will justify ethical claims in the strong sense to which constructivists aspire.

However, Kant does more than invoke an ungrounded 'supreme principle of practical reason'. He holds that an account of practical reason itself should be susceptible of justification: that ambition is implicit in the very titles of his major works. Critiques of pure and of practical reason are critiques not merely of the deployment of antecedently given, uncritically accepted conceptions of reason, but of those conceptions of reason. If Kant can do this, he may offer not a merely conditional but a deep vindication of ethical principles, which rests on vindicating a conception of practical reason. If in addition his vindication of reason is constructive, his constructivism will be not only deep but radical.

Rawls denied that Kant offered, or could offer, a constructive justification for his conception of practical reason. In 'Themes in Kant's moral philosophy' he posed and answered two questions:

> First, in moral constructivism, what is constructed? The answer is: the content of the doctrine... A second question is this. Is the CI-procedure itself constructed? No, it is not. Rather, it is simply laid out ... not everything can be constructed and every construction has a basis, certain materials, as it were, from which it begins. (*TKMP* 98–9)

On Rawls's view these materials include Kant's conception of free and equal persons as rational and reasonable, which is 'elicited from our moral experience' (*TKMP* 99). Ethical reasoning builds on the basis of these elicited conceptions; practical reason itself is not justified by any constructive procedure.

In the following section of *Themes in Kant's Moral Philosophy* Rawls argues that Kant's conception of practical reason is grounded in his difficult doctrine of the Fact of Reason, as set out in the *Critique of Practical Reason*. A quite common view of Kant's discussion of the Fact of Reason is that this is the given bed-rock for all moral reasoning: practical reason, and hence the Categorical Imperative procedure(s),[20] are simply given to human consciousness, hence not themselves constructed. This reading suggests that (despite himself) Kant fell back on some form of rational intuitionism, and even on moral realism.

However, Rawls does not construe Kant's doctrine of the Fact of Reason as an attempt to offer an unalterable datum (bed-rock, foundation) for the justification of ethics. Although the supreme principle of practical reason, which is the moral law, cannot be given any proof, although it cannot be derived from theoretical reason,[21] although it is not a regulative idea (*TKMP* 106–7), it can be authenticated as the principle needed for 'completing the constitution of reason as one unified body of principles' (*TKPM* 108). On Rawls's reading, the *Second Critique* confirms that reason is 'self authenticating as a whole' by offering 'not only a constructivist conception of practical reason but a coherentist account of its justification' (*TKPM* 108).

The distinction which Rawls draws here between Kant's constructive use of the Categorical Imperative to establish ethical principles and the merely coherentist character of its justification parallels his own strategy in *Theory of Justice*, where the principles of justice are constructed using OP, but OP receives only a coherentist justification.[22]

Kant on the construction of reason

Yet when we look at Kant's writing on the vindication of reason, it can seem very natural to read him not merely as arguing that the Categorical Imperative, the supreme principle of practical reason, coheres with other aspects of his conception of reason, but more specifically that it can itself be constructively justified. Towards the end of the *Critique of Pure Reason*, in the initial passages of the *Doctrine of Method*, Kant depicts the edifice of human reason as doomed to failure without a vindication of reason. Although 'materials' in plenty have been assembled in the course of the

---

[20] I leave open whether the various formulations of the Categorical Imperative are equivalent or not. My own view is that they are equivalent under a plausible reading, see Onora O'Neill, 'Universal laws and ends in themselves', in *Constructions of Reason*, 126–44. Thomas E. Hill, Jr., argues otherwise; see his 'Humanity as an end in itself', in his *Dignity and Practical Reason* (Ithaca, NY: Cornell University Press, 1992), 38–57.

[21] A strategy whose possibility Kant explored thoroughly before he rejected it. See Dieter Henrich, 'Der Begriff der sittlichen Einsicht und Kants Lehre vom Faktum der Vernunft' in G. Prauss (ed.), *Kant. Zur Deutung seiner Theorie von Erkennen und Handeln* (Cologne: Kiepenheuer und Witsch, 1973), 77–115.

[22] For arguments that, on the contrary, the Fact of Reason itself is constructed see Pawel Łukow, 'The Fact of Reason: Kant's passage to ordinary moral knowledge', *Kant-studien* 84 (1993), 204–21.

Critique of Pure Reason, we will fail like the uncoordinated builders of Babel if we cannot find a 'common plan' for putting them to use.

However, there is no independent order of reason that lays down a common plan or procedure that constitutes the principle(s) of practical reasoning: 'reason has no dictatorial authority' (*CPR* A 739 / B 767). Since reason is not provided from 'on high', we will either dispose *at most* of rationality, or must show how a conception of reasonableness can be constructed out of the capacities and materials that human agents actually have at their disposal.

Yet if there is no antecedently given 'plan of reason', no independent, external authority, why should *any* way of proceeding count as more reasonable than any other? Can agents who do not enjoy the benefit of a pre-established harmony that orients them to an independently given canon of reason view any way(s) of proceeding as requirements of reason? As Kant analyses the matter, the very predicament of a plurality of uncoordinated agents is all that we can presuppose in trying to identify principles of practical reason. Since reason's authority is not given, it must be instituted or constituted – constructed – by human agents.

Consider the predicament of uncoordinated agents more closely. They cannot take any particular faith or belief, tradition or norm, claim or proposition, in short any arbitrary premise, as having the sort of unrestricted authority which would entitle them to view it as a principle of reason. Yet they need if they are to do anything that amounts to reasoning to give and receive, exchange and evaluate one another's claims about knowledge and action. How are they to construct ways of doing this? Since all that they have in common is their lack of a given 'plan of reason', all that they can do is to refuse to treat any of the particular beliefs or norms that some of them hold as having more general authority. Those who do not regard any specific beliefs and norms as having an unrestricted authority in effect adopt the overarching principle of thinking and acting on principles which they regard as open to and followable by all.

Yet this limited discipline of rejecting ways of thinking and acting that cannot be followed by others with whom reasoning is undertaken is surprisingly constraining. If thoughts and knowledge claims are to be seen as reasoned, they must be followable by others, and so intelligible; if principles of action are to be offered as reasons for action to others, they must be followable by others, and so adoptable as principles of action by those others. Agents who accept the 'supreme principle of practical reason' must adopt principles which, they take it, can also be adopted by others: in short they must accept the principle expressed in the Formula of Universal Law formulation of the Categorical Imperative.

These thoughts about the grounds for thinking that the Categorical Imperative states the fundamental requirement of practical reason have several corollaries. First, if the discipline of reason requires the rejection of principles whenever (we take it) not all others can understand or adopt them, or view them as providing reasons, then any reasonable procedures must be in principle accessible to all. Reason cannot be anchored either in the norms of communities (as communitarians suppose) or in the agreement of citizens of an ethically diverse polity (as Rawls supposes): it must be accessible in principle even to 'outsiders'. 'Outsiders' would legitimately view any claim that principles of reason are to be identified with the beliefs or norms of specific groups from which they are excluded as fetishising some 'alien', arbitrary authority. By contrast, where all such 'authorities' are put in question, nobody will be told that some claim, that they cannot but view as arbitrary, constitutes a reason for them to believe or act. Ways of organising thinking and acting that appeal to such spurious 'authorities' – whether these are the edicts of church or state, of public opinion or of local powers – are simply arbitrary for those who do not accept the purported authority.

In a world of differing beings, reasoning is not complete, or we may say (and Kant said) not *fully* public when it rests on appeal to properties and beliefs, attitudes and desires, norms and commitments which are simply arbitrary from some points of view. Often incompletely, partly arbitrary stretches of thought are enough to the purposes at hand: but not always. When we seek deep justifications, that are to reach others who are not already like-minded, we are satisfied only with claims about what to believe and what to do if (we think) they can be followed by those others. The only strategy that can count as a reason for all is that of rejecting all unvindicated assumptions, all spurious authorities, however respectable and well trusted.

Of course, organising thought and action on principles that are accessible (can be followed in thought or adopted in action) by others may seem a minimal demand, and less than the presumptively weighty authority of reason should amount to. Can the universal accessibility of claims about what to think and what to do be all that constitutes reason? Will this conception of practical reason yield any significant conclusions? Will a constructivist account of reason provide an adequate constructive procedure for ethics (or for justice)? Does the Categorical Imperative have practical implications?

Can ethical principles, including principles of justice, be justified? These questions remain to be settled: they are about the construction of ethics on the basis of practical reason rather than about the construction of practical reason itself.[23]

However, even without any close consideration of its ethical and political implications, some corollaries of Kant's distinctive construction of practical reason can be considered. I list only a few. First, it shows why Kant came to view the principle of universalisability as 'the supreme principle of practical reason', and why he speaks of it in its practical role as 'the moral law'. Second, it highlights the difference between the conceptions of practical reason that Kant and Rawls adopt. Put briefly, the difference is that Rawls (in the later versions of his theory of justice) took a conception of democratic citizenship within a bounded society as the source and context of all practical reason, whereas Kant (although he uses the terms 'citizenship' and 'public' metaphorically) presupposed only a plurality of uncoordinated agents. Kant does not presuppose institutions, such as those of a bounded state, or of democracy: they too need justification, and invoking them without justification is no more than an argument from authority.[24] Third, the account shows that it is unsurprising that in the construction of justice Kant reaches for a cosmopolitan vision, within which states have their justification, rather than being in part constitutive of reasonableness, and differ from Rawls who views bounded societies as presuppositions of reason, and treats international justice as an appendix to domestic justice. Fourth, the approach explains why Rawls's constructivism, being fundamentally civic, while sensitive to pluralism within a society, is directed solely at an account of justice, while Kant's constructivism can aim at a fuller range of ethical justification.

[23] There has been much dispute whether universalisability is as fruitful a procedure as Kant believes it is for constructing substantive ethical principles. Putting the matter as briefly as possible, universalisability is not a merely formal demand, since it requires us to reject principles if they cannot even be adopted (not enacted!) by all, for example because they prescribe ways of acting – e.g. violence, coercion, deception – that if adopted by all, and hence successfully enacted at least by some, will disable or damage at least some others, hence preclude those others from adopting those (and perhaps other) principles, which are thereby demonstrably not principles for all.

[24] The fact that Kant does not tie the notions of citizenship and of the public use of reason to specific institutional structures is evident in *What Is Enlightenment?*, where he speaks of various sorts of civic communication as *private* uses of reason (because they presuppose some 'alien', rationally unvindicated, authority) and of the audience for public uses of reason not as the citizens of an already constituted state but as 'the world at large'. His example of such communication – that among men of learning – is naive, but the point is clear enough. For closer comments see 'Vindicating reason', Chapter 1 above, and 'Kant's conception of public reason', Chapter 3 above.

Constructivism of the more radical Kantian sort is, in the end, no more (but also no less) than the project of working, indeed building, from wherever a plurality of diverse agents with unspecified beliefs and situations begins, without presupposing the legitimacy of existing powers and institutions, beliefs or norms, and thereby addressing the task of seeking – constructing – principles that can count as reasons for all of them. Sceptics will probably not worry that such a constructive procedure will prove too constraining, and are more likely to suspect that it will turn out to be either the emptiest of formalisms, or one more covert form of rational intuitionism.

Some conclusions

In this chapter I have said little about the practicality either of Rawls's or of Kant's constructivism. Further arguments – there have been plenty – would be needed to show that either position has significant normative implications. I have concentrated on the concern that if practical reason has no external or transcendent source, then it must either reduce to rationality, or make do with a contextualised conception of the reasonable that builds on accepted norms or beliefs, powers or institutions. Kant and Rawls are highly distinctive in that they accept the challenge of showing that ethical justification is possible even if antecedent agreement on norms is not presupposed.

Both go beyond conceptions of justification as anchored in mere rationality or in community norms; both regard such approaches as reaching normative implications only by according value without good reason – whether to actual preferences or to historically contingent configurations of norms and institutions. Both regard these approaches as able to provide reasons only for correspondingly diminished audiences. Yet despite these similarities, Kant and Rawls offer very different conceptions of the reasonable, and so of the scope and limits of constructivism in ethics. The fundamental differences lie in their diverging views of the sources, the authority and ultimately the audiences for practical reasoning. Rawls sees Kant's procedure as 'too individualist', because (he claims) it invokes the idea of a domain of individual agents each of whom reasons on his or her own. This point may be apt if we are considering a use of the Categorical Imperative to test some ethical principle. But it is inaccurate as a claim about Kant's conception of practical reason, which starts from the conception of a plurality of agents not coordinated by any pre-established harmony, or even by the contingencies of shared ideology or citizenship.

Constructivism for Kant, as for Rawls, relies on the thought that a plurality of diverse beings lacking antecedent coordination is the source and the audience for reasoning. But Kant takes a more radical view of this lack of coordination: he does not presuppose determinate social or political structures, or even the nexus of fellow-citizenship within a bounded, democratic society. Kant's constructivism begins with weaker assumptions than Rawls's relies on: he begins simply with the thought that a plurality of agents may lack antecedent principles of coordination, yet aim to build an account of reason, of ethics, and specifically of justice on this basis. We are doers before we are reasoners or citizens.

Although there are many points to be made about what Rawls and others have deemed Kant's individualism, it is clear that Kant's conception of the construction of reason rests on the view that there are many agents who differ in many ways. The Formula of Universal Law proposes as the test of ethical adequacy simply that principles adopted not be ones that could not be willed by, adopted by, all others. It is, as Kant puts it, a conception of the reasonable that addresses an unrestricted audience – 'the world at large' – rather than the restricted public of a particular society or state. Kant's public is not the Rawlsian public, consisting only of fellow citizens in a bounded liberal democratic society: it is unrestricted. Hence Kant's conception of ethical method takes a cosmopolitan rather than a quasi-statist[25] view of the scope of ethical concern; correspondingly he takes a more demanding view of the construction of ethical principles, in that he conceives of justification as aiming to reach all others, without restriction.

These issues are, I believe, the key to the different conceptions of the reasonable to be found in Rawls and in Kant, and so to the differences between their versions of constructivism. Rawls, by the time that he wrote

---

[25] Rawls insists, especially in *The Law of Public Reason* (Cambridge, MA: Harvard University Press, 1999), that he does not take a statist view of the context of justice, which he anchors in the reasoning of peoples rather than of states. Yet a conception of justice that is designed to be shared among the citizens of a bounded, closed society assumes that there will be a power that keeps that society closed and bounded: such powers are states, under a standard Weberian definition. For discussions of Kant's cosmopolitanism see Martha Nussbaum, 'Kant and stoic cosmopolitanism', *Journal of Political Philosophy* 5 (1997), 1–25; Thomas Mertens, 'Cosmopolitanism and citizenship: Kant against Habermas', *European Journal of Philosophy* 4 (1996), 328–47; for further comments on Rawls's statism see Onora O'Neill, 'Political liberalism and public reason: a critical notice of John Rawls' *Political Liberalism*', *Philosophical Review* 106 (1997), 411–28; 'Bounded and cosmopolitan justice', *Review of International Studies* 26 (2000), 45–60, and in Onora O'Neill, *Justice across Boundaries: Whose Obligations?* (Cambridge University Press, forthcoming).

Political Liberalism, identified the reasonable with public reasoning within a given, bounded society; Kant was committed to establishing a conception of reasonableness or practical reason (which he too calls *public reason*) that would hold for any plurality of interacting beings. It is this difference that leaves room for Kant, unlike Rawls, to commit himself to a constructive account not only of justice, but more broadly of ethics, and more radically of practical reason itself.

CHAPTER 5

Changing constructions[1]

Contracts and constructions

The publication of John Rawls's *Political Liberalism*[2] surprised many of his admirers. It defended the same substantive principles of justice that Rawls had put forward in *A Theory of Justice*[3] in 1971, but introduced major changes in the arguments by which they were supported. There is of course nothing wrong about offering distinct considerations in support of a single set of claims, yet it startled many readers to find Rawls proposing such large revisions in justification of substantive claims about justice that he had put forward for many years. Here I shall reflect on some of the innovations and the continuities in *Political Liberalism* that seem to me of most interest, and address some of the problems that I think it leaves unresolved.

From the time of writing *A Theory of Justice*, Rawls saw his work as continuing the social contract tradition, while aiming to avoid its recurrent problems. In the preface to *A Theory of Justice* he writes that he aims to carry 'to a higher level of abstraction the familiar theory of the social contract as found, say, in Locke, Rousseau and Kant' (*TJ* viii) and in the opening paragraph that he aims to offer 'a theory of justice that generalizes and carries to a higher level of abstraction the traditional conception of the social contract' (*TJ* 3).[4] But whereas in *A Theory of Justice* Rawls had mainly described his work as *contractarian*, in *Political Liberalism* the metaphors of the social contract tradition were mostly replaced by the idea that principles of justice can be *constructed* by reasonable procedures.

---

[1] 'Changing constructions' in Thom Brooks and Martha Nussbaum (eds.), *Rawls's Political Liberalism* (New York: Columbia University Press, 2015), 57–72. This chapter offers no further comments on Kant's constructivism. It concentrates on the development of John Rawls's approach to constructivism.

[2] John Rawls, *Political Liberalism* (New York: Columbia University Press, 1993); abbreviated *PL* in notes and citations.

[3] John Rawls, *A Theory of Justice* (Cambridge, MA: Harvard University Press, 1971); abbreviated *TJ* in notes and citations.

[4] See also 'Justice as fairness is...a contract theory' (*TJ* 16) and 'there are many different contract theories. Justice as fairness is but one of these' (*TJ* 121).

The approach taken in *Political Liberalism* defends a form of *political constructivism* that seeks to identify principles of justice that would be reached by citizens who reasonably deliberate together, where reasonable citizens are seen as proposing and abiding by fair terms of social cooperation among equals (*PL* 93ff.).

This specific focus on citizens and their deliberation had not been prominent in *A Theory of Justice*, but can be seen as developing rather than replacing the earlier approach. *A Theory of Justice* proposes a theory of justice for a society that is thought of as 'a more or less self-sufficient association of persons' (*TJ* 4) and 'as a closed system isolated from other societies' (*TJ* 8). It was clear from its first pages that John Rawls had bracketed questions about international justice (*TJ* 8), despite assuming that there are many societies. Rereading his initial account of the context of justice with hindsight, it seems that many of the issues raised by his assumption that justice is internal to bounded societies, with their explicit inclusions and exclusions, were present and might have led to earlier questions about these aspects of his arguments.

Yet widespread discussion of the implications of these inclusions and exclusions began only after the publication of *Political Liberalism* in 1993, and of *The Law of Peoples*[5] in 1999. I shall argue that the assumption that we are dealing (at least in the first instance) with a *bounded* society of fellow citizens became more central to Rawls's approaches to justifying principles of justice in the years between *A Theory of Justice* and *Political Liberalism*, despite the reality that globalisation of many sorts was already underway, and that it was becoming less and less plausible to assume that issues of 'domestic' justice could be handled in isolation. A focus on citizens and citizenship incorporates specific views of *who counts* in matters of justice, and also of *who does not count*, or *counts for less*. Claims about the *scope* of justice are fundamental to arguments about its demands, and Rawls's views about who counts in various contexts are of central importance to understanding his changing position.

Who counts in the Original Position?[6]

Rawls claimed in *A Theory of Justice* that his method is 'more abstract' than that used in traditional social contract theories. In certain obvious ways

[5] John Rawls, *The Law of Peoples* (Cambridge, MA: Harvard University Press, 1999).
[6] This section draws on some of the arguments I used in discussing Rawls's reliance on abstraction and idealisation in Onora O'Neill, 'The method of *A Theory of Justice*' in *John Rawls: Eine Theorie der Gerechtigkeit*, ed. Otfried Höffe (Berlin: Akademie Verlag, 1998), 27–43.

this is true. For example, he does not assume that there was some historical moment at which the members of each society actually contracted, or that (by some unknown means) their successors are now bound by the terms of that original contract. However, denying that the social contract was an historical event would hardly have been an innovation: the point had been familiar since the Enlightenment. But if the terms of the social contract are not historical but hypothetical, how and why do they bind actual persons who have never agreed to them? (See *TJ* 21.) The more abstract approach that Rawls took in *A Theory of Justice* was intended to continue the social contract tradition by constructing an argument that provided reasons why members of *any* society of citizens should accept specific principles of justice,[7] without drawing on (or inventing?) fictitious accounts of past occasions when they or some of their predecessors agreed to do so, but also without assuming that actual persons have accepted or must accept the terms of a hypothetical agreement or contract. The approach was to be philosophical and constructive, rather than historical or quasi-legal.

Rawls aimed both in *A Theory of Justice* and later to show that members of any society had *reason* to accept certain principles of justice. He notes at the end of *A Theory of Justice* that 'proof is not justification' since 'proofs simply display logical relations between propositions', but justifications work only 'once the starting points are mutually recognised' (*TJ* 581). The thought that principles of justice must be *justified to those who will be bound by them* is present throughout Rawls's work on justice, but it takes different forms in *A Theory of Justice* and in his subsequent work.

In *A Theory of Justice* the first step that Rawls takes is to distance reasonable agreement on principles of justice from ordinary, real-world agreements and disagreements by setting out a distinctively characterised Original Position. Agreements in ordinary life reflect differentials in power and knowledge, so they don't offer a good basis for identifying principles of justice. Rawls seeks to correct for this problem by arguing that specific principles of justice would be chosen by rational agents[8] in a hypothetical Original Position in which

> no one knows his place in society, his class position, or social status, nor does anyone know his fortune in the distribution of natural assets and abilities,

---

[7] The argument depends in part on showing that the two principles of justice are 'the unique solution to the problem set by the original position' (*TJ* 119). This claim has been repeatedly queried, but I shall not discuss it here.

[8] In these arguments he takes it that they are rational 'in the narrow sense, standard in economic theory, of taking the most effective means to given ends' but does not introduce any wider conception of the reasonable. See *TJ* 14 and 143.

his intelligence, strength and the like . . . their conceptions of the good or their special psychological propensities. (*TJ* 12)

Despite Rawls's description of this approach as 'contractarian', the term cannot be taken literally. Any claim that parties in the Original Position 'agree' or 'contract', or even that they endorse a hypothetical 'agreement' or 'contract', is highly metaphorical because there is nothing to differentiate one person from another in the Original Position. Rawls points out that 'we can view the choice in the Original Position from the standpoint of one person selected at random' (*TJ* 139).[9] No actual persons take part in or count in the Original Position.

So this hypothetical 'agreement' cannot be understood as a solution to disagreements of the sort that in actual situations might be resolved by bargaining or contracting, since by hypothesis nothing differentiates the parties. There is nothing that they need to agree on, or that they can agree on, since the terms of the hypothetical 'contract' are reached simply by obliterating sources of disagreement. The Original Position provides a way of *generating* or *identifying* principles of justice that articulate an ideal of fairness, but it is not used to justify them to those who (supposedly) are to be bound by them.

Who counts in reflective equilibrium?

In *A Theory of Justice* Rawls deals with the limitations of the Original Position by embedding it in a conception of Reflective Equilibrium that specifically addresses questions of justification to actual people. The Original Position is a device for generating tentative principles of justice, but their justification to 'us', who are to live by or under them, is not that they would be chosen in a situation that we arguably should, but in fact may not, regard as fair, but that they are in *reflective equilibrium* with 'our' best-considered judgements about justice. 'We' confirm the claim that the principles hypothetically agreed in the Original Position are principles of justice because they are (supposedly) 'the same judgements about the basic structure of society that we now make intuitively and in which we have the greatest confidence' (*TJ* §4 19; cf. §87 579). Reflective Equilibrium rather than the Original Position is Rawls's fundamental strategy of justification in *A Theory of Justice*:

[9] Cf. John Rawls, 'Justice as fairness: political not metaphysical' (*JFPM*), *Philosophy and Public Affairs* 14 (1985), 223–51; reprinted in John Rawls, *Collected Papers*, ed. Samuel Freeman (Cambridge, MA: Harvard University Press, 1999).

> By going back and forth, sometimes altering the conditions of the contractual circumstances, at others withdrawing our judgements and conforming them to principle, I assume that eventually we shall find a description of the initial situation that both expresses reasonable conditions and yields principles that match our considered judgements duly pruned and adjusted. This state of affairs I refer to as reflective equilibrium. (*TJ* 20)

So justification in the end is *not* to be hypothetical, and we should (as Rawls was later to put it) view the Original Position merely as a 'device of representation' (*PL* 24ff.) or as an 'artifice of reason' (*PL* 75). This awareness of the limitations of the Original Position was something Rawls held to throughout his discussion of justification in *A Theory of Justice*, where he notes that 'Moral philosophy is Socratic: we may want to change our present considered judgements once their regulative principles are brought to light' (*TJ* 49; see also 578). The deep strategy of *A Theory of Justice* is coherentist, and the device of the Original Position is used to fix the content rather than the justification of principles of justice.

However, subordinating the Original Position to Reflective Equilibrium for purposes of justification comes at a price. This is not because coherentist justifications are invariably problematic. Many of Rawls's colleagues and contemporaries used coherentist strategies of justification for a variety of purposes. Noam Chomsky looked for coherence between his proposed deep principles of grammar and intuitive judgements of grammaticalness made by native speakers (cf. *TJ* 47); W. v O. Quine argued in many works that justification cannot be linear or foundationalist, but must aim to show coherence between a plurality of claims. However, introducing coherentist justificatory strategies unavoidably raises questions of scope: *whose* considered judgements are to be brought into reflective equilibrium with principles hypothetically generated by the device of the Original Position? Who exactly counts in Reflective Equilibrium? In *A Theory of Justice* Rawls left his answer to this question open: he appeals to 'our' considered judgements, but leaves it unclear whom he has in mind. In later works, including 'Justice as fairness: political not metaphysical' and *Political Liberalism*, he says more about who counts for justification.

Who counts in political liberalism?[10]

The view of justification that John Rawls introduced in 'Justice as fairness: political not metaphysical' and developed in *Political Liberalism*

---

[10] Some of the arguments in this section draw on my 'Political liberalism and public reason: a critical notice of John Rawls' *Political Liberalism*', *Philosophical Review* 106 (1998), 411–28.

is specifically *political*, and appeals to a distinctive conception of public reason. As Rawls argued from the mid-eighties onwards, when it comes to justification, citizens count and non-citizens do not. He summarised his revised position in the claim that

> Public reason is characteristic of a democratic people: it is the reason of its citizens, of those sharing the equal status of citizenship . . . [it] is public in three ways: as the reason of citizens as such, it is the reason of the public; its subject is the good of the public and matters of fundamental justice; and its nature and content is public, being given by the ideals and principles expressed by society's conception of political justice, and conducted open to view. *PL* 213[11]

This conception of public reasoning takes specific, distinctive and interconnected views of the *context*, the *subject matter* and the *procedures* of public reasoning. I shall discuss each in turn.

The context and audiences of public reasoning

The *context* and *audience* of public reason, as understood in *Political Liberalism*, is once again a society conceived of as one among many. However, the societies in which such reasoning is seen as possible are now explicitly confined to *bounded*, *liberal* and *democratic* political societies, each conceived of as a 'complete and closed social system . . . [where] entry into it is only by birth and exit from it is only by death' (*PL* 40–1, 68, 301).[12] These strikingly strong – and markedly unrealistic – restrictions on the *context* of public reasoning raise several problems, in particular because they ignore reasoning undertaken in nondemocratic societies and reasoning that crosses the borders between different societies. Both of these themes gained some importance in Rawls's later work, but both were marginalised in *Political Liberalism*, which is entirely clear about who counts for purposes of political justification: fellow citizens count and others do not.

The nature and content of public reasoning

The context of public reason that Rawls assumes in *Political Liberalism* has decisive implications for his claims about its nature and content. The thought that public reasoning takes place among fellow citizens in bounded

---

[11] See also 'The idea of public reason revisited' (*TIPRR*) in John Rawls, *Collected Papers*, 574ff.
[12] Rawls denied that this bounded society is a state. However, the fact that it has and defends its boundaries suggests that it is close to being a state.

societies is fruitful because those citizens can be taken to share certain fundamental commitments. Their shared civic commitments to liberalism, to democracy and to the continued existence of their bounded society provide a basis for debating or justifying its specific political arrangements.

Yet the very fact that citizens are assumed to share these commitments may also hamper the justification of fundamental political arrangements. If commitments to liberalism, to democracy and to the continued existence of a bounded society are taken as given, the answers to certain fundamental questions about justice, such as the justice of secession or annexation, or the justice of liberalism or democracy, are prejudged. Even coherentist justifications must do more than reiterate commitments. The thought that public reasoning can take place *only* among fellow citizens may seem inadequate because it excludes reasoning that crosses boundaries or engages with those who are not fellow citizens. It seems as if Rawls assumed *more* than is advisable if fundamental political arrangements are to be justified, but also *less* than is needed for justifying political arrangements in a globalising world.

However, Rawls's discussions of the nature and content of public reasoning in *Political Liberalism* focus not on the implications of assuming political boundaries, but on the importance of a quite different boundary between political and non-political questions, in particular religious questions. At the end of *The Idea of Public Reason Revisited* he wrote:

> Throughout, I have been concerned with a torturing question in the contemporary world, namely: Can democracy and comprehensive doctrines, religious or non-religious be compatible? And if so how? (*TIPRR*, in *Collected Papers*, 611)

Rawls was more worried by the threat to liberal democratic societies that can arise from within, when religious and cultural views threaten to eclipse the public domain, than he was by questions about the injustice created by external boundaries and the exclusions they maintain. He concludes that public reasoning among fellow citizens cannot resolve all questions on which they may disagree, but only those on which their fundamental political commitments bear. Citizens in pluralistic, liberal democratic societies may hold a great variety of religious, ethical and social views that remain impervious to processes of public reasoning. Consequently persisting pluralism of outlooks and ideologies within each society is a natural outcome of the free public use of reason.[13] In *Political Liberalism* Rawls therefore

---

[13] *PL* xv; Rawls, *TIPRR*, in *Collected Papers*, 573–615, see esp. 574ff.

explicitly sets aside aspirations to justify any comprehensive moral position, in favour of a strictly political view of what can be justified by public reason. For this reason *Political Liberalism* is *less* ambitious about the limits of justification than *A Theory of Justice* had been. Rawls now maintains that public reasoning can justify no more than *political liberalism*, which takes no position on broader questions about the good for man.

Rawls did not think that these limitations on the subject matter of *public* reasoning meant that nothing reasoned could be said about morality or religion, but only that neither was a matter for *public* reasoning. He takes it that other types of reasoning assume different contexts, and concludes that 'Not all reasons are public reasons, as there are the non-public reasons of Churches and universities and of many other associations in society' (*PL* 213, cf. 220–2). A natural way to read his discussions of non-public reasoning is to accept that reasoning that is addressed only to limited audiences can, perhaps must, reason within frameworks that those audiences understand and accept at least in part (for example, those assumed by specific ideological, moral, theological or nationalist doctrines), which others may not accept, indeed may not even understand. Non-public reasoning, on this account, is not *unreasoned*, but it is unfit to persuade the public at large, many of whom will (at best) see any justifications it offers as conditional on assumptions they reject or find incomprehensible.

Processes of public reasoning

However, the most interesting aspect of the revised justification of principles of justice offered in *Political Liberalism* is its explicit appeal to processes of public reason. Already in 'Justice as fairness: political not metaphysical' Rawls had argued that justifications could appeal to ideals that are constitutive of the identities of citizens of liberal societies. In *Political Liberalism* he lays less emphasis on citizens' ideals and more on their being *reasonable* in ways that go beyond rationality.

In *A Theory of Justice* he had relied on narrower conceptions of reason, seeing choice and action as rational if they take optimal, or at least adequate, means to preferred or chosen ends. He then used the device of the Original Position to deflect the self-interest that rational choice would otherwise ratify, by ensuring that principles that were blind to individuals' preferences and interests were selected. In *Political Liberalism* Rawls takes quite a different approach to reason, and relies on a substantive conception of the reasonable:

> Persons are reasonable . . . when . . . they are ready to propose principles and
> standards as fair terms of cooperation and to abide by them willingly, given
> the assurance that others will likewise do so. (*PL* 49)

Reasonable persons seek to cooperate fairly; the merely rational pursue
their own interests, often at others' expense (*PL* 51). This conception of
the reasonable provides a basis for justification to others, and in particular
a basis for justification within the context of common citizenship. Rawls
summarises this thought by saying that 'the reasonable, in contrast with
the rational, addresses the public world of others' (*PL* 62, cf. 53).

Like some other contemporary proponents of conceptions of public reason, Rawls says more about his conception of the *public*, than about his
conception of *reason*.[14] However, he does *not* see public reason merely as
debate and discussion – discourse – that takes place between and among
the members of the public, variously conceived, hence in the public sphere.
Nevertheless, his focus is less on the distinctive features of various conceptions of reason than on the relations between the participants among whom
reasoning and interaction take place.

This conception of reasonableness as fairness or reciprocity among citizens offers a broader conception of public reason as the basis for justifying
principles of justice. It leads Rawls to substantive conclusions that reflect
citizens' shared political allegiance and their common liberal democratic
culture. He concludes that 'public reason is characteristic of a democratic
people: it is the reason of its citizens, of those sharing the status of equal
citizenship' (*PL* 213), that 'Justice as fairness is a political conception in part
because it starts from within a certain political tradition' (*PL* 225), and that
we look 'to our public political culture . . . as the shared fund of implicitly
recognised basic ideas and principles' (*PL* 228).

Public reason: form and scope

Other contemporary accounts of public reasoning – notably that proposed
by Jürgen Habermas[15] – focus less on conceptions of reason, and more on
the public among whom reasoning, generally or conventionally conceived,

---

[14] See Onora O'Neill, 'Autonomy and public reason in Kant', forthcoming in Mark Timmons and
Robert Johnson (eds.), *Reason, Value, and Respect: Kantian Themes from the Philosophy of Thomas
E. Hill, Jr.* (Oxford University Press) and as 'Autonomy and public reason in Kant, Habermas and
Rawls', Chapter 8 below.

[15] Jürgen Habermas, *The Structural Transformation of the Public Sphere: An Inquiry into a Category of
Bourgeois Society* [1962]; trans. Thomas Burger (Cambridge: Polity Press, 1989).

takes place. Some see public reasoning simply as discourse, debate or discussion that takes place between and among the members of the public, variously conceived, hence in the 'public sphere'. Although Rawls insists that he is 'concerned with reason not simply with discourse' (*PL* 53), he too says more about the context than about the processes of public reasoning, and he increasingly emphasised its geographical bounds, political context and close links with democracy. Towards the end of his life, in the introductory words of *The Idea of Public Reason Revisited*, he wrote:

> The idea of public reason, as I understand it, belongs to a conception of a well-ordered constitutional democratic society. The form and content of this reason . . . are part of the idea of democracy itself. (*TIPRR* 573)

We may seem to be up against an impassable barrier. Normative content cannot be derived from nothing, but if it is derived from the norms that are taken to be shared by fellow citizens in liberal democracies, then justification will be relativised to those norms. On the other hand, if it wholly abstracts from actually accepted norms, and does not build on any determinate content, will it be possible to establish any principles of justice?

One option that seems to me worth exploring would be to drop restrictions and exclusions such as those introduced by assuming a bounded, liberal and democratic society. Doing this would have two advantages. In the first place, it might allow something to be said about the justice of specific institutional arrangements, including boundaries and forms of liberalism and democracy, since they would not be presupposed. In the second place it would answer the concern that starting with bounded societies, liberalism and democracy assumes that justice to or among outsiders is not an issue. However, a conception of public reasoning that is shorn of the constraints created by assuming boundaries, liberalism and democracy may be too weak to justify any determinate conception of justice. Perhaps any 'conversation of mankind' that does not assume a certain amount of institutional structure and ideological content – such as boundaries, liberalism and democracy – will degenerate into a babble of voices. The only way to find out whether a more inclusive conception of public reasoning is fruitful is to suggest how it might be constructed and used to justify principles of justice.

In normative discussion and (attempted) justification we propose and recommend claims and norms to others who may in turn accept, or query, amend or reject those claims and norms. Communication and justification are *interactive*. Speakers have to assume some audience and tailor their speech acts to be intelligible to that audience, and enable their audience to assess their claims and proposals. Audiences have to aim to grasp what speakers communicate, which they may accept or reject, query or revise. All communication, including any justification of norms, is intrinsically *relational*, and will fail if the necessary conditions for successful communication are not met. However this does not mean that it has to be restricted to communication among fellow citizens.

The most obvious and elementary of those conditions, which is as relevant to cognitive as to practical norms, is that speakers must seek to make their proposals *intelligible* to those to whom they are made and that hearers must seek to *understand* and *assess* others' proposals. I do not justify beliefs or proposals for action *to* others unless I take steps to ensure that my audiences can understand what I say and grasp what I do in saying it (speakers and hearers may of course fail to communicate, but I leave that case aside). In a pluralistic world, these elementary requirements for successful communication can be exacting. Not only must interlocutors find at least some elements of common language in the obvious, linguistic sense. They must also take steps to enable their intended audiences to follow, grasp and assess their claims and proposals, as well as seeking to follow, grasp and assess others' claims and proposals. Reciprocal respect for the norms that permit intelligible and assessable communication is an indispensable success condition for communicative action, and so also for justification.

However, satisfying requirements for intelligible and assessable communication will not *by itself* justify any norms or standards, so will not justify principles of justice. As novelists and social anthropologists repeatedly show, we can understand and assess countless norms that we find irrelevant or trivial, alien or abhorrent, or incompatible with other norms we take seriously. If we are to identify norms that bear on justice, meeting conditions for communication may be necessary, but is seemingly is not enough.

One thought that may seem tempting at this point is that if we are to justify principles of justice for a globalising but pluralistic world, they must be *universal* norms that set out *universal* entitlements or requirements, such as those found in Declarations and Conventions of Human Rights – or for that matter in the less popular genre of Declarations of Human Duties. However, the thought that norms must be universal can mean several things, and some interpretations make it a less weighty matter than is often supposed.

A norm, rule or standard is universal *in form* if it prescribes for all cases falling under whatever agent description it assumes or incorporates, that is if (to use a Kantian turn of phrase) it is *lawlike*.[16] However, many cognitive and practical norms of restricted scope or questionable justification (or both) are lawlike in form. Both the norm *bank tellers should assume that customers are innumerate* and the norm *failing students should miss all lectures* are of universal form, and each addresses a restricted audience: but neither is obviously justifiable – although both are quite often adopted. Other cognitive and practical norms of universal form have more to be said for them. The norm *avoid inconsistent beliefs* and the norm *choose some effective means to your ends* are of universal form and address an unrestricted audience; they may well be justifiable. But clearly, we cannot justify norms of any sort *merely* by showing that they are intelligible and lawlike *in form*.

So we should not be surprised that norms and principles with lawlike form, that some think morally or politically important, often conflict with other norms and principles with lawlike form others think morally or politically important. That, after all, is the predicament of pluralism that Rawls addresses in *Political Liberalism*. Nor should we be surprised that some norms of universal form prescribe morally abhorrent standards or requirements, or are relevant only to specific and restricted groups, or conflict with other seemingly important norms. The pluralism to which so much contemporary writing in moral and political philosophy, including *Political Liberalism*, responds is a genuine predicament that arises from the reality that individuals and groups who live by differing sets of norms, many of them of universal form, must share the world. By itself, a demand that norms be universal *in form* cannot resolve disagreements about which norms should be seen as principles of justice.

However, while universal *form* by itself is a *less* weighty matter than is often imagined, combining universal *form* with universal *scope* may provide a basis for a more useful conception of public reason that is clearly relevant to identifying proposals and principles that can be communicated and potentially justified to an unrestricted audience.[17] We have seen that Rawls's justification of principles of justice in *Political Liberalism* in fact depends markedly on his assumptions about the *scope* of justice. Contemporary

---

[16] Kant pointed out the limitations of appeals to lawlike form *on its own* when he distinguished *heteronomous* from *autonomous* principles: both are lawlike in form, but he thinks that only the latter can be fully justified. On Kant's account, the *formal* structure of norms or principles is not enough to determine which norms are of cognitive or practical importance.

[17] Kant explored this approach in his later writings, where he develops a conception of public reason that stresses not the context and conditions in which it is conducted, but the norms that must be respected if communication is to reach a potentially unrestricted audience. As he sees it, 'private' uses of reason rely on assumptions that are peculiar to limited audiences, while 'public' uses of reason do not, so can be used in communication with, even justification to, 'the world at large'.

discussions often assume that the content of principles of justice can be settled independently of questions about their scope. So we tell ourselves encouraging stories about long-accepted norms and principles whose scope was initially seen as narrow but which were later progressively widened: the extension of the franchise and full citizenship from a propertied elite to all men and then to all women; the extension of full civil rights to groups previously marginalised on grounds of race or caste; the increasing inclusion and protection of children, the disabled, immigrants, homosexuals and members of many other groups that used to be relegated to second-class status. However, the claim that scope is a secondary matter and that we can generally justify principles of justice and subsequently adjust their scope as an afterthought or corrective may be mistaken. Scope often also matters for justification.

So it is reasonable to ask whether a conception of public reason as reasoning designed to reach an unrestricted audience could justify at least some politically (and perhaps ethically) important norms. On the surface things do not look particularly promising. We cannot reasonably expect that everybody will be able to *act* on any proposed norm or principle: the defects of this proposal have been exhaustively and tediously documented. A demand that norms or principles be universally *enactable* (at all times? in all contexts?) is a demand too far. However, the point of seeking to justify principles or norms to an unrestricted audience is not in the first place that all should promptly enact these norms, but to ensure that all can understand them, and assess them, and see their point and perhaps more, even if they find and foresee little current prospect of living by them.

Yet this may still seem to offer too weak a criterion for demarcating morally and politically significant norms. If the criterion for morally or politically significant norms is that they *could be adopted by all*, how can we distinguish between norms that can be followed by all simply because they prescribe trivially permissible action and those that prescribe action that is not trivially or merely permissible, but required? It seems that this more Kantian aim for justification may fail not because it assumes too readily that justice presupposes specific institutions, but because it assumes and provides too little to identify or justify any politically (or morally) important norms.

However, although the combination of lawlike form and universal scope is met by many trivial norms and principles, it is also one that at least some seriously reprehensible laws and principles cannot meet. This suggests that a fruitful use of this approach might be indirect. It might ask whether certain principles should be *rejected* because they are *not* justifiable. If we ask not which norms or principles *can* be universally adopted, but which *cannot* be universally adopted, an interesting picture emerges. There are many practical principles that can readily be adopted by *some* agents, but that cannot be adopted by *all* agents, and so cannot be coherently proposed to or justified to an unrestricted audience.

Typically such principles cannot be universally adopted because their adoption *even by some*, let alone by all, agents would be reflected in action that would disable or prevent at least some others from like action. Principles of violence or coercion, of manipulation or deception, and many others, cannot coherently be proposed to or justified to *all* others since their adoption will be reflected in at least some action on these principles, and even occasional enactment *by some* will preclude at least *some* others from taking like action. Combining demands for lawlike form and universal scope leads to non-trivial conclusions. Broadly speaking, norms whose successful enactment would make at least some others into victims, who cannot act on like norms, cannot coherently be put forward as norms for all or justified to all. This suggests that the principles we can initially justify to all might be very general principles of respecting or protecting others' agency. Such principles are a far cry from the principles of liberalism or democracy, or from specific institutional arrangements.

Principles and institutions

Political Liberalism builds certain institutional assumptions into the very core of its justification of principles of justice. Boundaries and liberal democratic citizenship are there from the start, and are presupposed by the proposed justification of principles of justice. The institutional presuppositions are in some tension with the aims of the social contract tradition, which has generally sought to justify rather than to assume institutions of such political importance.

There is, I think, a lot to be said for trying to justify rather than to presuppose institutional arrangements, including fundamental political arrangements. A political philosophy that does not build on premature or unjustified institutional assumptions leaves scope for considering the full range of political problems that any account of justice should address. The most basic of political problems is surely disorder and the threat of disorder: those who live with anarchy and the threat of anarchy cannot aspire to any more ambitious conception of justice. But order is not enough. Even when order has emerged, it may be harsh and arbitrary, and those who live with it may then conclude that the rule of law is a fundamental requirement if any sustainable civic life or constitutional order is to be possible. The more specific concerns of political liberalism, including secure boundaries, individual protection and freedom (and perhaps further liberal rights) and self-government (and perhaps democratic process) can be addressed *only* in societies that enjoy both order and the rule of law. This, it seems to me, shows why principles of justice for a globalising world cannot be justified by the approach that Rawls takes in *Political Liberalism*. It is a long march through the arguments from a less civic conception of public reason than the one Rawls deploys to any account of justified political institutions, but I think there may be good reasons for taking the long route and beginning an account of justice without assuming that boundaries, liberalism and democracy are uncontroversial presuppositions of democracy, whose justification we can take for granted.

PART II

Authority, autonomy and public reason

CHAPTER 6

Autonomy: the Emperor's New Clothes[1]

In the last half-century appeals to autonomy have played a larger and larger part in ethical and political debate, as well as in popular and professional culture. It is fair to say that autonomy is seen as one of the dominant values of our times. Yet the advocates of autonomy still disagree about what it is, and why it matters. At times it seems that they agree only that autonomy has a noble, Kantian pedigree, and that it is somehow linked to morality.

They are certainly right that Kant linked autonomy to morality. For example, he claimed both that '*Morality* is thus the relation of actions to the autonomy of the will' (*G* 4:439) and that '*Autonomy* of the will is the sole principle of all moral laws and of duties in keeping with them' (*CPrR* 5:33). However, it is far from clear that there are strong connections between morality and contemporary conceptions of autonomy, or that so close a connection between morality and autonomy has survived radical transformations in conceptions of autonomy. When protagonists of contemporary views on autonomy claim Kantian ancestry they may exaggerate, and venerate a naked Emperor of questionable legitimacy.[2]

These negative points tell us nothing about Kantian autonomy, or about its supposed links to morality. However, before trying to set out what Kantian autonomy is, I shall offer a brief account of contemporary views of autonomy. I will then try to set out the connection that Kant saw between his conception of autonomy and morality, which will require a short canter through some Kantian texts. This will, I hope, reveal a more

---

[1] *Autonomy: the Emperor's New Clothes, the Inaugural Address, Proceedings of the Aristotelian Society,* Supp. Vol. 57 (2003), 1–21. The text has been revised and updated in minor ways.

[2] The differences between Kant's account of autonomy and contemporary views is hardly a new discovery. Thomas E. Hill, Jr., has emphasised some of the central differences across many years in a series of powerful papers. See 'The Kantian conception of autonomy' in his *Dignity and Practical Reason* (Ithaca, NY: Cornell University Press, 1992), 76–96. He notes that 'Autonomy is a central concept in contemporary moral debates as well as in the discussion of Kant; but the only thing that seems completely clear about autonomy in these contexts is that it means different things to different writers', 76, and that current conceptions of autonomy have been 'cut loose from their Kantian roots', 77.

interesting landscape than the limited terrain so energetically charted by protagonists of sundry conceptions of individual autonomy that became prominent in the post-WWII world.

Autonomy as individual independence

I first realised quite how bewildering the array of differing conceptions of autonomy in contemporary debates had become when I read Gerald Dworkin's *The Theory and Practice of Autonomy*. Dworkin listed about a dozen different conceptions of autonomy, which, he claimed, has variously been equated with

> liberty (positive or negative)...dignity, integrity, individuality, independence, responsibility and self-knowledge...self-assertion...critical reflection...freedom from obligation...absence of external causation...and knowledge of one's own interests.[3]

This list is far from complete. For example, Ruth Faden and Thomas Beauchamp in their much-cited work *A History and Theory of Informed Consent* note that autonomy has been equated with a quite different list of concepts, including 'privacy, voluntariness, self-mastery, choosing freely, choosing one's own moral position and accepting responsibility for one's choices'.[4]

Dworkin contends that, despite all these variations, all conceptions of autonomy share two features: 'The only features that are held constant from one author to another are that autonomy is a feature of persons and that it is a desirable quality to have.'[5] I doubt whether either claim is true. It is certainly not true that all conceptions of autonomy view it as a feature of persons. The original use of the term *autonomy* – literally *self-legislation* – in antiquity referred to a property not of persons, but of polities. Autonomous city-states made their own laws; colonies were given laws by their mother cities. And, as already noted, Kant ascribes autonomy not to persons, but to *willing* or to *determinations of the will*. Equally, some twentieth-century writers – structuralists, behaviourists – dismiss the very idea that autonomy could be a feature either of persons or of the will.

There is also no general agreement that autonomy is 'a desirable quality to have'. On the contrary, many distinguished writers dispute this view

---

[3] Gerald Dworkin, *The Theory and Practice of Autonomy* (Cambridge University Press, 1988), 6.

[4] Ruth Faden and Thomas Beauchamp, *A History and Theory of Informed Consent* (Oxford University Press, 1986), 7.

[5] Dworkin, *The Theory and Practice of Autonomy* .

and maintain that there is something morally unsavoury about autonomy. I offer just one example. Iris Murdoch (who unfortunately assimilated Kantian to twentieth-century autonomy) wrote:

> How recognisable, how familiar to us, is the man so beautifully portrayed in the *Grundlegung*, who confronted even with Christ turns away to consider the voice of his own conscience, and to hear the voice of his own reason . . . this man is with us still, free, independent, lonely, powerful, rational, responsible, brave, the hero of so many novels and books of moral philosophy. It is not such a very long step from Kant to Nietzsche, or from Nietzsche to existentialism and the Anglo-Saxon doctrines which in some ways resemble it. In fact Kant's man had already received a glorious incarnation nearly a century earlier in the work of Milton: his proper name is Lucifer.[6]

We could hardly have a stronger moral indictment of autonomy, or (as Murdoch supposes) of Kant. Murdoch is only one of many authors who assume that if autonomy is simply a form of *individual independence*, we should question its ethical importance. However (since arguments from authority are not particularly convincing) I will not list other eminent critics of autonomy as a form of individual independence who think that it is not invariably 'a desirable feature of persons'.

I cannot resist retelling a story to illustrate more concretely why autonomy, thought of as *individual independence*, has little to do with morally admirable action, and may not be a desirable feature of persons. I owe this story to a student whom I taught in New York in the now-distant 1970s. One spring Columbia University students (then all male) threw off their clothes, ran across Broadway to the Barnard College dormitories and invited the women living there to join them. One did. The campus newspaper duly published a photograph of many bare behinds, one of them female, leaping back across Broadway. As I knew the Barnard student quite well, I asked her why she had joined in. She explained that she had wanted to be sure that she was autonomous. I understood what she meant. She had shown a measure of individual independence. She had probably shown some independence from her parents' hopes, and from certain conventions. (On the other hand, hadn't she shown herself dependent on male initiative?) I think most would agree that her action was independent in some ways, but not that this independence gave it any distinctive ethical value. Nothing satanic, to be sure; equally nothing morally splendid or even admirable.

---

[6] Iris Murdoch, *The Sovereignty of Good* (London: Routledge, 1970), 80.

My student was not at all eccentric in holding this view of autonomy. Twentieth-century conceptions of autonomy typically see it either as, or as requiring, a degree of *individual independence*. Autonomy construed *merely* as individual independence is indeed a feature of some persons. Yet I doubt whether many people – pop Existentialists apart – think that individual independence *by itself* makes an action morally valuable. Mere independence in choosing and acting can lead to action that is good or bad, right or wrong, kind or callous, prudent or risky.

'Rational' autonomy

Many late twentieth-century protagonists of autonomy have taken this point, and have not identified autonomy with *mere* independence. Most have claimed that autonomous action must be not only chosen (so to some extent independent), but specifically rationally chosen. They have advocated a great variety of conceptions of *rational autonomy*. Rational autonomy, unlike autonomy that is simply a matter of mere, sheer independence, might be linked to morality.

John Stuart Mill's *On Liberty* is, I believe, a principal source for many contemporary conceptions of *rational autonomy*. He explicitly repudiated the thought that mere, sheer independence or choice is morally important. He ascribes value to intelligent and reflective choosing, characteristic of persons with well-developed *individuality* and *character*. He comments dismissively on other sorts of choice:

> A person whose desires and impulses are his own – are the expression of his own nature, as it has been developed and modified by his own culture – is said to have a character. One whose desires and impulses are not his own, has no character, no more than a steam engine has a character.[7]

Mill argues that the choosing of those with well-defined individuality and character benefits each and all, and so that Utilitarians have reason to promote and protect the liberties that foster individuality and character and thereby reflective and intelligent choosing: 'In proportion to the development of his individuality each person becomes more valuable to himself, and is therefore capable of being more valuable to others.'[8]

However, Mill does *not* call choosing that reflects individuality or character autonomous. So far as I can discover, he never speaks of the *autonomy*

---

[7] John Stuart Mill, 'On Liberty' in John Grey (ed.), *On Liberty and other Essays* (Oxford University Press, 1991), 67.
[8] *Ibid.* 70.

of persons, although I have found one reference in his work to the *autonomy of states*.[9] I suspect that for Mill the term *autonomy* was a term of art that belonged either in constitutional discussions, or in Kant's non-naturalistic accounts of action and ethics, so had no place in his own naturalistic accounts.

Despite this divergence in terminology, I think that twentieth-century advocates of 'rational autonomy' are not far from Mill when they say that what is ethically important is not *mere choosing*, or *mere independence*, but specifically some form of *rational choosing*, hence (some version of) *rational autonomy*.[10] However, unlike Mill, many recent admirers of rational autonomy are not Utilitarians. They do not view individuality, or the liberty that Mill sees as supporting it, as valuable only as a means to human happiness. Some of them are keen on versions of 'rational autonomy' not as an instrumental but as a fundamental human good or value in its own right.

However, the twentieth-century writers who follow Mill in claiming that some version of rational autonomy (rather than mere, sheer independence) is ethically important also disagree about what it is.[11] For example, Harry Frankfurt in a now classical paper[12] first published in 1970 distinguished between routine choosing and choosing that reflects *second order desires*, and argued that capacities for the latter sort of choosing set persons apart and are morally significant. His famous example contrasts the wanton addict who in choosing her fix is driven by mere desire, with the witting addict who also has second-order desires to be a person with certain immediate desires, and sees the witting addict as rationally autonomous in ways that the wanton addict is not. Autonomous choosing has been very variously characterised as choosing that is well informed, or fully informed, or reflective, or reflectively endorsed.

I will not linger here on the many ingenious variations that advocates of conceptions of rational autonomy have explored, and do not think that it would be easy to show that *choosing* that is rational in specific ways will always lead to ethically superior choices. 'Rational autonomy', variously

---

[9] John Stuart Mill, *Considerations on Representative Government*, in *ibid.* 428.

[10] Mill refers neither to *rational autonomy* nor to *autonomy*, yet many of his interpreters use both terms in describing his position. John Skorupski in his outstanding study of Mill's philosophy writes: 'Mill in whose philosophy naturalism and . . . rational autonomy are the two deepest convictions is committed to the assumption that they are indeed reconcilable.' See John Skorupski, *John Stuart Mill* (Routledge: London, 1989), 43.

[11] For an account of the variety of conceptions of rational autonomy see Onora O'Neill, *Autonomy and Trust in Bioethics* (Cambridge University Press, 2002).

[12] Harry G. Frankfurt, 'Freedom of the will and the concept of a person', *Journal of Philosophy* 68, no. 1 (1971), 5–20.

conceived, sets out standards for *procedures of choosing*, but following these procedures may not guarantee ethically superior choices. Rational procedures are more likely to be relevant to justifications than they are likely to be effective in practice, and sometimes other ways of choosing, that reflect affections or hunches, traditions or intuitions, may produce ethically better results. Mill himself recognised the limitations of calculation and process and famously remarked that

> Nobody argues that the art of navigation is not founded on astronomy because sailors cannot wait to calculate the Nautical Almanack. Being rational creatures, they go to sea with it already calculated; and all rational creatures go out upon the sea of life with their mind made up on the common questions of right and wrong, as well as on many of the far more difficult questions of wise and foolish.[13]

In particular, conceptions of rational autonomy that assume typical models of rational choice will see all choosing as preference-led or desire-driven. Rationally autonomous choosing will then be likely to endorse whatever individuals prefer, and to veer towards egotistical choosing, or at best towards more 'enlightened' self-interest. Many of the ethical objections that Iris Murdoch and others have raised about autonomy conceived of as mere, sheer independence will, it seems, also apply to conceptions of rational autonomy.

And there is worse to come. Proponents of rational autonomy can *at most* show that certain rational constraints on procedures for choosing *generally* lead to more valuable choices. But they will not be able to show even this much unless they invoke independent criteria for identifying valuable choices. In Mill's hands, where the value of choices is settled by Utilitarian arguments, there is a basis for arguing that certain ways of choosing are more likely to produce valuable choices. But without an independent account of valuable choices, it is unclear how we could show that one or another way of choosing, such as those favoured by various conceptions of rationally autonomous choice, is valuable. Attempts to promote rational autonomy as a *fundamental* rather than an *instrumental* value would need quite different sorts of support, and it is not obvious where it could be found. Like the merely independent, the rationally autonomous may be 'free, independent, lonely, powerful, rational, responsible [and] brave': but will they act well?

---

[13] John Stuart Mill, *Utilitarianism* in John Grey (ed.), *On Liberty and other Essays* (Oxford University Press, 1991), 157.

Kantian autonomy: context

Both Kant's admirers and his detractors agree that Kantian autonomy is distinctive. In my view it differs markedly *both* from mere, sheer individual independence *and* from contemporary conceptions of rational autonomy. Kant's views on autonomy were also innovative: no earlier writer had made such strong claims about the moral importance of *any* conception of autonomy. Jerry Schneewind was, I believe, correct when he wrote at the very beginning of his book *The Invention of Autonomy* that 'Kant invented the conception of morality as autonomy.'[14]

But what he invented has, I believe, little to do with twentieth-century conceptions of autonomy either as mere, sheer *individual independence* or as *rational autonomy*. The most convincing evidence that Kant was thinking about something quite different is that few of his central claims about autonomy make much sense if we equate Kantian autonomy *either* with mere individual independence *or* with current conceptions of rational autonomy.

On the surface, Kant may seem to be promoting some version of rational autonomy. For example, in the *Critique of Practical Reason*, and in many other works, he predicates autonomy of reason and links the autonomy of reason closely to morality. This is evident not only in the passages quoted at the start of this paper, but in many others. He claims, for example, that 'the moral law expresses nothing other than the *autonomy* of pure practical reason' (*CPrR*5:33), that 'the power to judge autonomously – that is, freely (according to principles of thought in general) – is called reason' (*CF*7:27). Taken out of context these claims could be – and often are – read as strong if obscure versions of the idea that autonomy is some form of rational choosing. To make sense of them they need to be set in the context of Kant's views on action.

Kant's account of action

The context of Kant's account of autonomy is a distinctive view of action. Kant looks at action from the agent's standpoint, that is from a practical point of view. He depicts rational agents as having a *power of choice* (*Willkür*), which they can use in innumerable ways. Agents exercise their

---

[14] J.B. Schneewind, *The Invention of Autonomy: A History of Modern Moral Philosophy* (Cambridge University Press, 1998), 3. For more extensive discussion of Schneewind's analysis of Kantian autonomy, see 'Autonomy, plurality and public reason in Kant, Habermas and Rawls', Chapter 8 below.

power of choice by adopting one or another *determination of the will*. They can freely adopt some practical principle, or rule, or law, or plan: in doing so they make it their maxim.[15] Maxims specify at a fairly general level some aspect of the way agents set about leading their lives: I may make it my maxim to build a mill (*CPrR* 5:26), to save for my old age (*CPrR* 5:20), to embezzle funds (*CPrR* 5:28), to avenge insults (*CPrR* 5:19), to overcharge gullible customers (*G* 4:397), to pursue my self-interest (*CPrR* 5:23–6)[16] or not to make false promises (*CPrR* 5:21; *G* 4:403). This heterogeneous sample includes maxims that Kant thinks of as matters of duty and others that he thinks of as morally unacceptable, and some that are merely optional or at most a matter of prudence.

In speaking of *determinations of the will* Kant is not making a claim about the efficient causes of action: the principle (law, plan) that an agent adopts does not cause him or her to do anything (how could abstract entities such as *principles* or *laws* or *plans* be efficient causes?). Rather the principle (law, plan) that is adopted is the formal cause of action: it articulates what the agent seeks to do. It does not follow that Kant thinks that action, looked at from a theoretical standpoint, cannot be causally explained: he says in many passages that acts have efficient causes. But in choosing what to do we do not offer a prediction of what we will be caused to do. Kant's account of action focuses on what is chosen, not on the efficient causes of action. Accordingly he predicates autonomy not of *agents* or *acts*, but of the *will* and *determinations of the will*, of *principles*, of *reason*. It is hardly surprising that his account of autonomy differs so markedly from contemporary accounts, which focus agents and their procedures for choosing.

Determinations of the will provide a promising focus for an account of reasons for action, and for connecting claims about morality and reasons. Since any principle, rule, law or plan that is or could be adopted as a determination of the will must have *propositional structure and content* it will be apt for reasoning. Moreover, this reasoning need not be confined to judging whether proposals for action are efficient or effective means to given ends: for Kant instrumental rationality is only one aspect of practical reasoning. Here I bracket his account of instrumental reasoning in order to concentrate on the basis of his distinction between heteronomous and autonomous reasons for action.

---

[15] Onora O'Neill, *Acting on Principle*, 2nd edn (Cambridge University Press, 2013); Jens Timmerman, 'Kant's puzzling Ethics of Maxims', *Harvard Review of Philosophy* 8, no. 1 (2000), 39–52.

[16] These are particularly informative passages, but there are many others where Kant discusses self-love and self-interest.

Kantian autonomy: heteronomy as a clue

The contrast between *heteronomy* and *autonomy* provides a useful way into understanding Kantian autonomy. Heteronomy is not a term we use in daily life, so may not seem a promising clue. However – for once! – Kant offers a helpfully simple account of the distinction he has in mind. He writes:

> If the will seeks the law that is to determine it *anywhere* else than in the fitness of its maxims for its own giving of *universal* law . . . heteronomy always results. (*G* 4:441)

The difference between heteronomous and autonomous choosing is a difference between the ways in which principles adopted as determinations of the will are supported or derived. Heteronomous choosing and Kantianly autonomous choosing are *both* a matter of *seeking, choosing, adopting* or *willing* some principle (law, plan), thereby adopting some *determination of the will.* The difference between them is *not* that those who choose heteronomously are not free agents, or not capable of any independence in action, or that they have no rational capacities, or that they cannot seek, choose, adopt or will laws or principles. Heteronomous choosing is choosing, and very often rational in a variety of ways. Agents with the *power to choose* (*Willkür*) are capable both of autonomous and of heteronomous choosing. The difference between them is that agents look in different directions in choosing autonomously and choosing heteronomously. The two types of principle are drawn or derived from different types of assumption.

Kant frequently contrasts heteronomous and autonomous principles by saying that the former take their justification *from elsewhere* (for example from the dogmas of a church, from the edicts of rulers, from immediate inclination, from the will of the majority), whereas autonomous principles take their justification *from nowhere else.* Yet here we may well lose patience. Surely justifications *must* begin somewhere *else*: isn't the whole point of justification to *derive* authority? And if a principle could be nonderivative, why would that make it morally special, as opposed to especially arbitrary? Why should a principle that is *merely* nonderivative have *any* standing, let alone be fundamental to a conception of reason? Have we not ended up with something worse than the fantasy that individual autonomy is the basis of morality? Have we descended from pop existentialism to postmodernism?

Kant's examples of the principles or laws adopted by those who choose heteronomously are extremely varied. The common core to all his examples is that the heteronomous chooser makes some *arbitrary*, hence unreasoned, move in justifying a determination of her will, whereas the autonomous chooser does not. A heteronomous principle is one that can only be spuriously 'justified' by imputing authority to something or other, for whose standing or authority either no reasons or (at most) incomplete reasons are given. Any reason to act on such principles *reflects arbitrary assumptions*, and heteronomous reasons for action are therefore always conditional upon those assumptions. Kant puts the point as follows:

> Wherever an object of the will has to be laid down as the basis for prescribing the rule that determines the will, there the rule is none other than heteronomy; the imperative is conditional, namely: *if* or *because* one wills this object, one ought to act in such and such a way; hence it can never command morally, that is, categorically. (*G* 4:444)

The principles that agents adopt heteronomously may be varied. Sometimes the arbitrary assumption simply asserts that some object is desired, or that acting in a specific way will satisfy some desire. But in other cases the arbitrary assumption may simply endorse the edicts of state or church, or the tide of public opinion (*WE* 8:35–42). The common core of all forms of heteronomous willing is that it relies on an appeal to something or other that is taken as having authority without reasons being given for that authority. Kant often depicts those who arbitrarily impute authority to such assumptions metaphorically as submitting to *alien* or *foreign* authorities.

Kant's account of heteronomous willing is useful for articulating the fundamental differences between lacking *individual autonomy*, lacking *rational autonomy* and lacking *Kantian autonomy*. Beings who wholly lack *individual* autonomy will not be able to choose *either* heteronomously *or* autonomously. In Kantian vocabulary, such beings lack the power of choice, so lack free will, and so lack a necessary condition for all action. Having the power of choice is a precondition for heteronomous as well as for Kantianly autonomous choosing, so cannot be equated with Kantian autonomy. Kant speaks of beings without a power of choice, who cannot act either heteronomously or autonomously, as having no more than animal capacities to choose, an *arbitrium brutum* as opposed to an *arbitrium liberum* (*MM* 6:211–14).

A person with power of choice may choose either autonomously or heteronomously. Heteronomous choosers defer to selected standards and authorities, and offer these as reasons for their actions. Such reasons have an essential place in technical and prudential choosing, and need not be capricious. However, heteronomy in ethics has its limitations. Heteronomous choosers may not always follow immediate inclinations, and may live with an eye to long-term personal advantage (egotism), or to the general happiness (Utilitarianism) or to the claims of a supposed moral sense, or to some conception of perfection (*G* 4:442–3; *CPrR* 5:39–41).

Kant would view twentieth-century proponents of rational autonomy as endorsing various forms of heteronomy in ethics. They do not indeed admire mere, sheer wilfulness, and think that agents should offer reasons for action, but what they offered need not itself meet standards. Heteronomous choosers ultimately simply appeal to supposed authorities – the claims of desire or of ideology, of public opinion or of the powers that be.

Although heteronomous choosers are arbitrary in according certain desires, demands and dogmas the status of reasons for action, they may have a good deal of moral luck. Their heteronomous choices are often expressed in morally acceptable action (the shopkeeper who is honest for the sake of his reputation, the self-interested chooser whose interests happen to coincide with others' interests). But in other situations heteronomous choosers may act in capricious, self-centred or even malign ways. Hitler and Stalin, for example, characteristically combined considerable individual autonomy and some forms of rational autonomy with total disregard for Kantian autonomy.

Kantian autonomy and self-legislation

The limitations of heteronomous reasons are easily seen. An agent chooses heteronomously by adopting a principle in order to achieve something for which he may offer no convincing reasons. Yet may we expect more? Kant thinks so. He claims that autonomous choosers adopt principles of action that are not conditional on matters for which no reason is given, so can offer unconditional reasons for action. In *Groundwork* he puts the matter as follows: '**Autonomy** of the will is the property of the will by which it is a law to itself (independently of any property of the objects of volition)' (*G* 4:440).

In this passage, and many similar passages, we meet the most difficult aspect of Kant's account of autonomy. What is a 'property of the will by which it is a law to itself (independently of any property of the objects of volition)'? How can the will adopt a determination simply on the basis of 'the fitness of its maxims for its own giving of universal law'? Kant's claims have a crabbed reflexivity that is often perplexing and hard to sort out. I offer a sketch.

A common approach to Kantian autonomy harks back to the etymology of the word *autonomy*, and identifies autonomous willing with some conception of *self-legislation*. What sense can we assign to Kant's use of this venerable phrase? A very popular way of looking at the matter is to interpret *self-legislation* as *legislation* done by a *self* or *subject*. On this individualistic reading we picture each of many wills as legislating for all. Two questions immediately arise. First, why should the legislative action of my will and your will point in the same direction? Second, why should we think that the legislative action of anybody's will must point in a morally acceptable direction, let alone that the 'principle of autonomy is the sole principle of morals' (*G* 4:440). If Kantian autonomy is pictured merely as *legislation by individual selves*, the convergence of individual wills on anything that should count as morality remains a mystery and the moral importance of autonomy remains obscure. Unsurprisingly, many passages in Kant's writings are reduced to nonsense, or at the very least to implausibility, if we equate his conception of autonomy with 'legislation' by individuals. Yet, this reading remains popular.

Could this problem be resolved if Kantian autonomy were pictured as legislation *by coordinated individual selves*? This is the strategy of Rousseau's famous account of self-legislation, where the problem of possible divergence between numerous self-legislating wills is resolved by positing an extraneous source of convergence. On Rousseau's view, 'The general will is always for the common good'[17] and 'The general will is always upright and always tends to the public utility.'[18]

Of course, Rousseau did not think that every individual actually wills as the General Will demands. On the contrary, any convergence of particular wills on the General Will is a contingent convergence of 'corrected' wills, not necessarily, or even generally, mirrored in real time by the will of each or the will of all. As Kant would see it, Rousseauian self-legislation is a form of heteronomy: it assigns authority to a conception of the general good, and claims that 'corrected' wills all point in this direction. Even if the problem of divergence were solved by this strategy – I personally think that Rousseau defines the problem out of existence rather than solving it – we have not been shown any reason to think that the supposed point of convergence defines morality, or is morally significant. Rousseau's account of *legislation by co-ordinated selves* resolves indeterminacy and disagreement by positing the authority of the general will. For Kant, despite his profound respect for Rousseau, this is heteronomy.

---

[17] J.-J. Rousseau, *Political Economy*, trans. and ed. Victor Gourevitch (Cambridge University Press, 1997), 8.

[18] J.-J. Rousseau, *Social Contract* II iii, trans. and ed. Victor Gourevitch (Cambridge University Press, 1997), 58.

Kantian autonomy: lawlike and lawless willing

Can an alternative interpretation of the idea of self-legislation make better sense of Kant's claims, and avoid conflating autonomy and heteronomy? It may seem that we are faced with a dilemma. If we view self-legislation simply as a matter of choosing or willing for oneself (independently, using some rational process), then the very distinction between heteronomy and Kantian autonomy is erased. If we view self-legislation as a matter of choosing or willing principles *with a certain sort of content* we apparently fall into *heteronomy* by arbitrarily ascribing moral weight to that content.

Kant avoids this dilemma by viewing autonomy neither as a requirement on *procedures for choosing*, nor as a requirement on the *content of choices*. Kantian autonomy cannot be identified simply with specific *procedures for choosing*, of the sort admired by contemporary fans of rational autonomy. But it also cannot be identified with choices with specified *content* or *objects*, since that would be a form of heteronomy in willing. So Kantian autonomy is more than a constraint on *procedures for choosing*, but less than a requirement to accept principles with *determinate content*. By elimination it then seems that Kantian autonomy must be a matter of adopting principles with a certain *structure or form*.

As is apparent from countless passages, Kant thinks that autonomous willing is expressed in choices that have the *form of law* or are *lawlike*. He contrasts *lawlike* choosing with choosing determinations of the will that are literally *lawless*. What, we may wonder, is the problem with lawless choosing? Why shouldn't we embrace the most extreme forms of lawlessness or lack of structure both in thought and in action? Isn't any claim that thought or action *must* meet certain requirements intrinsically dogmatic?

It is fascinating to find Kant engaging with the postmodernists of his day – the advocates of spiritual enthusiasm or *Schwärmerei* – to show why the postmodernist fantasy of dispensing with all authorities, with all reasons, with all principles or laws for organising thinking or action, is deceptive. Like postmodernists, Kant sees clearly why people *imagine* that 'lawless' thinking is not merely feasible but attractive; but he also sees what it threatens. He depicts the pleasures of the advocates of lawless thinking with pointed irony:

> First *genius* is very pleased with its bold flights, since it has cast off the thread by which reason used to steer it. Soon it enchants others with its triumphant pronouncements and great expectations and now seems to have set itself on a throne, which was so badly graced by slow and ponderous reason, whose language, however, it always employs. Then its maxim is that

reason's superior law-giving is invalid – we common human beings call this **enthusiasm**, while those favoured by beneficent nature call it *illumination*. (*WOT* 8:145)

Kant believes that this heady liberation ends not merely in confusion but in cognitive and practical disaster: 'Since reason alone can command validly for everyone, a confusion of language must soon arise among them; each one now follows his own inspiration' (*WOT* 8:145). Communication breaks down and superstition rides high; morality, even civil society, fails. Attempts to achieve total freedom in thinking prove self-defeating, and do nothing for morality.

As Kant sees it, freedom in thinking and in acting properly culminates not in *lawlessness*, but in *lawfulness* that does not assume or defer to any external authority or 'lawgiver':

> freedom in thinking signifies the subjection of reason to no laws except *those which it gives itself*; and its opposite is the maxim of a **lawless use** of reason (in order, as genius supposes, to see further than one can under the limitation of laws). The natural consequence of declared lawlessness is that if reason will not subject itself to the laws it gives itself, it has to bow under the yoke of laws given by another; for without any law, nothing – not even nonsense – can play its game for long. Thus the unavoidable consequence of *declared* lawlessness in thinking (of a liberation from all the limitations of reason) is that freedom to think will ultimately be forfeited and – because it is not misfortune but arrogance which is to blame for it – will be trifled *away* (*verschertzt*) in the proper sense of the word. (*WOT* 8:145)

Lawlessness undermines reasoning. It undercuts the very possibility of offering others reasons for believing or for acting. Thought and action alike depend on offering others with whom we seek to live and communicate, think or interact, proposals that they can follow. Whatever else reasons are, they must be *followable by others*, and so the sorts of things that we can offer and refuse, accept and challenge. This is why practical reasoning cannot cut loose from lawlike determinations of the will. If we are cavalier about these considerations, we no longer deal in reasons for acting or reasons for believing.

Needless to say, the demand that we act on lawlike principles is an extremely weak constraint. Many whose principles of action are heteronomous through and through also act on lawlike principles. Even if Kant is right in diagnosing lawlessness in thought and action as catastrophic, heteronomy might be the *only* other option for conducting our thinking and acting. Perhaps, contra Kant, morality can be at most a system of hypothetical imperatives. Perhaps all reasons for action are ultimately conditional.

Kantian autonomy: lawlike form, universal scope

If a distinction between autonomous and heteronomous action is to make any sense, there must be *two* sorts of lawlike principles. Kant's constant refrain in his practical philosophy, from the beginning of the *Groundwork* onwards, is that morally important principles not only must be *lawlike*, but must have universal *scope*. Since heteronomous principles arbitrarily take for granted the desires, convictions, interests or demands of specific others, they do not have universal scope. They are not capable of being principles for all. By contrast, lawlike principles of universal scope are autonomous principles.

Kant connects the demands of scope and lawlike form as follows:

> it is requisite to reason's lawgiving that it should need to presuppose only *itself*, because a rule is objectively and universally valid only when it holds without the contingent, subjective conditions that distinguish one rational being from another. (*CPrR* 5:20)[19]

Kantian autonomy is not a matter of persons being independent (although of course Kant holds that persons are independent to a degree, since they have a power of choice). Rather Kantian autonomy is a matter of adopting *lawlike principles that are independent of extraneous assumptions that can only be grasped by or hold for some, and not for all.* Kant often encapsulates this requirement in phrases such as 'a lawgiving that needs to presuppose only itself' or in compressed references to the notion of 'a lawgiving of its own' or 'nonderivative lawgiving'. Principles that meet this standard are not merely lawlike, but 'hold without the contingent, subjective conditions that distinguish one rational being from another'. They are potentially principles for all, and not merely for those who uncritically assume the authority of some desire or a local dogma or the powers that be, who can at most converge on heteronomous principles.

The idea of a 'lawgiving that needs to presuppose only itself' is I think the key to Kant's distinctive understanding of self-legislation. As he sees the matter, it is the *principle* or the *willing*, and not the agent, that 'presupposes only itself'. For Kant the term *self-legislation* cannot mean that there are some terrific acts of the self (or terrific acts of the terrific self?)

---

[19] Freedom in the positive sense, as we know from *Groundwork* III, is another term for Kantian autonomy.

that are morally important, or definitive of morality, but only that there are some principles of action that are not derivative from supposed, but ultimately arbitrary, 'authorities', and that these are morally important. The element 'self' in the notion of 'self-legislation' is *reflexive rather than individualistic*; it applies to certain justifications of principles rather than to certain agents or 'legislators'. Kant takes himself to be giving an account of the sort of lawgiving that is reason's own, and not an account of law-givings that are an agent's own. Kantian autonomy is *reason's lawgiving* rather than the *lawgiving of individual agents* (whatever that might mean).

Reason's lawgiving is not merely a matter of adopting one or another lawlike determination of the will: heteronomous action often does as much. Kantian autonomy is expressed in adopting principles, willings, reasonings that both are lawlike in structure or form and do not derive that lawlikeness from arbitrary assumptions that are open to some but not to others. Heteronomous reasoning, by contrast, even when lawlike in form, relies on some specific and restricted assumption about the scope. Heteronomous principles may be widely shared: those who take for granted the authority of church or state, public opinion or local ideology, will have plenty of company. Unlike postmodernist gestures, heteronomous practical reasoning does not always tend to incomprehension or cognitive shipwreck. Its defect is only that its intelligibility coasts on assumptions that some others cannot share, so cannot provide reasons for action to them. Heteronomous reasons do not aspire to be '*a lawgiving of its own* on the part of pure and, as such, practical reason [which] is freedom in the *positive* sense' (*CPrR* 5:33).[20]

This is why, on Kant's view, heteronomous reasons are ultimately incomplete reasons. Reasons need to be in principle *followable* by their presumed audiences. That is why they must be lawlike, or have the form of law. Heteronomous reasons do not fully meet this standard, so can at most be used where some common desire, belief or other source of agreement can be assumed. They may provide in-group reasons to others who have deferred (heteronomously) to the same 'authority': but they offer no basis for reasoning among those who do not share allegiance to the same desire, dogma or doctrine, hence no basis for reasoning with 'the world at large', no basis for fully public reason, hence in Kant's view no sufficient basis for morals or politics. This is perhaps quite a weak conception of practical reason: but it is not covert reversion to heteronomy.

---

[20] The German text reads 'diese *eigene Gesetzgebung* . . . der reinen und als solche praktischen Vernunft ist Freiheit im *positiven* Verstande'.

Correspondingly, the phrase 'a lawgiving of its own' (*eine eigene Gesetzgebung*) is no mere awkwardness of locution. It expresses the requirement that anything that can count as the self-legislation of practical reason must be not only *lawgiving* (*gesetzgebend*) but also *nonderivative* (*eigen*). It is this demand for living by principles that could be described as *lawgivings of reason*, so fit for all (regardless of their particular faith or ideology, allegiance or citizenship, desires or culture), that underpins Kant's distinctive use of the metaphor of self-legislation and that links his conception of autonomy to fitness for universal law. It is this picture that allows him to claim that autonomy and universalisability are alternative formulations of the Categorical Imperative, inseparable from one another and equally, indeed equivalently, fundamental to morality:

> The principle of autonomy is, therefore: to choose only in such a way that the maxims of your choice are included as universal laws in the same volition. (*G* 4:439)

As Kant sees it, combining a *formal* requirement (lawlikeness) with a *scope* requirement (universality) allows us to derive certain substantive constraints, which he views as basic principles of morality. Morality is fundamentally a matter of setting aside principles of action that could not be adopted by all, so could not be laws for all. If we aim to adopt only lawlike determinations of the will that could be universal laws, we must adopt only principles that (we judge) all and any others too could adopt, and so must reject many tempting and interesting principles of action. Kantian autonomy bypasses the problem of possible divergence of individual choices, that has to be resolved if we think of self-legislation as a matter of each individual legislating for all. The key to Kant's thought is the identification of self-legislation or autonomy with adopting only principles that 'hold without the contingent, subjective conditions that distinguish one rational being from another'.

Once we have shifted our conceptions of self-legislation in the way that a coherent reading of the Kantian texts requires, it is no longer so hard to see why he thinks that autonomy is a demand of practical reason. If we think of reasons as given and received, exchanged or refused, accepted or challenged, putative reasons that *cannot* be followed by some are defective or incomplete: they are not really, or not fully, complete reasons for action.

From practical reason to morality

Practical reason is a matter of ensuring that what we offer to one another as reasons for action are indeed fit to be reasons for others. That is what it is for them to meet the requirements of autonomy. Kant, I think, assumes that once we have an adequate account of practical reason, an account of morality will not be far away. He wrote optimistically in the *Groundwork* 'that the above principle of autonomy is the sole principle of morals can well be shown'.[21] I think this a bit optimistic; and it is certainly a task for another day. Although I hope I have set out why the Kantian principle of autonomy is fundamental to reason giving, this does not show whether it is the *sole* or fundamental principle of morals. This task of showing that it is the sole and fundamental principle sets the programme of Kant's ethical and political writings, in which he aims to show that

> *Autonomy* of the will is the sole principle of all moral laws and of duties in keeping with them; *heteronomy* of choice, on the other hand, not only does not ground any obligation at all but is instead opposed to the principle of obligation and to the morality of the will. That is to say, the sole principle of morality consists in independence from all matter of the law (namely, from a desired object) and at the same time in the determination of choice through the mere form of giving universal law that a maxim must be capable of. (*CPrR* 5:33)

In the fairy tale the Emperor processed stark naked, and only a child dared to point this out. As I see it, the newer versions of autonomy that have played so large a part in discussions of morality and politics since the mid twentieth century, and that have penetrated the innermost and outermost reaches of public and professional life (especially in the English-speaking world) are pretty scantily clad. Neither mere, sheer independence nor so-called rational autonomy has much to commend it – though no doubt each can be contrasted with even nastier possibilities. We face a choice. Either we accept some contemporary conception of autonomy, and must conclude that it is at best a minor (and sometimes suspect) aspect of the moral life. Or we take the Kantian conception of autonomy seriously, and have at least reason to consider whether it just might be 'the sole principle of all moral laws and of duties in keeping with them'.

[21] In German, 'Allein daß gedachtes Princip der Autonomie das alleinige Princip der Moral sei, läßt sich gar wohl darthun.'

CHAPTER 7

Self-legislation, autonomy and the form of law[1]

Legacy and loss

Kant's ethical and political legacies have never been more widely revered than they are today. Yet central parts of that legacy are in danger of slipping beyond the understanding of many who claim to revere it, and are often equated with views that Kant would have rejected. This drift in standard readings of Kantian themes gives those who care about his philosophy good reason to pay close attention to its current reception.

This might be done in several ways. One approach – it may seem particularly appropriate in the year of the 200th anniversary of Kant's death – is to see ourselves as custodians of a precious heritage. We could make it our mission to clarify and present Kant's claims or arguments, to correct (mis)appropriations, to promote textual rigour, to rescue travestied arguments and to set them in their proper context. But a merely retrospective and corrective stance rejects or overlooks the efforts of colleagues who try to keep versions or descendants of Kant's ideas in wider circulation and in contention. A purely custodial approach to Kant's legacy might have little impact on contemporary debates and fail to keep Kant's thought alive.

A second, more constructive, way of engaging with contemporary (mis)appropriations of Kantian ideas would respond to their selective approach to topics and to texts by paying extra attention to those Kantian ideas that have the greatest contemporary resonance. In ethics and political philosophy this approach might lead us to concentrate selectively on topics such as ethical universalism, respect for persons, human dignity, autonomy and cosmopolitan justice. A selective approach needs a certain

---

[1] 'Self-legislation, autonomy and the form of law', *Sonderband der Deutschen Zeitschrift für Philosophie* (Berlin: Akademie Verlag, 2004), 13–26; first presented at a conference held in Vienna in 2004 to mark the 200th anniversary of Kant's death. Since it is more textually detailed than other papers in this collection, quotations from Kant's writings are also given in German.

sympathy with work that is often not based on close reading of Kant. It will unavoidably do less than justice to topics that would be indispensable in a full treatment of Kant's claims and arguments, yet lack contemporary resonance.

Yet if the aim is to prevent a gulf opening between current work in philosophy and close engagement with Kant's writings, this sympathy with contemporary concerns must also be kept in check. After two centuries, a close relationship between contemporary would-be Kantian writing and the original texts must be cultivated rather than taken for granted. So much by way of preamble and excuse. My intention here is to explore some ideas that are central to Kant's practical philosophy and supposedly still resonant, yet frequently obscured and distorted. The Kantian notions to which I shall attend are those of *self-legislation* or *autonomy*, of the *form of law* and of *universality*.

Some paradoxes of self-legislation and autonomy

The ideas of *self-legislation* and *autonomy* are seemingly closely, indeed etymologically, linked. Both terms apparently connect the ideas of a *choosing self* and of *chosen laws or principles of action*, which have the *form of law*. Both terms are rightly taken to have impeccable Kantian ancestry. Yet their subsequent careers have diverged. Self-legislation has become philosopher's term of art; autonomy has become a pop star.

Taken literally, the very ideas of *self-legislation* and of *autonomy* may seem paradoxical. How can an individual, a self, legislate? *Laws or principles* are not mere decisions: they are designed for many agents and many cases. Laws and principles are *types*, which might be adopted or rejected as maxims by one or many or all agents, at some or many or all times. They set out the content of possible maxims, just as propositions set out the content of possible beliefs.[2] *Legislation* promulgates or prescribes laws or principles as authoritative or binding for certain agents. If individuals could promulgate or prescribe laws for others, those others would be subject to that law, so could not it seems be self-legislators. If individuals could prescribe laws or principles only for themselves, the metaphor of *self-legislation* would inflate what is only a process of choice or decision. So it is difficult to make literal sense of the standard, personal reading of the reflexive idea of *self-legislation* that sees it as *legislation by a self*.

---

[2] For a fuller version of this sketchy account of Kant's theory of action see 'Kant: rationality as practical reason', Chapter 2 above.

An initial response to these obvious difficulties in the idea of self-legislation might point out that Kant barely uses the reflexive terms *self-legislation, self-legislating* etc.[3] By contrast he constantly uses the non-reflexive terms *lawgiver, lawgiving, legislation* and *law*. Equally, Kant uses the less obviously reflexive term *autonomy* quite selectively.[4] Yet, noting that Kant does not emphasise these particular reflexive terms much may not be very helpful. The texts support the common use of the reflexive term *self-legislation* to explicate his position, since he regularly introduces a range of reflexive notions, using a variety of phrases. He speaks of the human being 'as subject *only to laws given by himself but still universal*' (G 4:432).[5] He deploys the image of a kingdom of ends, which combines the dual perspective of each and every will as giving law and subject to law given by all.[6] It is very natural, even if we set aside literal readings of the reflexive terms and downplay the picture of individuals enacting law, to read Kant as saying that morality is a matter not simply of adopting principles or laws, but specifically of adopting or conforming to *self-imposed* principles or laws, or of *self-legislation*.

However, it is not obvious that all the passages in which Kant combines notions of legislation and reflexivity invoke the image of a self that 'legislates'. Numerous passages use impersonal rather than personal reflexive phrases, such as the notion of 'the representation of a law for [in?] itself',[7] of representing an 'action that is objectively necessary of [for?] itself'[8] and of 'a practical law that commands absolutely of [for?] itself'.[9] Such passages are particularly important to an understanding of the connections

---

[3] He does not use the terms *Selbstgesetzgebung* and *Selbstgesetzgeber*, and rarely uses *selbstgesetzgebend*. One instance is at *G* 4:431, where he writes: 'In accordance with this principle all maxims are repudiated that are inconsistent with the will's own giving of universal law. Hence the will is not merely subject to the law, but subject to it in such a way that it must be viewed as also giving the law to itself and just because of this as first a subject to the law (of which it can regard itself as the author).' 'Alle Maximen werden nach diesem Prinzip verworfen, die mit der eigenen allgemeinen Gesetzgebung des Willens nicht zusammen bestehen können. Der Wille wird also nicht lediglich dem Gesetze unterworfen, sondern so unterworfen, daß er auch *als selbstgesetzgebend*, und eben um deswillen allererst dem Gesteze (davon er selbst sich als Urheber betrachten kann) unterworfen, angesehen werden muß.'

[4] In Kant's main works in practical philosophy, the terms *autonomy* and *heteronomy* occur mainly in two patches: at the end of Chapter 2 and beginning of Chapter 3 of *Groundwork*; and sparingly in the *Critique of Practical Reason*.

[5] 'daß er nur *seiner eigenen* und dennoch *allgemeinen Gesetzgebung* unterworfen sei'.

[6] *G* 4:438: 'Now in this way a world of rational beings (*mundus intelligibilis*) as a kingdom of ends is possible, through the giving of their own laws [lawgiving] by all persons as members' 'Nun ist auf solche Weise eine Welt vernünftiger Wesen (*mundus intelligibilis*) als ein Reich der Zwecke möglich, und zwar durch die eigene Gesetzgebung aller Personen als Glieder.'

[7] *G* 4:401: 'die Vorstellung eines Gesetzes an sich selbst'.

[8] *G* 4:414: 'eine Handlung als für sich selbst ... als objektiv-notwendig vorstellte'.

[9] *G* 4:425: 'ein praktisches Gesetz, welches schlechterdings ... für sich gebietet'.

that Kant draws between autonomy, reason and morality, and I shall return to them.

Even if we set aside literal conceptions of commanding 'legislators' and obedient 'subjects', an air of paradox persists in any attempt to make self-legislation basic to morality. Allen Wood has put the matter clearly:

> Autonomy of the will as the ground of moral obligation is arguably Kant's most original ethical discovery (or invention). But it is also easy to regard Kant's conception of autonomy as either incoherent or fraudulent. To make my own will the author of my obligations seems to leave both their content and their bindingness at my discretion, which contradicts the idea that I am *obligated* by them. If we reply to this objection by emphasising the *rationality* of these laws as what binds me, then we seem to be transferring the source of obligation from my will to the canons of rationality. The notion of *self-legislation* becomes a deception or at best a euphemism.[10]

As Wood articulates the problem in this passage, we find ourselves compelled to emphasise the authority *either* of the choosing self as the author of laws *or* of the rationally chosen, lawlike principles. Whichever reading we prefer, both self-legislation and autonomy appear to lead to problems and paradoxes for any account of morality as self-legislation. If we stress the role of the self as *author* of laws, we seem to dissolve moral claims in some form of individualism.[11] If we stress the *rationality* of the laws that are chosen, the choosing self and the notion of self-legislation are no longer seen as the key to morality.

Minimalist readings of self-legislation

A determinedly minimalist reading of the notions of self-legislation and autonomy might reduce the air of paradox. Kant's theory of action allows us to make ready sense of the idea of a *choosing self* and of its *chosen principles or laws*. Free agents can adopt principles of action that have the form of law. Just as the content of an individual's belief can be a proposition whose logical form is that of a universal generalization, so the content of an individual's maxim can be a practical principle whose form is lawlike. No paradox here.

On this minimalist reading of self-legislation, the lingering air of paradox might be attributed to Kant's habit of embedding the rich vocabulary of *law* and *legislation* in a range of reflexive metaphors, and to others' tendency to take these reflexive turns of phrase rather too literally. A minimalist

---

[10] Allen Wood, *Kant's Ethical Thought* (Cambridge University Press, 1999), 156.

[11] As exemplified in the way interpretations of autonomy have developed in the past fifty years. See 'Autonomy: the Emperor's New Clothes', Chapter 6 above.

reading would accept that there is no real possibility of everybody being simultaneously a lawgiver, accept that we can use 'the Idea *of the will of every rational being as a will giving universal law*',[12] but insist that there is no need to take this vocabulary too literally.

Yet a minimalist reading of Kant's use of the vocabularies of law and (self)-legislation avoids paradox only at considerable cost. If we try to read Kant's claims about self-legislation and autonomy as meaning only that choosing selves act on chosen, lawlike principles we will find ourselves catapulted from the frying pan into the fire. For on this weak reading of self-legislation, much heteronomous willing counts as self-legislation, and as a result Kant's distinction between autonomy and heteronomy collapses. So a minimalist reading offers a poor basis for understanding Kant's insistence that self-legislation and autonomy provide the key to morality.

Agents whose choices are heteronomous are not unfree: if they were, their action would not be imputable and there would be nothing wrong about heteronomy. Moreover, agents whose choices are heteronomous often act on principles that have the form of law: their action typically does not reflect mere, 'lawless' spontaneity. So agents whose choices are heteronomous exemplify the pattern of a choosing self adopting a chosen law or principle. The problem is that they adopt morally inadequate lawlike principles (their action on those principles may, of course, conform to duty, in which case they do nothing wrong). So there must be more to Kantian self-legislation and autonomy than the minimalist account of choosing selves adopting and acting on chosen, lawlike principles can allow for. A minimalist reading of self-legislation averts the sense of paradox, at the cost of obscuring Kant's distinction between autonomy and heteronomy as well as the connections that he draws between autonomy or self-legislation and morality.

Contemporary autonomy

Another and more radical approach to Kant's claims about self-legislation and autonomy might take the subsequent history of autonomy as a guide to untangling Kant's thoughts. Contemporary conceptions of autonomy are prominent in ethical and political discussions. They have apparently shed the air of paradox that still troubles the notion of self-legislation.[13]

---

[12] *G* 4:431: '[die] Idee des Willens eines jeden vernünftigen Wesens als *allgemeingesetzgebenden Willens*'; cf. *G* 4:432.

[13] For some of the earlier non-Kantian philosophical work on autonomy see Gerald Dworkin, *The Theory and Practice of Autonomy* (Cambridge University Press, 1988); John Christman, *The Inner Citadel: Essays on Individual Autonomy* (Oxford University Press, 1989); J.B. Schneewind, *The Invention of Autonomy: A History of Modern Moral Philosophy* (Cambridge University Press, 1998).

A minority of contemporary views of autonomy stress the choosing self, but downplay all reference to chosen laws or principles. Autonomous action is then seen as expressing personal choice or preference, and the requirement that such choice or preference be incorporated into a law or into a principle that has the form of law, is quietly – perhaps brazenly – set aside. On such radically individualistic views, autonomous action is a matter of mere, sheer choice, and need not be based on *any* law or principle. It has proved hard, and many would think impossible, to show that radically antinomian conceptions of autonomy are significant aspects of ethical and political life, let alone the only significant value. Even its advocates do not see this conception of autonomy as (a version of) the supreme principle of ethics. They reject Kant's robust claims that 'Morality is thus the relation of actions to the autonomy of the will' (*G* 4:439) and that '*Autonomy* of the will is the sole principle of all moral laws and of duties in keeping with them' (*CPrR* 5:33). Although some existentialists and libertarians have made bold (if implausible) claims about the moral significance of such antinomian conceptions of autonomy, which they see as mere, sheer individual choice, most contemporary advocates of autonomy see it as one important moral value among others.

A second range of contemporary conceptions of autonomy emphasises not only the choosing self but its chosen laws or principles. Contemporary advocates of so-called *rational autonomy* see it as requiring individuals to choose laws or principles rationally. Conceptions of *rational autonomy* may seem more Kantian than conceptions of mere, sheer choice, since they tie autonomy to a (thin) conception of practical reason. However, they diverge greatly from Kant in their conceptions of practical reason, which are generally more or less Humean.

Rationally autonomous action, as currently conceived, differs from radically individualistic autonomous action because it is based not on the preference of the moment, but on deeper and more stable features of an agent's desires, character or life, so can provide a basis not only for particular choices but also for choosing more general principles that will serve for a range of cases. Advocates of rational autonomy typically see it as more than instrumentally rational action undertaken to satisfy happenstantial desires or preferences. Rationally autonomous action has been variously characterised as seeking to satisfy desires and preferences that are well ordered,[14] to

---

[14] For example, in work that assumes that models of rational choice provide adequate accounts of rationality, hence in large parts of economics and some parts of other social sciences.

which the agent accords second-order endorsement;[15] which survive reflective evaluation;[16] which express stable individuality or character;[17] or which are constitutive of an agent's life projects, sense of self or even of identity. Although contemporary conceptions of rational autonomy are highly varied, they generally owe more to John Stuart Mill than to Kant. They see autonomous choosing not merely as instrumentally rational pursuit of the desire or preference of the moment, but as the rational expression of deeper, more lasting and more integrated aspects of the self that will typically be exemplified by adopting stably internalised, lawlike principles.

So rationally autonomous action as currently understood is done on principles that indeed have the form of law, and explicitly links the ideas of a choosing self and of chosen laws or principles. Yet, while contemporary accounts of rational autonomy reject radically antinomian forms of individualism, they too view choosing, hence autonomous choosing, in markedly individualistic terms. They rely on background theories that see rational action as guided by individuals' desires, preferences, beliefs and 'identities'. Rationally autonomous choosing differs from autonomy conceived of as mere, sheer choice in ways that might provide reason for replacing egoism with enlightened self-interest, or for preferring long-term to short-term advantage. But there is no general reason to suppose that rationally autonomous agents will always adopt morally acceptable principles (as is evident in every discussion of the prisoner's dilemma). Some rationally autonomous action may conform to moral requirements; some may violate moral standards. The advocates of rational autonomy are not likely to support Kant's claims that '*Morality* is thus the relation of actions to the autonomy of the will' (*G* 4:439)[18] or that '*Autonomy* of the will is the sole principle of all moral laws and of duties in keeping with them' (*CPrR* 5:33).[19]

In my view, neither contemporary approach to autonomy can be equated with Kantian autonomy. Mere, sheer choice is only what Kant sometimes

15 Harry G. Frankfurt, 'Freedom of the will and the concept of a person', *Journal of Philosophy* 68 (1971), 5–20.
16 For example, Charles Taylor's conception of strong evaluation deploys more than the formal notion of a second-ordered endorsement. See his 'What is human agency?' in his *Human Agency and Language: Philosophical Papers*, Vol. I (Cambridge University Press, 1985), 15–44.
17 John Stuart Mill, 'On Liberty' in John Grey (ed.), *On Liberty and other Essays* (Oxford University Press, 1991), 67. For discussion of Mill and autonomy (a word Mill does not use) see John Skorupski, *John Stuart Mill* (London: Routledge, 1989), who writes: 'Mill in whose philosophy naturalism and ... rational autonomy are the two deepest convictions is committed to the assumption that they are indeed reconcilable', 43.
18 'Moralität ist also das Verhältnis der Handlungen zur Autonomie des Willens.'
19 'Die Autonomie des Willens ist das alleinige Prinzip aller moralischen Gesetze und der ihnen gemäßen Pflichten.'

calls a '*lawless use of reason*': agents who choose spontaneously need not act on *any* principle or law. As Kant sees it, their willing is *lawless* rather than *lawlike*: it lacks the very *form of law* (*WOT* 8:144). In Kant's terminology it manifests spontaneity, but not autonomy (or equivalently negative but not positive freedom). There are no sufficient reasons for thinking that whatever is spontaneously chosen is well chosen, or that it meets moral standards. Some spontaneous choices may conform to moral requirements, others may violate moral standards. Some contemporary discussions of autonomy as radical spontaneity, particularly by existentialists and libertarians, read their own views back into Kant. Some critics of autonomy as radical spontaneity (including Iris Murdoch, in a memorable passage in which she likens Kant to Lucifer[20]) ascribe forms of hyper-individualism into Kant. But since such readings have to shed all attempts to connect autonomy to principles or laws, let alone to reason, they have little bearing on Kant's arguments.

Contemporary conceptions of *rational autonomy* do not view mere spontaneity or *lawless uses of reason* as exercises of autonomy, so come closer to advocating some conception of self-legislation. They combine the notions of a choosing self and of a rationally chosen law or principle that has the form of law. Minimal notions of *self-legislation* can, it seems, gain a foothold in discussions of rational autonomy. However, rational autonomy too cannot be equated with Kantian autonomy, because the principles Kant classifies as heteronomous would also count as rationally autonomous – although they are by definition not autonomous in Kant's view. Heteronomous willing, as the etymology of the term makes plain, also embodies principles or laws, so has the form of law. Clearly it is impossible to understand Kant's position without clarity about the difference between heteronomy and autonomy.

Kant offers at least three ranges of examples of heteronomy. In one range of examples, heteronomous action is seen as pursuit of desires or preferences,[21] and will be principled (and so rationally autonomous in the contemporary sense) if, but only if, it pursues stable and lasting desires or preferences. In a second range of examples, heteronomous action is seen as conformity to principles that are embedded in institutions, conventions and ideologies, such as the forms of deference discussed in the first pages of *What Is Enlightenment?*[22] or the interpretative strategies of 'biblical

---

[20] Iris Murdoch, *The Sovereignty of Good* (London: Routledge & Kegan Paul, 1970), 80. Quoted above on p. 105.

[21] See *G* 4:441 and other discussions of hypothetical imperatives.

[22] See *WOT* 8:36–7. Kant's examples include deference to the written word, to doctors, to spiritual advisers, to military command, to tax collectors and to clerical fiat.

theologians' that he discusses both in *Religion within the Limits of Mere Reason* and in *The Conflict of the Faculties*. In a third range of examples, heteronomous action is exemplified by action on well-known ethical theories, such as those based on principles of happiness or perfection (*G* 4:441–5; *CPrR* 5:25–40). In all these cases, agents exhibit a form of rational autonomy, yet in Kant's view 'these principles set up nothing other than heteronomy of the will as the first ground of morality' (*G* 4:443).[23] Since contemporary conceptions of rational autonomy do not rule out action that Kant would class as heteronomous, the conception of autonomy they endorse must be weaker than Kant's conception of autonomy.

Heteronomy and autonomy

Kant characterises the heteronomous positions that he rejects not as failing to prescribe laws or principles that have the form of law, but as prescribing laws or principles that indeed have the form of law *yet are nevertheless of the wrong sort*. Those who both adopt heteronomous ethical theories, and adopt less systematically organised heteronomous principles, freely choose principles of action that often (though not invariably) have the form of law. Yet they may choose morally inadequate principles. To understand the requirements of Kantian autonomy it is essential to see why he thinks even lawlike heteronomy is morally inadequate, and why he concludes that autonomy is not merely a matter of adopting principles that have the form of law.

On Kant's account, heteronomous willing adopts principles without sufficient *grounds* or *justification*. Its principles, even when formally lawlike, are based on arbitrary or extraneous assumptions. Action both on Kantianly autonomous and on heteronomous principles is chosen by individuals, and the latter too can be principled. Yet heteronomous willing does not meet the requirements of morality because its prescriptions are no more than conditional, and will appear arbitrary to those who do not satisfy or accept the assumed condition:

> If the will seeks the law that is to determine it *anywhere else* than in the fitness of its maxims for its own giving of universal law – consequently if in going beyond itself it seeks this law in any of its objects – heteronomy always results. The will in this case does not give itself the law; instead the

---

[23] 'daß diese Prinzipien überall nichts als Heteronomie des Willens zum ersten Grunde der Sittlichkeit aufstellen'.

object by means of its relation to the will, gives the law to it. (*G* 4:441; cf. 4:433)[24]

Heteronomous willing often has the form of law, but it seeks or takes its principles or laws from 'somewhere else'. It relies on some further but unvindicated assumption as a basis for selecting principles. Consequently heteronomous willing is not a matter of willing 'laws for themselves'. It is a matter of willing principles of action that are contingent on various rationally ungrounded assumptions: that is why it can ground no more than *hypothetical imperatives.*

For example, agents may assume that their own desires or preferences always count as reasons for action (egoism), or that the general happiness always counts as reason for action (eudaimonism), or that divine commands always count as reasons for action (theological perfectionism) (*G* 4:441–5; *CPrR* 5:25–41). Heteronomous reasoning claims that agents ought to do something *because of something else*: heteronomous willing introduces 'one thought too many'. That appeal to *something else* is basic to heteronomous willing, and is Kant's reason for claiming that in willing heteronomously an agent allows some *object* to give it the law and 'the will . . . does not give itself the law'. Kant does not use this reflexive phrase to suggest that agents whose willing is heteronomous do not choose their principles of action: heteronomous choice is choice all right, and often principled choice. He means that the choice rests on some further but unvindicated assumption about reasons for action. Heteronomous willing is *chosen* and can be *principled* (*hence law like*), but it is not autonomous in Kant's sense, because it assumes some further, unvindicated claim.

Is this position coherent? Perhaps those who think that morality must in the end amount to a system of hypothetical imperatives, or that some form of rational autonomy is the most we could aspire to, are right. What could it possibly be to choose laws or principles without deriving reasons for action 'from anywhere else'? What does Kant mean when he characterises autonomous willing as a matter of adopting *a law for itself*? Does he perhaps mean that the distinguishing, reflexive character of autonomous action is no more than negative? Is it just the absence of any extraneous, unvindicated premises, which would introduce heteronomy, that is the basis of willing a 'law for itself' and the hallmark of Kantian autonomy?

---

24   'Wenn der Wille irgend *worin anders* als in der Tauglichkeit seiner Maximen zu seiner eigenen allgemeinen Gesetzgebung, mithin wenn er, indem er über sich selbst hinausgeht, in der Beschaffenheit irgend eines seiner Objekte das Gesetz sucht, das ihn bestimmen soll, so kommt jederzeit *Heteronomie* heraus. Der Wille gibt alsdann sich nicht selbst, sondern das Objekt durch sein Verhältnis zum Willen gibt diesem das Gesetz.'

Yet how is such independence from other assumptions to be achieved? Isn't *some* additional assumption always needed, even if not explicitly articulated, if an agent is to choose one rather than another lawlike principle of action? It may seem that Kantianly autonomous willing is impossible: an agent who invokes *any* consideration to choose one rather than another principle of action will slide into heteronomy; an agent who does not do so will be unable to choose any determinate principle of action. The ancient accusation that rejection of heteronomy leads to empty formalism may hold.

Personal and impersonal reflexivity

Kant seeks to turn this tight corner to advantage by arguing that it is precisely the *absence* of any appeal to extraneous features or considerations that provides the key to understanding autonomous willing or self-legislation. An agent who does not 'seek the law that is to determine it *anywhere else*' (*G* 4:441; see note 23 for German text) cannot assign weight to features that distinguish some agents from others: to do so would be to revert to heteronomy. By elimination, Kant concludes, 'The principle of autonomy is therefore: to choose only in such a way that the maxims of your choice are also included as universal laws in the same volition' (*G* 4:440).[25] The lack of a rational basis for distinguishing among principles that appeal to features that distinguish one agent from another (desires, ideology, social status, the demands of the powerful) drives the conclusion that adopting principles that are not fit to be universally adopted is unreasoned. The principles which unrestricted practical reasoning justifies do not introduce arbitrary assumptions that do not or cannot hold for some agents: they can be adopted by anyone, and so by everyone.

So Kantian autonomy is a matter not merely of choosing principles of action that have the form of law, but of choosing principles of action that both have the *form of law* and *could be principles for all* – and so of rejecting those heteronomous principles that have the form of law, but cannot be principles for all. *It is a matter of choosing principles that combine universal form and universal scope.*

In some passages Kant elides his comments on universal form and universal scope, writing as if having the form of law guaranteed universal scope. However, he usually distinguishes them; he argues for both; and he

---

[25] 'Das Prinzip der Autonomie ist also: nicht anders zu wählen als so, daß die Maximen seiner Wahl in demselben Wollen zugleich als allgmeines Gesetz mit begriffen seien.'

needs to argue for both if he is to ground a distinction between heteronomy and autonomy. Accordingly, Kantian autonomy is a matter not merely of a choosing self and its chosen principles: it also relies on impersonal rather than personal conceptions of 'self-legislation'.

Kant's use of impersonal reflexive idioms cannot be grasped without taking these points seriously. Only because he defines autonomy *reflexively but impersonally* as 'the will's property of being a law to itself'[26] can he offer reasons for thinking that autonomy is reasoned in a way that heteronomy is not. Only because he thinks of autonomy as a 'lawgiving of its own on the part of pure practical reason' (rather than as a 'lawgiving' by an individual self)[27] can he reach conclusions that link autonomy, reason and morality. These appeals to impersonal reflexivity are fundamental to the claims that 'Morality is thus the relation of actions to the autonomy of the will' (*G* 4:439; for German text see note 18) and that '*Autonomy* of the will is the sole principle of all moral laws and of duties in keeping with them' (*CPrR* 5:33; for German text see note 19).

In speaking of autonomy as basic to practical reasoning and to morality, Kant therefore does not mean just that reasoned action, or morally acceptable action, is based on principles that can be chosen or adopted by agents. *All* morally imputable action is chosen by agents: freedom of choice is the basis of wrongdoing, of mere conformity to moral requirements and also of action on moral principles. Nor does he mean just that the will adopts some principle of action that has the form of law: heteronomous willing may achieve as much. He means that the will adopts a principle that is lawlike in form *and* is not based on any unvindicated assumption, so is a 'law for itself' and may be thought of as a '*lawgiving of its own* on the part of pure and, as such, practical reason' (*CPrR* 5:33; for German text see note 27).

Unsurprisingly, given the structure of Kant's writing on practical reason and ethics, this conception of autonomy as a matter of choosing principles that can be 'laws for themselves' is latent in the earliest discussion of self-legislation in *Groundwork* and in the *Critique of Practical Reason*. Even in Book I of the *Groundwork*, with its restricted framework of a common understanding of morality, Kant expresses (a version of) the Categorical Imperative with the thought that since he has (by hypothesis) deprived the will of every other source of reasons for action '*nothing is left* [my italics] but conformity of its actions as such with universal law, which alone is to serve

---

[26] *G* 4:447: 'die Eigenschaft des Willens, sich selbst ein Gesetz zu sein'. See also *G* 4:400; *CPrR* 5:72, 5:128; *MM* 6:446.

[27] *CPrR* 5:33: 'diese eigene Gesetzgebung . . . der reinen und als solche praktischen Vernunft'.

the will as its principle'.[28] In his subsequent discussion of the Formula of Universal Law he again stresses the elimination of all other bases for selecting a principle of action and points out that 'since the imperative contains... only the necessity that the maxim be in conformity with this law, while the law contains no condition to which it would be limited, *nothing is left* [my italics] with which the maxim is to conform but the universality of a law as such'.[29]

The key to the ways in which Kant connects autonomy, reason and morality lies in his impersonal conception of reflexivity, which underlies this transition from the broader notion of *conformity to law* – having the form of law – to the more specific notion of *conformity to law that has universal scope*. Conformity to law is a matter of adopting some principle of action that has the form of law. Much heteronomous action meets this standard. But heteronomous principles do not combine conformity to law with universal scope, so offer incomplete justifications.

The incompleteness of justification is clearest in those more theoretical forms of heteronomy in ethics that Kant classifies as *perfectionism*, where fundamental assumptions requiring powerful but unavailable justification (a theory of the good) are introduced. However, in many less theorised contexts heteronomy arises because the principles chosen cannot be 'included as universal law in the same volition'.[30] The difference between autonomy and heteronomy is a difference between a formal requirement without any scope requirement, and a formal requirement combined with a scope requirement. Mere adherence to the form of law without attention to the scope of the laws or principles adopted can be achieved by action on principles which cannot have universal scope, because it is impossible for all others to adopt them, or *a fortiori* to have reason to adopt them.

Heteronomous principles are often *excluding* principles: the various assumptions or conditions on which they are based exclude those who do not meet a specified condition, and this creates an overt or covert restriction on their scope. For example, principles of enslaving, of exploiting, of killing and of coercing others can be adopted by many: but they cannot be principles for all. We can establish this by trying to imagine a possible

[28] *G* 4:402: 'so bleibt nichts als die allgemeine Gesetzmäßigkeit der Handlungen überhaupt übrig'.

[29] *G* 4:420–1: 'Denn da... diesem Gesetze gemäß zu sein, das Gesetz aber keine Bedingungen enthält auf die es eingeschränkt war, so bleibt nichts als die Allgemeinheit eines Gesetzes überhaupt übrig, welchem die Maxime der Handlung gemäß sein soll.' See also 'Gründen, die fur jedes vernünftige Wesen als ein solches gültig sind', *G* 4.413; 'die Notwendigkeit [bei dem Imperativ der Sittlichkeit] sich auf keine Voraussetzung stützen kann', *G* 4.419.

[30] *G* 4:440: '[nicht anders zu wählen als]... in demselben Wollen zugleich als allgemeines Gesetz mit begriffen seien'.

world in which they were adopted by all. In such a world, we must assume, at least some would act on these principles successfully, so there would be at least some others who in consequence would be unable to adopt those principles: such principles *cannot* be principles for all. Heteronomous principles of this sort are based on assumptions that preclude their universal adoption. Whether their rejection provides a sufficient framework for a full or adequate range of substantive moral principles is a further and large question: but these points are enough to show that a general objection of formalism fails.

Heteronomy is expressed in action on chosen principles that have the form of law, but that also rely on further, substantive assumptions for which no full rational vindication is provided. Hence heteronomous principles make no claims on agents whom they exclude, or for whom the assumptions on which the principles are based are inapplicable. Principles of action that are predicated on agents having specific sorts of status, desires, beliefs, or ideology can offer reasons to some, but not to all. By elimination, autonomy is expressed in action on principles that not only have the form of law, but can hold universally because they do not depend on further assumptions or conditions that cannot hold for all.

Kant regards this as showing that autonomy is the basis of unconditional practical reasoning, while heteronomous principles, which introduce extraneous, unjustified assumptions, can be deployed only where those further assumptions happen to hold or be accepted. He describes the principle of autonomy as 'reason's lawgiving' because it meets the negative demand of not introducing or relying on unvindicated assumptions. This rejection of unvindicated assumptions can be seen as setting a requirement for *impersonal* reflexivity:

> it is requisite to reason's lawgiving that it should need to presuppose only *itself*, because a rule is objectively and universally valid only when it holds without the contingent, subjective conditions that distinguish one rational being from another.[31]

This passage shows that Kant's use of reflexive notions such as *self-legislation* and *autonomy* does not identify morality with the choice, nor even with the rational choice, of individuals. Kant sees morality as anchored not in *some reasoner's lawgiving* but in *reason's lawgiving*. In these passages he does not

---

[31] *CPrR* 5:21: 'Zu ihrer [d.h. der Vernunft] Gesetzgebung aber wird erfordert, daß sie bloß *sich selbst* vorrauszusetzen bedürfe, weil die Regel nur alsdann objektiv und allgemein gültig ist, wenn sie ohne zufällige subjektive Bedingungen gilt, die ein vernünftiges Wesen von dem anderen unterscheiden.' Cf. *G* 4:427.

rely on a personal reflexive notion of *self-legislation*. He does not identify autonomy either with mere, sheer choice ('legislation' by a self) or with rational choice ('legislation' by a self that acts on lawlike principles). He assigns authority neither to individual choice, nor to choice combined with lawlike form, but to arguments that make no arbitrary assumptions, hence are impersonally reflexive, so have a universal rather than a restricted scope and potential audience. Hence his thought that morality is based on 'a law for itself', and that it is '[reason's] own universal legislation'. The shift from a personal to an impersonal view of the reflexive element in the idea of self-legislation dispels the air of paradox discussed in the beginning of this chapter.

Kant sets out the links that he makes between autonomy, morality and practical reason in the claim that

> the sole principle of morality consists in independence from all matter of the law ... and at the same time in the determination of choice through the mere form of giving universal law that a maxim must be capable of. That *independence*, however, is freedom in the *negative* sense whereas this *lawgiving of its own* on the part of pure and, as such, practical reason is freedom in the *positive* sense. Thus the moral law expresses nothing other than the *autonomy* of pure practical reason.[32]

Kant's conception of autonomy sees agents as adopting principles that are not based on and do not incorporate arbitrary assumptions. The first two marks of autonomy are common to autonomy and to heteronomous action: the third differentiates them and distinguishes Kantian from contemporary views on autonomy. On Kant's account, autonomy is not a matter of action that expresses some striking or independent individual decision or attitude. Nor is it a matter of action done on principles that reflect some rational calculation, a shared ideology, or an ethical theory. The basic idea, without which the Kantian notion of autonomy would collapse into heteronomy, is simply that autonomous principles are *not derived from elsewhere*. Their universality is a corollary of this requirement. He sees the principle of autonomy as 'the sole principle of all moral laws'[33] because any other (non-equivalent) principle could have at most conditional vindication,

---

[32] *CPrR* 5:33: 'In der Unabhängigkeit nämlich von aller Materie des Gesetzes ... und zugleich doch Bestimmung der Willkür durch die bloße allgemeine gesetzgebende Form, deren eine Maxime fähig sein muß, betsteht das alleinige Prinzip der Sittlichkeit. *Jene Unabhängigkeit* aber ist Freiheit im *negativen*, diese eigene Gesetzgebung aber der reine und als solche praktischen Vernunft ist Freiheit im positiven Verstande. Also drückt das moralische Gesetz nichts anderes aus als die Autonomie der reinen praktischen Vernunft.'

[33] *G* 4:440. This reading takes it that other formulations of the Categorical Imperative can be shown equivalent.

and could hold only for the range of cases that meet some ungrounded condition. Kant's frequently repeated impersonal and reflexive claims that morality is based on a 'law for itself', that moral worth is to be found in 'the representation of a law for itself',[34] are all corollaries of this basic assumption. These impersonal reflexive considerations also lie behind his claims that morality is *not a system of hypothetical imperatives*, that *its claims are unconditional* and that its highest principle must be *formulated as a categorical imperative*.

Once the role of impersonal reflexivity in Kant's approach to the justification of moral principles is clear, his occasional uses of personal reflexive constructions in his writing on ethics and politics fall into place. Kant never loses sight of the fact that agents adopt the principles on which they act *for themselves*; hence also adopt their moral principles *for themselves*. Equally he never loses sight of the fact that agents may choose principles that flout or ignore moral claims: I may make it my maxim to pursue self-love at the expense of morality. So the implausible, if not paradoxical, thought that principles can be justified *merely* by the fact that agents adopt or 'legislate' them is far from Kant's views. By contrast, twentieth-century discussions of autonomy have laid great weight on the thought that agents choose their own principles, and have sometimes even sought moral justification in this fact alone. The cost has been high. Moral justification has been allied to extreme forms of individualism and to weak conceptions of practical reason. Self-expression and self-interest have played an increasing (and allegedly legitimate) role in ethical reasoning. Individual autonomy has acquired celebrity status far beyond the ethical writings from which it emerged. How long will the new celebrity last?

---

[34]   G 4:401: 'die *Vorstellung des Gesetzes* an sich selbst'.

CHAPTER 8

Autonomy and public reason in Kant, Habermas and Rawls[1]

In a striking and convincing comment on Kant's view of autonomy, Thomas Hill observed some twenty-five years ago that 'Autonomy is a central concept in contemporary moral debates as well as in the discussion of Kant; but the only thing that seems completely clear about autonomy in these contexts is that it means different things to different writers.'[2] Until I read this remark, I had assumed – in the face of considerable textual evidence to the contrary! – that Kant's discussions of autonomy deal with some variant of the topics discussed in contemporary writing on autonomy.

Contemporary views of autonomy see it as some form of individual independence, but disagree about which sort of independence it requires. Views range from existentialist or quasi-existentialist conceptions of autonomy, that identify it with mere, sheer independence in choosing and acting, to a wide range of positions that see autonomy as independence in choosing and acting that meets the demands of one or another conception of rationality. Although Kant too assumes both that agents are capable of independence (they can choose and refuse freely) and that they are rational, his claims about autonomy introduce very different considerations.

The textual evidence for the negative claim that Kant does not identify autonomy with any version of individual independence is abundant. In *What Is Enlightenment?* – possibly his most popular discussion of autonomy – Kant identifies it with a distinctive conception of the *public use of reason* (WE 8:33–42). In *Groundwork of the Metaphysics of Morals* he introduces the *Formula of Autonomy* as a version of the Categorical Imperative that articulates '*the idea of the will of every rational being as a will giving universal law*', and claims 'that the above principle of autonomy is

---

[1] This chapter was first published with the title 'Autonomy and public reason in Kant' in Mark Timmons and Robert Johnson (eds.), *Reason, Value, and Respect: Kantian Themes from the Philosophy of Thomas E. Hill, Jr.* (Oxford University Press, 2015), pp. 119–31.
[2] Thomas E. Hill, Jr. (1989), 'The Kantian conception of autonomy', reprinted in his *Dignity and Practical Reason in Kant's Moral Theory* (Ithaca, NY: Cornell University Press, 1992), 76–96, 76.

the sole principle of morals can well be shown' (*G* 4:440). In the *Critique of Practical Reason* he asserts that 'the moral law expresses nothing other than the autonomy of pure practical reason' (*CPrR* 5:33). In the *Conflict of the Faculties* he states that 'the power to judge autonomously – that is freely (according to principles of thought in general) – is called reason' (*CF* 7:27). In these and many other passages Kant links autonomy with *reason* rather than with *independence*. He neither construes autonomy merely as a form of individual independence, nor speaks of autonomous persons or selves. The conception of principled autonomy that he proposes and defends requires the adoption of principles that combine *lawlike form* and *universal scope*, so are fit to be offered as *reasons* to all others.[3] Kant identifies autonomy with a specific conception of *public reason*, rather than with a specific conception of *individual independence*.

Yet this has been obscured both by the very different accounts of autonomy that became popular in the late twentieth century, and by the very different articulations of public reason proposed by political philosophers in the same period. Here I shall approach Kant's account of autonomy by a roundabout path, first contrasting his account of public reason with contemporary conceptions of public reason, and then commenting on the considerations that lead Kant to link his conceptions of public reason and of autonomy.

Public reason and deliberative democracy: Habermas and Rawls

Conceptions of public reason are among the big, bold legacies of the European Enlightenment that regained lustre in the political thought of the late twentieth century. Despite this renewed prominence, there is still little agreement about conceptions of public reason, or about its importance. So I shall begin with a sketch of two well-known contemporary ways of thinking about public reason, and then look at some of their implications and limitations, and gesture to the conceptions of democracy to which they are linked.

Jürgen Habermas and John Rawls advanced the two best-known contemporary discussions of public reason.[4] Their approaches focus on the *public* among whom reasoning is to take place, but say remarkably little about *reason*. Public reason is seen simply as debate and discussion,

---

[3] For further textual detail see 'Self-legislation, autonomy and the form of law', Chapter 7 above.

[4] For an overview and comparisons see Thomas McCarthy, 'Kantian constructivism and reconstructivism: Rawls and Habermas in dialogue', *Ethics* 105 (1994), 44–63.

discourse and deliberation, that take place between and among the members of the public, variously conceived, hence in the public sphere.

In *The Structural Transformation of the Public Sphere*[5] Habermas had offered an account of the emergence during the European Enlightenment of a public sphere no longer dominated, if still harassed, by the power of church and state. In this world, communication could take place with a measure of freedom in salons and coffee houses, in conversation and correspondence, in newspapers and periodicals. This public sphere was not democratic, since participation was open only to those with education and means, but it was politically significant because its swirling discourses were not tightly subordinated to church, state or other authorities. Questions of more sorts could be raised and debated by more people in more ways. Habermas saw this Enlightenment world as *precursor* to a world that supports participation in debate by all competent persons within (perhaps beyond) states, so as precursor to an increasingly democratic (perhaps global) conception of public reasoning that is free from coercion.

In later writings Habermas elaborates a dialogical account of reasoning, which he sees as taking place in inclusive, non-coercive discourse among free and equal participants.[6] He holds that such dialogue counts as reasoned, provided that certain minimal conditions are met. All competent subjects must be free both internally and externally to take part in discourse, to introduce their own assertions and question others' assertions, and to express their attitudes, desires and needs. This account of the conditions of participation in dialogue says little about norms of reasoning: the requirements on which Habermas focuses are the requirements for *participating*. This focus on conditions for participation underpins the close links he draws between public reason and deliberative conceptions of democracy, in which, as he sees it, citizens exchange views and seek agreement (however, agreement is neither the only aim of democratic deliberation, nor its invariable result). While any agreement reached by citizens in such deliberation can presumably count as *democratically legitimated*, it is unclear why, given the lack of any account of norms of reasoning, it should count as *justified* (a consensus may, after all, be iniquitous, or false). Habermas says little about norms of reasoning or their justification, and nothing about the connections between reason and autonomy of the sort Kant explored

[5] Jürgen Habermas, *The Structural Transformation of the Public Sphere: An Inquiry into a Category of Bourgeois Society* [1962]; trans. Thomas Burger (Cambridge: Polity Press, 1989).
[6] See for example Jürgen Habermas, 'Reconciliation through the public use of reason: remarks on John Rawls's *Political Liberalism*', *Journal of Philosophy* 92 (1995), 109–31.

in his account of public reason, let alone about contemporary conceptions of autonomy.

In his later work John Rawls also put forward an explicitly *political* conception of public reason. His account embodies certain substantive political norms, but he too is largely silent about norms of reasoning. In *Political Liberalism* he wrote:

> Public reason, then, is public in three ways: as the reason of citizens as such, it is the reason of the public; its subject is the good of the public and matters of fundamental justice; and its nature and content is public, being given by the ideals and principles expressed by society's conception of political justice, and conducted open to view.[7]

Rawls sees public reason as taking place among the *citizens* of a *bounded*, *liberal* and *democratic* political society, who 'enter by birth and leave by death' and are willing to accept constraints, provided others too will accept and abide by them.[8] Public reasoning as he conceives it is not internal to a specific social or religious group. It addresses 'the public world of others',[9] and can be deployed by fellow citizens with varying comprehensive ethical and political views. The substantive norms presupposed in this account of public reason are commitments to a bounded society and (the search for) its good, to liberalism and to democracy.[10] Rawls too says little about norms of reasoning or about connections between reason and autonomy of the sort Kant explored in his account of public reason, let alone about contemporary conceptions of autonomy.

Rawls does not see public reason as the only form of reason, and notes that other stretches of reasoning (conceived of in quite general and conventional terms) may have more restricted contexts and assumptions, so cannot count as *public* reasoning:

---

[7] John Rawls, *Political Liberalism* (New York: Columbia University Press, 1993). See also John Rawls 'The idea of public reason revisited' in *Collected Papers*, ed. Samuel Freeman (Cambridge, MA: Harvard University Press, 2002), 573–615, esp. 574ff.

[8] Rawls denied that this bounded society is a state. However, the fact that he depicts it as having and defending geographical boundaries puts pressure on this claim. See Onora O'Neill, 'Political liberalism and public reason: a critical notice of John Rawls' *Political Liberalism*' in *Philosophical Review* 106 (1998), 411–28.

[9] See Rawls, *Political Liberalism*, 53.

[10] Nor is this a limitation to be overcome at some future time, when processes of public reasoning have led all to a shared outlook. Rawls sees persisting pluralism of outlooks and ideologies within societies as the natural outcome of the free public use of reason, and sets aside aspirations to justify a comprehensive moral outlook. That is why he characterises his liberalism specifically as *political* liberalism, and why his conception of public reason offers not only a basis for legitimation but (arguably) a coherentist justification of principles of justice that is relativised to the political sphere in which it takes place. See Rawls, *Political Liberalism*, xv; and *The Law of Peoples*, 578.

> Not all reasons are public reasons, as there are the non-public reasons of Churches and universities and of many other associations in society.[11]

Interestingly Rawls does not see non-public reasoning as defective *reasoning:* it is not *unreasoned.* It cannot, however, offer reasons to the public at large, since many will (at best) see non-public reasoning as conditional on assumptions they reject, indeed may not understand. In his later works, Rawls increasingly emphasised both the geographical bounds and the political context of public reason, and followed Habermas in linking public reason to democratic legitimation. His late essay *The Idea of Public Reason Revisited* begins with the forthright assertion that:

> The idea of public reason, as I understand it, belongs to a conception of a well ordered constitutional democratic society. The form and content of this reason . . . are part of the idea of democracy itself.[12]

These prominent accounts of public reason say almost nothing about *norms of reasoning*, as opposed to *requirements for participating in reasoning.* Each conceives of reason generically and conventionally, and focuses on necessary conditions for individuals, thought of as citizens, to participate. Each approach has been influential in contemporary discussions of democracy, and in particular of deliberative democracy. It is a small step from these accounts of public reason to accounts of deliberative democracy, in which policy and decisions about public affairs are to be shaped by inclusive deliberation among citizens.

However, inclusive deliberation about public affairs is difficult, if not impossible. Citizens have limited time and energy, and many demands on both. Constant deliberation about 'the good of the public and matters of fundamental justice' demands a lot. One trouble with deliberative democracy, it has been said, is that it takes too many evenings,[13] even if deployed only for limited or local decision making. Deliberation and dialogue may offer an attractive, even compelling, model for organising the affairs of small associations, but are not feasible at great or even at medium scale.[14] Perhaps deliberative forms of democracy can be achieved in the smallest polities, or for a few fundamental decisions, but aspiring to deliberative democracy in large polities looks like fruitless nostalgia for small

---

[11] Rawls, *Political LIberalism*, 220.   [12] Rawls, *The Law of Peoples*, 573.

[13] The quip, originally about socialism rather than deliberative democracy, has been variously ascribed to Oscar Wilde, George Bernard Shaw and George Orwell.

[14] See Andrew Kuper, *Democracy beyond Borders: Justice and Representation in Global Institutions* (Oxford University Press, 2006). For a more optimistic view of global public reasoning see Ingrid Volkmer, *The Global Public Sphere: Public Communication in the Age of Reflective Interdependence* (Cambridge: Polity Press, 2014).

communities and times past. Real world democracies cannot rest much on inclusive public reasoning. Or so it seems.

Technological fixes and quasi-communication

Some optimists think that new communications technologies may overcome these problems and make deliberative democracy possible for larger associations and polities. This is implausible, for many reasons. First, the rapid expansion of access to these technologies in the richer parts of the world may not be matched on a global scale: a digital divide persists. Second, the dearth of evenings, and the many other uses people have for them, are unlikely to end. Third, even those who are free to spend many hours communicating with many others across great distances often prefer to spend that time on social, cultural, educational, professional or business communication with selected others, rather than on political communication with all others.

Some of these problems might be overcome in part, but the deeper difficulties with supposed technological solutions to the limitations of deliberation among large publics arise because they secure only some aspects of communication. Communication technologies, old and new, indeed make it possible to *transmit content* to many others. This has been possible since the invention of printing, and greatly extended by broadcasting and the internet. But transmitting content need not and often does not secure communication: it is necessary but not sufficient for communication. The new technologies cannot secure global communication or dialogue, because they cannot ensure that inclusive (or even less-than-inclusive!) audiences grasp or even notice what others seek to communicate, let alone participate in discussions of public affairs. Communicative speech remains, as it always has been, vulnerable to failure: it works only when speech acts are not merely accessible to intended audiences, but intelligible to and assessable by them. And where dialogue is the aim, those audiences must be able to respond and be heard, and must actually do so. Indeed, since effective communication nearly always has to be differentiated for differing audiences, neither dialogue nor deliberation can hope to be fully inclusive, whatever technologies they use. Where standards for effective communication are ignored, the dissemination of speech content amounts only to quasi-communication.[15]

---

[15] On the other hand, *non-inclusive* communication and deliberation among *selected* members of the public is feasible. Activities such as deliberative polling, focus groups and citizens' juries can secure

These points may seem so obvious that they should not need making. And yet they do. We live in a public culture in which we all too often speak of communicating, even when referring to speech that is not grasped by intended, let alone unrestricted, audiences, indeed may not be comprehensible to them, so *does not and cannot communicate with them*. Thinking that ignores the needs of audiences is likely to overlook the necessary conditions for effective communication, deliberation or dialogue, including the necessary conditions for offering others anything that can count as reasons.

A selective focus on the *production* of speech acts that ignores the conditions for their *reception*, and overlooks the demands of genuine interaction and communication between participants, is apparent in many contemporary discussions of the ethics of speech and communication. Some discussion, and quite a lot of legislation and regulation, focuses on standards that can be satisfied by speech acts that need not communicate with anybody, such as *self-expression*, *dissemination* or *disclosure*; or on norms that do not require successful communication, such as norms of *transparency* or *openness*.[16] Other discussions do not focus on speech acts at all, but only on requirements for *handling or processing* speech content, or for *data protection*. In such discussions, norms that must be observed if communication with audiences is to be effective, among them norms of reasoning, are easily ignored and marginalised.

The necessary conditions of public reason

Superficially Habermas and Rawls appear to draw on Kant's account of public reason. Their central demand that 'the public use of one's reason must always be free' echoes, indeed quotes, Kant's very words (*WE* 8:37). However, Kant's account of public reason is very different from those offered by Habermas and Rawls. Rather than equating public reason with *actual* inclusive participation in communication or dialogue, Kant sees it

---

limited and focused communication and engagement among small groups. These exercises typically ask a *limited* sample of the public to take a *limited* amount of time to address a *limited* range of questions in the light of a *limited* amount of information provided and formatted by the organisers. The results can be informative and useful, both for those who organise and for those who take part. Such exercises are probably most useful in addressing fairly specific questions, for example about consumer preferences, or about local environmental or recreational priorities. They exclude most citizens, usually pass unnoticed by those excluded, and cannot be scaled up to achieve deliberative democratic governance.

[16] Transparency limits secrecy, but often does not secure communication. See Archon Fung, Mary Graham and David Weil, *Full Disclosure: The Perils and Promise of Transparency* (Cambridge University Press, 2007); David Heald and Christopher Hood (eds.), *Transparency: The Key to Better Governance?* (Proceedings of the British Academy 135; Oxford University Press, 2006).

as a commitment not to preclude the *possibility* of reasoning with others. Public reasoning, on Kant's account, may not rely on principles that others *cannot* follow. His conception of public reasoning is *normative* and *modal*, and is put forward as a basis for ethical justification rather than for democratic legitimation (which requires *actual* deliberation and (some) agreement).

Kant articulated these points by proposing a surprising way of distinguishing between public and private uses of reason. He characterises uses of reason that rely on ungrounded assumptions, such as the edicts of church or state, or theological or ideological dogma, not as *public* but as *private*. In *What Is Enlightenment?* he (disconcertingly) classifies the reasoning of those who hold *public* office (military officers, pastors of the established church, civil servants) as *private* uses of reason. As he sees it, these public officials derive their authority from their office, and when their communication assumes that authority, it is not (fully) reasoned so cannot count as *public* reasoning.[17] He contrasts such *private* uses of reason with 'the public use of one's own reason . . . which someone makes of it *as a scholar* before the entire public of the *world of readers* . . . who in his capacity of a scholar by his writings . . . speaks to a public in the proper sense of the word' (*WE* 8:37). The image of scholarly communication as a paradigm of fully reasoned communication may be self-flattering, but provides a suggestive metaphor for the idea of communicating in ways that do not preclude the *possibility of reaching an unrestricted audience*. Kant's distinction between public and private uses of reason is a distinction between *private* uses of reason that assume but do not justify authority, so may seem pointless or unreasoned to some audiences, and *public* uses of reason that do not assume authority without justification, which could in principle be followed by an unrestricted audience.[18]

So Kant sees public reason not as achieved by universal participation, but as a matter of respecting norms that enable claims to be intelligible and assessable to all. His focus on what is possible, rather than on what is actually done, has profound implications. It supports an account of public reason that focuses not on the *context and conditions* of actual discourse, but on the *normative conditions required if discourse is to communicate with*

---

[17] 'What I call the private use of reason is that which one may make of it in a certain *civil* post or office with which he is entrusted' (*WE* 8:37).

[18] A corollary of this use of the distinction between public and private uses of reason is that Kant would see contemporary exercises in deliberative democracy as *private* uses of reason, because they presuppose the boundaries and authority of civilly and socially constituted institutions and practices.

unrestricted audiences. His view is that reasoning among pluralities of agents can work only if participants can offer others reasons, and those to whom they are offered can accept, challenge or refuse what they are offered, and can offer reasons in their turn. Public reasoning fails if the conditions for giving *and* receiving, accepting *and* rejecting others' claims are ignored, damaged or flouted. Reasoned discourse of all sorts must therefore be structured so that others can follow it in thought, and practical reasoning must be structured so that others can adopt its recommendations and act on them in suitable circumstances – although, of course, they may decide not to act on reasons that they can follow in thought, or find no occasion to act on principles of action that they have adopted.

It is a curious feature of the accounts of public reason put forward by Habermas and Rawls that they say so little to show why freely entered into dialogue and engagement among citizens should count as *reasoned*. By contrast, Kant's approach to public reason articulates essential normative requirements not for participation, but for reason giving. If we follow Habermas and Rawls, we have to regard all unfettered speech acts that are made publicly available, however they are constructed or structured, as reasoned. Kant evidently does not accept this line of thought. He insists that public reason demands more than freedom to participate in dialogue or discourse, and depicts those who make public use of their reason not merely as free from constraint, but as deploying cognitive and normative disciplines that permit their speech to reach an unrestricted audiences.

Consequently Kant can distinguish between acceptable and unacceptable uses of freedom to reason. He does so in many writings, using many different images. One interesting account can be found in *What Does It Mean to Orient Oneself in Thinking?*, published soon after *What Is Enlightenment?* While the earlier essay argued that rulers should accord freedom to those whose reasoning is fit to be public in Kant's distinctive sense of the term, the later one focuses on standards or norms that must be respected if discourse is to count as reasoned.

The first of these standards is the demand that reasoning be *lawlike*, and so in principle followable by others: discourse that lacks the structure and discipline necessary for others to follow it does not offer reasons to others. Kant challenges sceptics about reason, who imagine that freedom from constraint is enough for discourse to count as reasoning, asking 'have you thought about . . . where your attacks on reason will lead?' (*WOT* 8:144). He argues against those who think that reason requires *no more* than free, unconstrained discourse, and claims that enthusiasts for this form of liberation from discipline lose that very freedom that they claim to prize, by adopting principles that actually stand in the way of *communicating* with others: we cannot communicate our thoughts or offer one another reasons for belief or action without *imposing* sufficient structure or discipline on our discourse to enable intended audiences to follow our communication. *Lawless* thinking simply ignores necessary conditions for reaching possible audiences. Even a *private* use of reason must enable intended audiences to follow it, so must be (in some respects) lawlike.

Although a demand that communication be based on lawlike principles is quite minimal, and leaves many possibilities open, its justification is not simple. Any direct argument for norms of reason would descend into circularity, and in *What Is Orientation?* Kant takes a more indirect approach, using fiercely sarcastic rhetoric[19] to deride those who suggest that reasoning can do without structure or discipline, or that a 'lawless' absence of structure could be liberating. He had clear contemporary targets in mind, including purveyors of religious enthusiasm, superstition and exaggerated views of the powers of genius. Today his targets might include postmodernists, sceptics and deconstructionists. Such sceptics about reason, he suggests, simply fail to see where unstructured, lawless 'liberation' of thought and action *by itself* will lead:

> if reason will not subject itself to the laws it gives itself, it has to bow under the yoke of laws given by another; for without law, nothing – not even nonsense – can play its game for long. Thus the unavoidable consequence of *declared* lawlessness in thinking (of liberation from the limitations of reason) is that the freedom to think will ultimately be forfeited and – because it is not misfortune but arrogance which is to blame for it – . . . will be *trifled away*. (*WOT* 8:145)

The hubris that expresses itself in such 'lawless' thinking leads, Kant suggests, not only to confusion but to cognitive disasters:

> First genius is very pleased with its bold flight, since it has cast off the thread by which reason used to steer it. Soon it enchants others with its triumphant pronouncements and great expectations and now seems to have set itself on a throne which was so badly graced by slow and ponderous reason. Then its maxim is that reason's superior law-giving is invalid – We common human beings call this **enthusiasm**, while those favoured by beneficent nature call it illumination. Since reason alone can command validly for everyone, a confusion of language must soon arise among them; each one now follows his own inspiration. (*WOT* 8:145; and see also *CPR* A 707 / B 735)

---

[19] A reasoned rebuttal of deniers of reason is not possible – as those who tried to engage reasonably with postmodernists often discovered.

Such anarchic, 'lawless' discourse lacks resources for reasoned responses to the claims of dogma, rabble rousing and public relations, spin and superstition, and risks confusion and anarchy in thought and action.

However, if reason required *only* reliance on lawlike principles, its capacity would be quite limited. A requirement to avoid 'lawlessness' can be met by many sorts of reasoning, among them reasoning that defers to the categories and norms of particular political, social, cultural or religious institutions and practices. Private reasoning too is reasoning. Although reasoning that relies on local categories and norms will inevitably be what Kant calls heteronomous reasoning, and can have no more than local or conditional authority and normative force, it is nevertheless reasoned *up to a point*. However, on Kant's account, heteronomous reasoning does not count as a fully *public* use of reason.

Heteronomy and autonomy: the form and scope of public reason[20]

As Kant sees it lawlikeness is not enough for fully public reasoning. Fully public reasoning cannot assume the authority of some arbitrary ('alien') norm, standard or power. It must *both* be lawlike *and* meet further standards. Here, it seems Kant must face difficulties: how are any norms of reasoning to be identified, if they are not to be or defer to the norms promulgated by one or another political, social, religious or other 'authority'?

Kant addresses this issue by arguing that *fully* public reasoning requires agents to think, act and communicate on principles that *not only are lawlike in form but have universal scope*. Failure to adopt principles with lawlike form undermines all reasoned communication, including that which rests on heteronomous considerations; failure to adopt principles that could be principles for all indeed offers reasons (it is after all a *private* use of reason) – but only to the like-minded:

> If the will seeks the law that is to determine it *anywhere* else than in the fitness of its maxims for its own giving of *universal* law . . . heteronomy always results. (*GMS* 4:441)[21]

Those who *seek* to make public use of their reason must meet a more exacting standard:

> To make use of one's own reason means no more than to ask oneself, whenever one is supposed to assume something, whether one could find

---

[20] For further discussion of heteronomy see 'Self-legislation, autonomy and the form of law', Chapter 7 above.

[21] See also 'Self-legislation, autonomy and the form of law', Chapter 7 above, pp. 121–36.

> it feasible to make the ground or the rule on which one assumes it into a
> universal principle for the use of reason. (*WOT* 8: 146n)

Public reasoning, as Kant conceives it, indeed cannot rely on 'lawless' freedom in thinking, doing or communicating. But it also cannot rely on lawlike principles of restricted scope, which can support heteronomous but not autonomous reasoning. Thinking, discourse and action are fully reasoned, so count as public reasoning, only if they are based on principles that *could* be followed in thought or adopted for action by all. As is well known, Kant formulates this combination of demands on the form and scope of reasoning – with more compression than would be ideal! – in the strictest formulation of the Categorical Imperative: *act only on that principle through which you can at the same time will that it be a universal law* (*G* 4:421).

By approaching the nature and authority of reason in this way Kant takes a specific view of the *normative* requirements for reasoned thought, action and discourse. Anything that is reasoned must offer reasons *to others* – which they may or may not consider or accept. *Lawless* discourse fails to offer others reasons. *Lawlike* but heteronomous discourse offers reasons that are directed to and can be grasped by restricted audiences, so at least achieves a *private* use of reason. Only lawlike and autonomous discourse can offer reasons to 'the world at large' and provides a basis for fully public uses of reason. Kant's conception of autonomous reasoning is a conception of the conditions for fully public reasoning, rather than for real-time, *actual* discourse. His arguments are about *the necessary conditions for anything to count as reason giving*, and his most basic claim about reasoning might be put quite crudely as the thought that if we offer others only considerations that they cannot follow, we simply fail to reason with them. On this reading, Kant's account of public reason is neither individualistic nor anchored in a philosophy of consciousness, and seeks to articulate minimal conditions for reasoned thought, action and discourse.

It may still seem puzzling that Kant chose the term *Selbstgesetzgebung* – literally *self-legislation*, and by etymological affinity and convention *autonomy* – for the idea of ensuring that what are offered as reasons can be reasons for all, and are not contingent on specific or variable features of agents. Where is the legislating self in this picture? I would suggest that this question reflects a problem in reading and translating Kant more than it reflects his thinking. As I read the texts, Kant *cannot* be referring to a 'self' who (miraculously?) legislates: if that were his thought, those who adopt heteronomous principles would also be 'self-legislators', since they too adopt lawlike principles. Indeed, it might seem that they would have a stronger claim to be called self-legislators, since the principles they adopt or propose may be *self-serving* or incorporate *self-affecting* considerations. But that is not Kant's thought. The point of the reflexive element *selbst* in *Selbstgesetzgebung* is not to suggest that there is some self that legislates, but to indicate that a 'law' or principle that gives reasons for all cannot be conditional on or dependent on features found in some but not in others. It is therefore a law *to* or *for* itself: not the law of some very special individual self.[22] The image of 'self-legislation' suggests not that selves can legislate, but that legislation or principles can be *nonderivative*: they can be independent of features that are found in some but not in others – and if so can have unrestricted scope. Self-legislation means not *legislation by a self*, but (as Kant often puts it) *legislation that is for itself*, that is a possible 'law for itself' that combines lawlike form and universal scope.

Public reason today

Kant's modal conception of public reason is ostensibly less directly political than its contemporary successors. Those successors link public reason closely with the public and political processes of democracies. Yet the conceptions of public reason that they advocate are not feasible at great, or even at moderate scale. As is well known, these approaches have not proved helpful for thinking about justice at a global scale, and offer an insufficient basis for reasoning that could be received by an open-ended, universal audience.

Could a modal conception of public reason – a more direct descendant of Kant's line of thought – be relevant to public life today? To test this thought we need to ask how communication might secure the possibility of reasoning with all and any others. Broadly speaking, I think that today this would require the shaping of communicative practices to provide unrestricted audiences the possibility of grasping and testing what others, including institutions, claim and the commitments that others, including institutions, make. This agenda is not wholly absent in current aspirations for public communication put forward by governments, companies, the media and other institutions, but its patchy implementation reflects, among other things, a failure to consider what reason-giving for an unrestricted audience would demand.

---

[22] Cf. 'Autonomy of the will is a property of the will by which it is a law to itself (independently of the objects of volition' (*G* 4:440).

Too often it is said that we need more and better communication in some area of life, yet the remedies proposed are not adequate for communication even with restricted audiences, let alone with an open-ended audience. Simplified, let alone dumbed-down, streams of information formatted for wide public 'consumption' may not offer an unrestricted audience the possibility of understanding what is communicated, and will not provide genuine opportunities for response and interaction, for check or challenge, or adequate ways of judging truthfulness or trustworthiness. This is one reason why so many claims 'to communicate with the public' simply fail. Sometimes they offer considerations that go over the heads of many members of the public; on other occasions they oversimplify and distort; sometimes their glossy presentation raises suspicions that realities and prospects are not as depicted, without offering adequate means to check or challenge what is said; sometimes they invoke considerations that owe more to the demands of public relations than to the needs of genuine communication.[23]

But there are also examples of effective communication that genuinely seek to be followable and assessable for unrestricted audiences. Such attempts at public reasoning may include: plain speech, openness about sources; straightforward reporting of the limitations of what is communicated; provision of ready ways of replying and of dealing with communicative failures; ensuring that responses reach the appropriate destinations, rather than 'communications officers' and recorded messages, and a gamut of other possibilities. Incompletely reasoned communication and quasi-communication may now dominate public discourse, but this is not inevitable and we could secure greater respect for the epistemic and ethical norms that matter for reasoned communication that is fit to reach an unrestricted audience.

---

[23] Problematic types of quasi-communication are often deployed in the name of securing better communication, but are unfit to do so. This is often apparent in company reports, promotional literature, press releases, as well as the 'creative' use of small print, league tables, opinion polling, and much more.

PART III

Authority in politics

CHAPTER 9

Orientation in thinking: geographical problems, political solutions[1]

Kant often uses geographical and political ideas and images to articulate philosophical questions and their resolution. There has been a lot of discussion of his use of each range of images, but the links between them are less obvious and less explored.[2] Here I shall consider some links he draws in his 1786 essay *What Is Orientation in Thinking?*, and their philosophical significance.[3] The shift from geographical to political imagery within this essay, I shall argue, is no superficial matter of style. The extensive geographical images in the first part of the essay articulate problems that arise in the ordinary use of human cognitive capacities, which seem inadequate for addressing many questions to which we seek answers. The political images in its closing pages are used to articulate an approach to norms of reasoning that could be used to resolve some of those questions. This interplay of geographical and political imagery recurs in many of Kant's writings, but I shall concentrate on this essay, leaving aside other writings in which he uses

---

[1] 'Orientation in thinking: geographical problems, political solutions', published in Eduardo Mendiata and Stuart Elden (eds.), *Reading Kant's Geography* (New York: Stony Brook Press, 2011). References to Kant's works use the abbreviations given in the Bibliographical Note with the Academy pagination; where I quote the translations in Immanuel Kant, *Kant's Political Writings*, trans. B. Nisbet, ed. H. Reiss, 2nd edn (Cambridge University Press, 1991), page references to that work are also given. Where it may be helpful I cite the German text in the footnotes.

[2] For some discussion of Kant's use of geographical imagery beyond his writings on geography see David W. Tarbet, 'The fabric of metaphor in Kant's *Critique of Pure Reason*', *Journal of the History of Philosophy* 6 (1968), 257–70. For some discussion of his uses of political imagery beyond his writings on politics see Hans Saner, *Kants Weg vom Krieg zum Frieden. Bd. 1: Widerstreit und Einheit* (Basel, 1967), trans. as *Kant's Political Thought: Its Origins and Development* by E.B. Ashton (translator imposed title!) (University of Chicago Press, 1973); Ronald Beiner, *Political Judgment* (University of Chicago Press, 1983); Hannah Arendt, *Lectures on Kant's Political Philosophy*, ed. Ronald Beiner (University of Chicago Press, 1982); Onora O'Neill, 'Reason and politics in the Kantian enterprise' in *Constructions of Reason: Explorations of Kant's Practical Philosophy* (Cambridge University Press, 1989), 3–27; Natalie Brender, 'What is disorientation in thought' in Natalie Brender and Larry Krasnoff (eds.), *New Essays on the History of Autonomy: A Collection Honouring J. B. Schneewind* (Cambridge University Press, 2004), 154–80.

[3] This is the conventional English translation of the title, but a more accurate one, that preserves the reference to agents that is central to Kant's argument, might run 'What Is It to Orient Oneself in Thought?'

geographical and political imagery, as well as works in which he addresses substantive geographical and political questions.

Even the discussion of *What Is Orientation in Thinking?* will have a limited focus. The essay is usually seen mainly as a discussion of rational theology. In it Kant disputes claims put forward by Moses Mendlessohn and others that human reason can deliver *knowledge* of God.[4] Yet, profound as this theme is, it is not the fundamental issue at stake in the essay. *What Is Orientation in Thinking?* is mainly of interest not because it is a notable contribution to eighteenth-century debates about knowledge of God (which it is), but because Kant approaches this debate by trying to articulate and delimit the powers of human reason. Only if this task can be addressed successfully can we find reasons for accepting – or rejecting – the theological claims advanced by Mendelssohn and others. So it is with some daring that I offer an account of this essay that skirts its discussion of theological claims, including its adumbrations of Kant's own views which allow for reasoned faith but not for knowledge of God.

The essay approaches deep questions about the powers of human reason by way of an extended comparison between terrestrial orientation, orientation in an arbitrary space and orientation in thought. In each of these passages Kant's reliance on geographical ideas and imagery is manifest. But it is less obvious, and certainly less remarked, that the later pages of the essay mainly use political ideas and imagery. As I see it, Kant's view of human reason as the capacity to orient ourselves in thought cannot be properly articulated without taking seriously his claims that this is a shared rather than a solitary task, so must meet any necessary conditions for coordination among a plurality of agents. These conditions are also necessary conditions for political coordination. So it should not surprise us that Kant articulates them using political ideas and imagery. The core of his conception of orientation is that it requires *action*, and if orientation in thought is to be possible not only for individuals taken separately but for a plurality of individuals, it must have striking parallels with the necessary conditions of *political action*.

Geographical imagery and philosophical perplexity

Philosophers and others have often used geographical images to set out their most basic questions. The thought is quite intuitive: philosophical perplexity is like the experience of being lost, of not knowing the right

---

[4] Moses Mendelssohn [1785], *Morgenstunden oder Vorlesungen über das Dasein Gottes* (Berlin: Christian Friedrich Boß, 1786) (*Morning Hours or Lectures on the Existence of God*).

way to go. This geographical picture of the starting point for inquiry, and specifically for philosophical inquiry, is built into our language. When we are lost we stray or wander, hence miss the right way, so may err morally, intellectually or theologically.[5] Unsurprisingly, these thoughts are not unique to philosophers. They also occur again and again in religious and ethical writings, in poetry and in other literature.[6]

Philosophers have used various geographical images to articulate this predicament. Human beings may be thought of as lost or in the dark (a cave, a deep wood, a thicket), at sea (out of their depth, drowning), imprisoned or trapped (in a fly bottle). We can find such images in Plato's great myth of the cave, and in Descartes' *Meditations*, where he likens philosophical perplexity to drowning:

> So serious are the doubts into which I have been thrown by yesterday's meditation that I can neither put them out of my mind nor see any way of resolving them. It feels as if I have fallen unexpectedly into a deep whirlpool which tumbles me around so that I can neither stand on the bottom nor swim up to the top. Nevertheless, I will make an effort, and once more attempt the same path which I started on yesterday.[7]

Philosophical and other solutions to this predicament also reveal recurrent patterns. Often the solution is seen as a matter of finding a *guide* (a still small voice; the word of God; a knowledgeable stranger; a guiding thread); an *instruction* (Augustine hearing the words *tolle lege*); a *landmark* (the right way, the path); or a source of *illumination* (the light of reason; light dawning). These images suggest that when we are lost we can find our way only by reference to some authoritative *external* source, which providentially supplies what we need.

Orientation without providential assistance

The background to *What Is Orientation in Thinking?* can be found in Kant's comments on the limits of human reason in the prefaces and introduction

---

[5] The Anglican General Confession compresses several of these images: 'Almighty and most merciful Father, We have erred and strayed from your ways like lost sheep . . .', *Book of Common Prayer*.

[6] Two famous and striking twentieth-century uses of this range of imagery: 'We shall not cease from exploration / And the end of all our exploring / Will be to arrive where we started/And know the place for the first time', T.S. Elliot, 'Little Gidding' in *Four Quartets* (London: Faber, 1944); 'When we first learn to believe anything, what we believe is not a single proposition, it is a whole system of propositions. (Light dawns gradually over the whole.)', Ludwig Wittgenstein, *On Certainty*, ed. G.E.M. Anscombe and G.H. von Wright, trans. Denis Paul and G.E.M. Anscombe (Oxford: Basil Blackwell, 1969), para. 141.

[7] René Descartes, *Meditations on First Philosophy*, trans. John Cottingham (Cambridge University Press, 1996). See *Meditation* II, 16.

of the *Critique of Pure Reason*, where he uses geographical images to characterise the starting point and difficulties of philosophical inquiry. In those passages he insists that human reason – here just the ordinary use of human cognitive capacities – leads us on, then lets us down. 'The procedure of metaphysics', he complains, 'has hitherto been a merely random groping, and what is worst of all, a groping among concepts' (*CPR* B xv).[8] Consequently reason 'not merely fails us, but lures us on by deceitful promises, and in the end betrays us' (*CPR* B xv). This betrayal threatens to stymie our thinking, including our philosophical thinking; 'it precipitates itself into darkness and contradiction' (*CPR* A viii), with the result that 'ever and again we have to retrace our steps' (*CPR* B xiv). If ordinary human reason is unreliable, will not our thinking, including our attempts to address philosophical questions, be disoriented, perhaps impossible?

What Is Orientation in Thinking? returns to these themes. The historical context of the essay is an extended set of disputes about the possibility of rational theology that were exercising several of Kant's contemporaries. In particular, parts of the essay comment on Moses Mendelssohn's assertion in his essay *Morgenstunden* that 'healthy human reason'[9] enables us to know the existence of God. Kant rejects this position as fundamentally dogmatic. 'Healthy human reason', as Kant sees it, is simply Mendlessohn's comforting term for an unconvincing *deus ex machina*.

However, Kant's essay is philosophically interesting less for its critique of Mendelssohn, or of others engaged in these debates, than for its constructive attempt to show how we can orient ourselves in thought without relying on dogmatic claims about the powers of reason. It is a swirling, suggestive, over-compressed essay, in which he often switches abruptly from discussion of rational theology to discussion of the method of reason, and many important points are made in footnotes or asides rather than integrated into the argument. Yet it is clear that the essay is *fundamentally* a discussion of the method of reason, which is to provide the context for reconsidering the debates of rational theology.

As we know from the vast demolition of rationalist metaphysics that we find in the *Transcendental Dialectic* sections of the *Critique of Pure Reason*, Kant's claims about the limitations of ordinary human reasoning

---

[8] I quote these four short passages using the very well known and more resonant words of the older translation by Norman Kemp Smith.

[9] Kant points out that Mendelssohn used various equally vague terms in different writings: 'a certain guideline which he sometimes described as *common sense* (in his *Morgenstunden*), sometimes as *healthy reason*, and sometimes as *plain understanding* (in *An Lessings Freunde*)' (*WOT* 8:133; Reiss, 237).

are entirely serious. So is his refusal to reinstate any form of divine guarantee or providential assistance. He offers a more modest view of what it takes to find one's way – to orient oneself – than those that hold that we can or must find an authoritative external guide or source of illumination that shows us 'the right way'. As he sees it, we need and can have no access to a transcendent reality that can end our disorientation, and would not be helped by the illusory guidance of any *deus ex machina*. *What Is Orientation in Thinking?* proposes a more modest account of orientation in thinking, and thereby of reason.

Varieties of disorientation

The essay begins with extended analogies between geographical and spatial orientation, and then moves on to consider orientation in thinking. *If* we could find an authoritative method of conducting thinking and action, which we could use to overcome confusion and disorientation in thought, we would gain at least some understanding of the method of reason. Yet how can we hope to find a method of conducting thinking and action that moves beyond an account of ordinary, fallible uses of human cognitive capacities, and offers an account of the *proper* use of those capacities? Kant approaches this daunting task by comparing orientation in thought with the more manageable tasks of geographical and spatial orientation.

Near the beginning of the essay three extended passages focus on the task that must be undertaken if one is lost or disoriented. In the first passage Kant offers an account of being lost and orienting oneself that is straightforwardly geographical (*WOT* 8: 134–5; Reiss 238–9). What must we do if we find ourselves in some unfamiliar terrestrial domain and want to work out which direction is which?

> A. To orientate oneself, in the proper sense of the word, means to use a given direction – and we divide the horizon into four of these – in order to find the others, and in particular that of the *sunrise*. If I see the sun in the sky and know that is now midday, I know how to find the south, west, north, and east. For this purpose, however, I must necessarily be able to feel a difference within my own *subject*, namely that between my right and left hands.[10] I call this a *feeling* because these two sides display no perceptible difference as far as external intuition is concerned. If I were not able, in describing a circle, to distinguish between movement from left to right and movement from right to left without reference to any differences between objects within

---

[10] 'Zu diesem Behuf bedarf ich aber durchaus das Gefühl eines Unterschiedes an meinem eigenen *Subject*.'

the circle, and hence to define the different positions of such objects by *a priori* means, I would not know whether to locate west to the right or to the left of the southernmost point of the horizon in order to complete the circle through north and east and so back to south. Thus, in spite of all the objective data in the sky, I orientate myself *geographically* purely by means of a *subjective* distinction;[11] and if all the constellations, while in other respects retaining the same shape and same position in relation to one another, were one day miraculously transposed so that the former easterly direction now became west, no human eye would notice the slightest change on the next clear night, and even the astronomer, if he heeded only what he saw and not at the same time what he felt[12], would inevitably become *disorientated*.

The most unusual feature of this account is Kant's insistence that 'I orientate myself *geographically* purely by means of a *subjective* distinction.' His line of thought draws on his critical accounts both of spatial and of causal knowledge.

Kant held that we cannot coherently think of space either as *absolute* (Newtonian) or as *relational*. Absolute space – as Leibniz had already argued – would be inaccessible except to beings with transcendent cognitive capacities that humans lack and cannot comprehend. Relational conceptions of space cannot allow for incongruent counterparts (left hand/right hand, spirals, snail shells etc.), where the spatial structure of distinct objects is internally the same, yet they cannot fill the same space because they differ in their orientation. Only if we *inhabit* a space – if, as Kant puts it, space is the form of outer sense for human knowers – can we orient ourselves within it while allowing for the possibility of incongruent counterparts.[13]

Kant had argued in the Second Analogy of the *Critique of Pure Reason* that human knowledge of events in the world depends on an ability to distinguish objective from merely subjective sequences of perceptions. Unless we can distinguish changes that are beyond our control from those that we bring about, we cannot identify events in the world that may be candidates for causal investigation. This move is echoed in the passage on terrestrial

---

[11] 'nur durch einen *subjectiven* Unterscheidungsgrund' (*WOT* 8:135; Reiss 239). The claim that I orientate myself *only* by reference to a subjective distinction is too strong. Kant in fact argues that orientation requires a subjective distinction, but not that a subjective distinction is sufficient. He evidently thinks that terrestrial (in his example terrestrial orientation in mid latitudes) also requires perceptual data, remembered information and bodily knowledge. But it also requires movement by which the subject creates the 'subjective distinction' needed for orientation.

[12] 'wenn er bloß auf das, was er sieht, und nicht zugleich was er fühlt, Acht gäbe' (*WOT* 8:135; Reiss 239). Here Kant clearly makes the more plausible claim that orientation requires both a subjective distinction and other information.

[13] We can, of course, distinguish locations in spaces we do not inhabit – for example, within imagined spaces – provided that we also imagine a frame of reference that allows us to do so.

orientation when Kant states that it is by 'distinguishing between movement from left to right and movement from right to left without reference
to any differences between objects within the circle' that I can tell whether
a sequence of perceptions is or is not a perception of change in the world.
Human beings rely on their abilities to draw such distinctions in order to
separate reality from dream, events from fantasies: otherwise they could
not identify events in the world, support causal claims, let alone locate
themselves by reference to the points of the compass.

Two further comments may be useful. First, the phrase 'subjective distinction' in this passage means simply 'a distinction in the subject'. The
intended distinction is neither merely mental, nor epistemically merely
subjective as opposed to objective. My ability to distinguish which way I
am facing, travelling or turning in the world I inhabit allows me to orient
myself in that world and to make my way through it, and to distinguish
changes that I bring about from others that I do not. These necessary
conditions of orientation in a terrestrial space constitute transcendental
conditions of everyday geographical knowledge.

Secondly, orientation in space need not use a terrestrial, if abstract,
frame of reference, such as the one structured by the points of the compass.
Often orientation is good enough for immediate purposes if I can identify
directions and changes in terms of quite local landmarks, and make claims
such as 'I am looking towards the steeple of St Mary's', or 'the lake is
on my left'. In the passage on geographical orientation Kant discusses the
abstract frame of reference conventionally used for terrestrial directions,
which defines the points of the compass, so focuses on orientation 'in the
proper sense of the word' (*WOT* 8:134; Reiss 238), but his argument also
works for more local and limited frames of reference.

So the transition from the case of orientation in a terrestrial space by
reference to the points of the compass to orientation in any given physical
space is easy. Given an appropriate range of information and provided
we can draw the necessary subjective distinction, we can orient ourselves
within any sufficiently structured and differentiated space within which
we find ourselves, whether or not it allows us to use the terrestrial frame
of reference constituted by the points of the compass. The passage on
orientation in any given space reads:

> B. I can now extend this geographical concept of the process of orientation
> to signify any kind of orientation within a given space, i.e. orientation in
> a purely *mathematical* sense.[14] In the darkness, I can orientate myself in

---

[14] 'sich in einem gegebenen Raum überhaupt, mithin bloß *mathematisch* orientiren'.

a familiar room so long as I can touch any one object whose position I remember. But it is obvious that the only thing which assists me here is an ability to define the position of the objects by means of a *subjective* distinction[15]: for I cannot see the objects whose position I am supposed to find; and if, for a joke, someone had shifted all the objects round in such a way that their relative positions remained the same but what was previously on the right was on the left, I would be quite unable to find my way around in a room whose walls were in other respects identical. But in fact, I can orientate myself simply by the feeling of difference between my two sides, my right and my left.[16] This is what happens if I have to walk, and take the correct turnings at night on streets with which I am otherwise familiar but in which I cannot at present distinguish any of the houses. [We must remember how dark Königsberg would have been on moonless nights!] (*WOT* 8:135; Reiss 239)

This argument seems to me essentially the same as that in the discussion of terrestrial orientation. The difference is that the frame of reference is adjusted to the situation of an agent in a space that offers local landmarks that are not enough to identify the points of the compass. In this instance too, what is necessary is that I can tell how I am facing, turning and moving in the space I inhabit.

Orientation in thinking: maxims as subjective distinctions

Kant extends this line of thought by abstracting entirely from geographical or spatial orientation to consider the transcendental conditions of orientation in thinking in general. The third passage on orientation runs:

C. Finally, I can extend this concept even further if I equate it with the ability to orientate oneself not just in space, i.e. mathematically, but also in *thought*, i.e. *logically*. It is easy to guess by analogy that this will be the means by which pure reason regulates its use when, taking leave of known objects (of experience), it seeks to extend its sphere beyond the frontiers of experience and no longer encounters any objects of intuition whatsoever, but merely a space for the latter to operate in.[17] It will then no longer be in a position,

---

[15] 'nach einem *subjectiven* Unterscheidungsgrunde'. Once again the subjective distinction is not the only thing that is needed; but it is needed.

[16] ' das bloße Gefühl eines Unterschiedes meiner zwei Seiten, der rechten und der linken'. Once again Kant can be read as if he held that the 'subjective distinction' were sufficient for orientation, but a moment's thought shows that his claim is that it is necessary rather than sufficient.

[17] In speaking of 'a sphere beyond the frontiers of experience' Kant indicates only that it is a 'sphere' within which spatial, *a fortiori* geographical, orientation is not possible. That 'sphere' would include not only any domain of transcendent objects (to which Kant thinks we have no access), but also more relevantly the domains of transcendental presuppositions and normative claims about which we can think.

in determining its own faculty of judgement, to subsume its judgements under a specific maxim with the help of objective criteria of knowledge, but only with the help of a subjective distinction. This subjective means which remains available to it is simply the feeling of a need which is inherent in reason itself... if it is not just a matter of indifference whether one wishes to make a definite judgement on something or not, if this judgement is made necessary by a real *need* (in fact by a need that reason imposes on itself), and if we are at the same time limited by lack of knowledge in respect of factors essential to the judgement, we require a maxim in the light of which this judgement can be passed. (*WOT* 8:136; Reiss 239–40)

The analogy with the preceding passages on terrestrial and spatial orientation lies in the insufficiency of objective criteria for organising our thinking and action, and the consequent need to have recourse to a 'subjective distinction'. However, orientation *in thought* is evidently not just a matter of being able to distinguish, face, turn or move in one rather than another direction in the space one inhabits, or of developing a frame of reference for terrestrial or other spaces. Consequently it is harder to see what can provide the necessary 'subjective distinction'. Kant asserts that the 'subjective distinction' is created by agents *who adopt maxims in order to make good a deficiency or need in their ordinary cognitive capacities, so that they can regulate their thought and action*. Agents who do not by nature have cognitive capacities of the sort to which they might aspire 'require a maxim in the light of which [this] judgement can be passed'. The maxim is to provide a *standard* or *norm* for a subject to use in organising her thinking and acting (*WOT* 8:136; Reiss 240).

As a first step in trying to see how maxims can provide the necessary 'subjective distinctions' it is useful to remember that Kant characterises maxims as *subjective* principles of volition, where once again 'subjective' means neither merely mental nor epistemically merely subjective, but rather something that belongs to, indeed is chosen by, subjects or agents as a norm to guide what they do (cf. *G* 4:421, note). However, this seemingly creates a further problem. Kant insists that such choices cannot be guided by 'objective' or 'external' criteria or maxims: that is his objection to Mendlessohn, and to rationalist thought in general. But if choices of maxims cannot be guided by such a criterion, will they not be arbitrary? How can a maxim that is adopted in order to create a point of reference or norm for making judgements be justified?

As a first move Kant points out that although human capacities to reason are defective and unreliable, we are at least aware of their deficiency: 'reason... perceives its own deficiency and produces a feeling of need'.[18] Our ordinary cognitive capacities alert us to their own deficiencies and the threat of persistent disorientation, in which 'ever and again we have to retrace our steps' in thinking. Only if we can move beyond this predicament can the 'need of reason' be met. Yet how can this be done? Can recognising a need help to meet that need? Can we perhaps choose to live with unmet needs?

Kant is alert to these problems, but aims to show that while agents are free to choose maxims arbitrarily, they need not do so. He claims that 'a rational belief which is based on the need of reason for practical purposes could be described as a postulate of reason' (*WOT* 8:140; Reiss 245) and could provide a

> signpost or compass by means of which the speculative thinker can orientate himself on his rational wanderings . . . and the man of ordinary . . . reason can use it to plan his course, for both theoretical and practical purposes. (*WOT* 8:142; Reiss 245)[19]

The problem is to understand how freely chosen maxims can provide a compass rather than a will-o'-the-wisp for orienting thinking.

Lawlessness and plurality

In the final pages of *What Is Orientation in Thinking?* Kant shifts his focus from the case of an individual agent who chooses a maxim to provide a subjective distinction or standard to orient his own thinking, to the case of human agents whose lives are linked to others' lives, and whose choice of maxims will affect others. This is not an arbitrary widening of focus. In many other writings Kant argues that human beings *inevitably* find themselves living in juxtaposition with others, because the world they inhabit is a finite sphere that offers only a limited arena for human life. As human numbers grow, we are bound to have contact with others.[20] Our

---

[18] Cf. 'Reason does not feel. It perceives its own deficiency and produces a feeling of need through the *cognitive impulse*. The same applies in this case as in the case of moral feeling, which is not the source of the moral law, for this is entirely a product of reason; on the contrary, moral feeling is itself produced or occasioned by the moral laws and hence by reason, because the active yet free will needs specific grounds [on which to act]' (*WOT* 8:139–40, note; Reiss 243, note). Compare the discussion of moral feeling – 'reverence' – at *G* 4:401, note.

[19] 'Ein reiner Vernunftglaube ist also der Wegweiser oder Compaß, wodurch der speculative Denker sich auf seinen Vernunftstreifereien im Felde übersinnlicher Gegenstände orientiren, der Mensch von gemeiner, doch (moralisch) gesunder Vernunft aber seinen Weg sowohl in theoretischer als praktischer Absicht dem ganzen Zwecke seiner Bestimmung völlig angemessen vorzeichnen kann.'

[20] For discussion of the theme see Katrin Flikschuh, *Kant and Modern Political Philosophy* (Cambridge University Press, 2000).

relations with them may range from peaceful cooperation, to conflict and enmity, to deep incomprehension. However, Kant rules out the possibility of human beings remaining solitary wanderers on the face of the earth, leading the life that Rousseau depicted in the first part of his essay on the origins of human inequality as 'the earliest state of nature'.[21] Our *geographical* situation inevitably raises *political* questions about the forms of association that a plurality of human beings can have, given that they cannot indefinitely continue to lead dispersed and solitary lives.

As Kant sees it, adequate accounts both of reason and of politics need to take account of human plurality. Both in reasoning and in politics we need to adopt principles that can be principles for all, and to reject *lawlessness*. The importance of law for any adequate polity is obvious enough: societies that lack the rule of law suffer either the imperious rule of some despot, or the uncertainties of anarchy. In either case their inhabitants will be exposed to arbitrary demands. Analogously, those who either defer to the dogmatic claims of some alleged supreme principle of reason, or rely on arbitrarily chosen maxims to orient their thinking, will be exposed to one another's arbitrary claims and demands. Just as we are condemned to lawlessness in politics unless we can avoid both *despotism* and *anarchy*, so Kant thinks we are condemned to lawlessness in thinking unless we can avoid both *dogmatism* and *scepticism* about reason.

Kant's use of the term *lawless* to characterise defective conceptions of reason forms part of a rich range of political imagery in his writing on reason, in which he repeatedly likens defective conceptions of reason to defective forms of political association. *What Is Orientation in Thinking?* does not use the full range of political imagery that Kant deploys elsewhere. It focuses entirely on the thought that reasoning among a plurality of agents will fail unless they shun *lawlessness in thinking*. In the first half of the essay Kant exposes *dogmatic* conceptions of reason by showing that their supposedly reasoned claims would have to be seen as arbitrary, since they have only the illusory backing of an 'argument' from authority. (We simply lack an 'external' guide or source of illumination of the sort that Mendelssohn and many others (wrongly) imagined was available.) In the last pages of the essay Kant exposes *sceptical* approaches, which see what passes for reasoning only as a reflection of individual choice, so once again risk arbitrariness or 'lawlessness'. Just as *despotism* and *anarchy* are both of

---

[21] Jean-Jacques Rousseau (1754), 'What is the origin of inequality among men, and is it authorised by the natural law?' in Victor Gourevitch (trans. and ed.), *Rousseau: 'The Discourses' and Other Early Political Writings* (Cambridge University Press, 1997).

them lawless and defective forms of human association, so *dogmatism* and *scepticism* about reason are lawless and defective ways of orienting thinking.

Since a reasoned proof of a supreme maxim of reason that can orient human thinking is in principle impossible, there is no way of proving that the other maxims agents may choose to orient their thinking are all of them unreasoned. Nevertheless, it is possible to show the calamitous costs of assuming that if there is no supreme maxim of reason – if reason is not a 'dictator' (*CPR* A 738 / B 767) – anything goes. In the last pages of *What Is Orientation in Thinking?* Kant does this by mounting a polemical attack on sceptics who maintain that since no supreme principle of reason is given, we may choose whichever maxims we like to orient thought and action. In particular, he challenges those who think in this way to reconsider where their attack on reason is leading, and to take the implications of living with others seriously:

> Men of intellectual ability and breadth of mind!...have you also fully considered what you are doing and where your attacks on reason are likely to lead?...how much and how accurately would we *think* if we did not think, so to speak, in community with others to whom we *communicate* our thoughts and who communicate their thoughts to us! (*WOT* 8:144; Reiss 247)

Those whose lives are connected to others' lives need to realise that by viewing the choice of maxims to orient interaction and communication as arbitrary, they risk undermining not only interaction and communication, but thinking itself. Such lawless views of reason lead not to emancipation, but to disorientation. Kant writes with biting sarcasm about the catastrophic results of supposing that thinking can be adequately oriented by some arbitrary choice of maxims to serve as standards for orienting thinking:

> The sequence of events is roughly as follows. The *genius* is at first delighted with its daring flights, having cast aside the thread by which reason formerly guided it. It soon captivates others in turn with its authoritative pronouncements and great expectations, and now appears to have set itself up on a throne on which slow and ponderous reason looked so out of place. It then adopts the maxim that the supreme legislation of reason is invalid, a maxim which we ordinary mortals describe as **zealotry**, but which those favourites of benevolent nature describe as *illumination*. Meanwhile a confusion of tongues must soon arise among them, for while reason alone can issue instructions that are valid for everyone, each individual now follows his own inspiration. (*WOT* 8:145; Reiss 248)

Thinking in ways that are arbitrary does not lead to the liberation of thought: it costs us the possibility of thinking with others, and of working out with or communicating to others what we have reason to think or to do. Kant points to protagonists of this catastrophic strategy, including purveyors of religious enthusiasm, of superstition and of exaggerated conceptions of the powers of genius. Today he might also have pointed to postmodernists, sceptics or deconstructionists. All of these opponents of reason disregard the disasters that will arise when agents adopt a strategy of taking just *any* maxim they choose as a basis for reason. They ignore the risk that

> if reason does not wish to be subject to the laws which it imposes on itself, it must bow beneath the yoke of laws which somebody else imposes upon it: for nothing – not even the greatest absurdity – can continue to operate for long without some kind of law. Thus the inevitable result of *self-confessed* lawlessness in thinking (of emancipation from the restrictions of reason) is this: that the freedom of thought is thereby ultimately forfeited and, since the fault lies not with misfortune, but with genuine presumption, this freedom is in the true sense of the word *thrown away*. (*WOT* 8:145; Reiss 248)

Lawless, lawlike and lawful thinking

But is it enough for reasoners to 'operate. . . [with] some kind of law'? Adopting *lawlike* principles or maxims, rather than making singular choices or edicts for particular cases, is hardly demanding. Mere lawlikeness appears to set a very minimal standard. Innumerable cognitive and practical principles (including heteronomous principles) are formally lawlike. Different agents could all adopt formally lawlike maxims that varied in many ways, yet fail to light on 'subjective distinctions' by which they could orient their thinking or action in ways that made it accessible to all others. Action on *lawlike* principles is simply not enough to ensure that communication is possible, and will not preclude cognitive or practical disorientation, in which a Babel of voices speak past one another (*CPR* A 707 / B 735). Agents who seek to reason with others need rather to adopt principles that combine *lawlike form* with *universal scope*.[22] Failure to adopt maxims that are *both lawlike in form and universal in scope* will amount to *lawlessness*, and will prove inadequate to orient the thinking of a plurality of agents.

---

[22] For present proposes I shall not say anything about the *scope* of these lawlike principles. This is an important and difficult topic, to which one can gesture by indicating that their scope must include all relevant agents, but that differing understandings of relevance may be needed in different contexts. See 'Self-legislation, autonomy and the form of law', Chapter 7 above.

This demand may seem excessive. Kant is well enough aware that we often manage to communicate on the basis of principles that are formally lawlike, but that could not be universally adopted, so could not be principles for all, and could not offer reasons that all others could follow in thought or action, consider, accept or reject. But adopting either incoherent or heteronomous principles has costs. Principles that prescribe forms of epistemic or logical incoherence may be formally lawlike, yet cannot be universally adopted in thinking. Principles that prescribe violence, monopolising material resources, wholesale coercion or the destruction of agents may be formally lawlike, but cannot be universally adopted in action.

In limited contexts a requirement to orient thinking by maxims that combine the form of law with universal scope may not be needed. Often we organise our thinking and action on the basis of maxims that have and can have no more than parochial scope. Just as local landmarks can be enough to orient ourselves in limited spaces for specific purposes, so parochial maxims can be used to orient aspects of thinking, acting or communicating in specific contexts. Kant does not view all reliance on maxims that could not be adopted by all human agents as wholly unreasoned, but he sees it as *incompletely* reasoned, so prone to error, confusion and failure and likely to exclude some others. Merely adopting *some lawlike maxim or other* for thought or action, while disregarding restrictions on its scope, may not take us beyond what Kant elsewhere[23] calls *private uses of reason*. Such incomplete reasoning is typically premised on forms of cognitive and practical deference, and provides a basis for thinking and acting that remains *in certain respects* arbitrary and unreasoned, and can reach only a limited audience.

Kant is emphatic that 'private' uses of reason are not enough. In the last paragraphs of *What Is Orientation in Thinking?* he offers some vivid illustrations of the baleful effects of relying on lawlike principles with restricted scope in attempting to organise thought or action. If we assume that *all* that is relevant to reasoning is to adopt lawlike maxims, *whether or not they can be principles for all*, then thinking and acting will be inadequately oriented, and may still amount to no more than 'a lawless use of reason' (*WOT* 8:145; Reiss, 247). The consequence will not be a wonderful liberation of thought and action, but their subjugation 'beneath the yoke of laws which somebody else imposes' (*WOT* 8:146; Reiss, 248). If we seek to reason, we must settle not for just any formally lawlike principle,

---

[23] See especially WE 8:35–42. For more detailed textual analysis see 'Vindicating reason', Chapter 1 above, and 'Kant's conception of public reason', Chapter 3 above.

but rather for ways of organising thinking and acting that are both lawlike and could be followed by all, which others too could choose to accept or reject. We must beware that mere 'freedom of thought if it tries to act independently even of the laws of reason, eventually destroys itself' (*WOT* 8:146; Reiss 249).

Anything that can count as fully reasoned must therefore be fit to be given or received, exchanged or refused among all agents. Fully reasoned claims and proposals must be *followable* in thought or *adoptable* for action by any others who are to consider, entertain, adopt and reject them. Only when a plurality of agents organise their thinking and acting on maxims that they could *in principle* communicate and share do they rely on a 'subjective distinction' that sets a standard that is fully fit to orient thinking. The 'subjective distinctions' that lawful maxims provide have to offer more than a 'subjective distinction' for *each subject*: they must be able to serve as a common point of reference for a *plurality of subjects*. Unless agents adopt maxims that can provide distinctions that meet these standards, they will not be able to organise their thinking in ways that others can follow in thought or in action, so will not be able to offer, accept, criticise or refuse others' specific reasons for thinking and acting.

Reasoning as a negative strategy

These considerations seemingly do not tell us what the 'supreme' principle or other principles of reason are, nor do they identify determinate and detailed maxims for conducting thinking. Rather they make plain to any-one who needs to overcome the deficiencies of ordinary human cognition that this can be done only by adopting a *negative strategy*. The negative strategy is to reject principles that are unfit to serve as principles for all. But can this be *all* that reasoning requires?

At the end of *What Is Orientation in Thinking?* Kant asserts forthrightly in a remarkable (if compressed) footnote that rejecting maxims that cannot be followed by others is *all* that is basic to orienting both practical and theoretical reasoning. In both domains those who seek to offer and receive reasons must orient their thinking by rejecting maxims that cannot serve for all. Reasoning, as Kant sees it, is not a matter of cleaving to some canonical list of principles of reason, but a strategy of refusing to rely on principles that do not combine *lawlike form* with *universal scope*:

> To think for oneself means to look within oneself (i.e. in one's own reason) for the supreme touchstone of truth: the maxim of thinking for oneself at all

times is enlightenment. Now this requires less [note less, not more!] effort than is imagined by those who equate enlightenment with knowledge, for enlightenment consists rather in a negative principle in the use of one's own cognitive power,[24] and those who are exceedingly rich in knowledge are often least enlightened in their use of it. *To employ one's own reason means simply to ask oneself, whenever one is urged to accept something, whether one finds it possible to transform the reason for accepting it, or the rule that follows from what is accepted, into a universal principle governing the use of one's reason.*[25] [my italics]

Anything that can count as reasoning must be based not solely on adopting opinions, conventions or superstitions that may be accepted by some but disputed by others – let alone on one or another individual's idiosyncratic maxims. It must be oriented by the negative strategy of refusing to base one's thinking on lawless principles that are unfit to be principles for all.[26] This strategy provides the starting point for reasoned thinking, and can be used to pick out more determinate principles that can serve for theoretical and practical reasoning in specific domains.

This, I think, is why Kant's discussions of reason – of the most general standards or norms relevant to orienting thought and action – shift from geographical to political imagery. When we look more widely in the Kantian texts we find again and again that a range of political images is used to articulate the thought that reasoning must be anchored in principles that can potentially serve not just for an individual, but for all members of a plurality. Reasoning is no more than a strategy by which a plurality can keep open the *possibility* of discussing, and of converging on, more specific claims and proposals. It cannot guarantee actual convergence, let alone agreement: but cutting off the possibility of convergence guarantees that there cannot be communication, agreement – or disagreement. If the possibility of communication is undermined, individual agents will not be able to engage with others' claims or proposals, and will have no response to the claims and proposals of those who fancy 'lawless uses of reason'. By refusing to rely on claims that others with whom we seek to interact

---

[24] 'ein negativer Grundsatz im Gebrauche seines Erkenntnißvermögens'.

[25] *WOT* 8: 146 and 147 note (Reiss 249 note). The italicised passage runs: 'Sich seiner eigenen Vernunft bedienen, will nichts weiter sagen, als bei allem dem, was man annehmen soll, sich selbst fragen: ob man es wohl thunlich finde, den Grund, warum man etwas annimmt, oder auch die Regel, die aus dem, was man annimmt, folgt, zum allgemeinen Grundsatze seines Vernunftgebrauchs zu machen.'

[26] Some may worry that this inserts Kant's supposedly exigent account of duty into the heart of cognitive and practical life. This is an unnecessary worry. In refusing to base thought or action on principles that others who are to follow what is claimed or proposed cannot follow we indeed discard certain ways of thinking or acting, but are generally left with a wide area of freedom.

or communicate may not be able to follow, we keep open the possibility that those others may follow and consider our reasons for believing and for acting, and accept or refuse our claims and proposals.

Our ordinary cognitive capacities are indeed limited. They provide us (as Kant puts the matter elsewhere) with 'just enough for the most pressing needs for the beginning of existence' (*IUH* 8:19–20; Reiss 43), and it is up to human agents to provide the rest. What distinguishes uses of human cognitive capacities that begin and end in disorientation from uses that can orient the thinking of a plurality of agents is just that the latter systematically reject principles for thought or action that could not be followed by all.

In a number of other works Kant uses more specific political imagery to characterise reasoning. He writes, for example, of establishing a 'tribunal of reason' or a 'lasting peace', and of being 'governed' by 'reason's laws'. But while his choice of institutional imagery varies, its common core is that the rejection of lawlessness is central. The task of reasoning is to adopt a negative strategy of avoiding lawlessness in thinking, as in politics.

Reason's fundamental task, as Kant sees it, is normative rather than receptive. Reason is not given by any external source: it is a standard that thinkers can adopt by rejecting maxims that would undermine the possibility of a plurality of free agents articulating and communicating their beliefs and proposals for action. That task parallels the political task of establishing institutions (whatever specific features they may need in actual historical circumstances) that can constitute a polity in which a plurality of otherwise uncoordinated agents can seek to enact common laws.

Kant does not argue for a unique, substantive formulation of a 'supreme' principle of reason – indeed he offers a number of formulations of the Categorical Imperative, and says less than one would hope or expect about the shared structure of theoretical and practical reasoning. But it is clear that he argues that would-be reasoners should reject maxims for thinking or acting that cannot be adopted by all, and rely only on maxims for thinking and acting that can be adopted by all. This limited principle is a far cry from the supposedly powerful principles that rationalists commend, and also from those vaguer standards that Mendelssohn (and others) invoked. However, unlike grander proposals that cannot be justified, it can perhaps be vindicated as a transcendental condition for orienting thought and action among a plurality of agents.

CHAPTER 10

Kant and the Social Contract tradition[1]

In memory of Pierre Laberge

The fundamental idea of the Social Contract tradition is that consent or agreement can justify basic social and political institutions: just societies are based on the consent of the governed, unjust societies are not. As is well known, the tradition has had many forms, notably in political philosophies of the early modern period and in the luxuriant variety of contemporary contractualisms. As is equally well known, a discouraging list of standard difficulties stands in the way of the thought that consent can justify fundamental political and social arrangements.

One long-standing dispute is about the sort of consent needed for justification: should it be the actual consent of those involved, or the hypothetical consent that would be given by beings with a distinctive (e.g. reasoned, informed, disinterested) view of the matter? If actual consent is needed, should it be explicit or is tacit consent enough? Neither view of actual consent seems satisfactory for purposes of justification: we consent explicitly to too little, but (as it seems) tacitly to far too much. If, on the other hand, consent is only hypothetical, then it is quite obscure why it justifies. Why should the consent of hypothetical idealised rational agents, or of hypothetical beings in an ideal speech situation, or of persons in an artfully tailored hypothetical Original Position, justify the principles by which we are to live, who have never been any of these supposedly ideal beings, and probably cannot and do not aspire to become any of them? Moreover, even if hypothetical consent could justify, how should we choose among the many versions of hypothetical consent that have been proposed? And if there is a choice to be made, does not this very fact suggest that considerations other than consent are basic to justification?

---

[1] 'Kant and the Social Contract tradition', first published in François Duchesneau, Guy Lafrance and Claude Piché (eds.), *Kant actuel: hommage à Pierre Laberge* (Montreal: Bellarmin, 2000), 185–200; slightly revised version in Elisabeth Ellis (ed.), *Kant's Political Theory: Interpretations and Applications* (University Park: Penn State University Press, 2012).

On the surface it seems that Kant too must encounter these difficulties. He is generally taken to be a Social Contract theorist, and a good one. In the most distinguished formulation of twentieth-century contractualism John Rawls writes that 'My aim is to present a conception of justice which generalises and carries to a higher level of abstraction the familiar theory of the Social Contract as found, say, in Locke, Rousseau and Kant.'[2] Many knowledgeable writers on Kant's political philosophy during the eighties and nineties spoke confidently of him as a Social Contract theorist.[3] Patrick Riley even titled an article 'On Kant as the most adequate of the Social Contract theorists'.[4] However, others do not see Kant as a Social Contract theorist.

In his great political writings of the 1790s – *Theory and Practice*, *Perpetual Peace* and *The Doctrine of Right* (which forms the first part of *The Metaphysic of Morals*) – Kant provides a fair amount of evidence for the view that he is a Social Contract theorist. Numerous passages in *Theory and Practice*, in *The Metaphysic of Morals*, and some in the other political writings, discuss and apparently endorse a conception of the Social Contract. Yet Kant's basic justification of political institutions appeals not to the Social Contract but to the 'Universal Principle of Justice (Right)'. This principle is stated at the beginning of section 2 of *Theory and Practice* and in the opening passages of *The Doctrine of Right*: 'Any action is *right* if it can coexist with everyone's freedom in accordance with a universal law, or if on its maxim the freedom of choice of each can coexist with everyone's freedom in accordance with a universal law' (*MM* 6:230; cf. *TP* 8:289).

The Universal Principle of Justice makes no obvious reference to consent, and Kant does not identify it with the Social Contract. Indeed, many of his central writings on justice, and specifically on the justification of state power, barely refer to the notion of a Social Contract.

So it is not wholly surprising that some writers argue that Kant does not fall within the Social Contract tradition at all. For example, Reinhardt Brandt has stressed both premodern elements in Kant's political philosophy and the importance of the so-called *lex permissiva* rather than of consent in justifying coercive state power.[5] Leslie Mulholland argues in *Kant's System*

---

[2] John Rawls, *A Theory of Justice* (Cambridge, MA: Harvard University Press, 1971), 11.

[3] For example, Susan Meld Shell, *The Rights of Reason: A Study of Kant's Philosophy and Politics* (Toronto University Press, 1980), 152; Howard Williams, *Kant's Political Philosophy* (Oxford: Blackwell, 1983): 'Kant's theory of justice is, substantially, a theory of contract', 94.

[4] Patrick Riley, 'On Kant as the most adequate of the Social Contract theorists', *Political Theory* 1 (1973), 450–70.

[5] See Reinhardt Brandt, 'Das Erlaubnisgesetz' in Brandt (ed.), *Rechtsphilosophie der Aufklärung* (Berlin: de Gruyter, 1982), 233–85, esp. 235ff.; see also Heinrich Bockerstette, *Aporien der Freiheit und ihre Aufklärung durch Kant* (Stuttgart: Frommann-Holzboog, 1982).

of Rights that his account of justice belongs not in the Social Contract tradition, but in the early modern Natural Law tradition.[6] Katrin Flikschuh argues that he belongs in neither.[7] Arthur Ripstein also emphasises the Universal Principle of Justice rather than contractualist elements in Kant's thought.[8]

Clearly, if Kant is a Social Contract theorist he is a peculiar one. Here I shall look at some of the peculiarities, and suggest that they may enable Kant to avoid some standard difficulties both of Social Contract theory and of contemporary contractualism. If I am right about the distinctiveness of Kant's relationship to the Social Contract tradition, it may not be feasible to see his position as fundamentally contractualist.

Justification by actual and hypothetical consent

Before turning to Kant, I shall consider some of the underlying claims of consent theories, including classical Social Contract theories and contemporary contractualist positions. Their basic thought is that consent can justify basic principles for social and political structures, hence indirectly those structures and even the coercion they inflict. This thought may seem intuitively plausible. When we have consented to something, we have no basis for objecting; we are not wronged when it happens; we have authorised what is done: *volenti non fit iniuria*.

On second thoughts, matters are far more complex. A start can be made by looking at the role of actual consent in justification. There are some cases where actual consent is not sufficient to justify and others where it is not necessary. Its importance is nevertheless not hard to discern.

Consider first how ordinary it is for us to think that actual consent is not sufficient to justify because it has been given to an action or policy of an unacceptable type. Suppose that A agrees that B may practise surgery on him; or to sell B one of his body organs (a kidney, say); or to let B push him from a dangerous height in return for payment, or to let B bully him, or to be B's slave. In these and countless similar cases we are likely to think that, all legalities apart, consent does not provide sufficient justification. We may be tempted to 'save' the claim that actual consent justifies by arguing that in such cases there was something defective about

---

[6] Leslie A. Mulholland, *Kant's System of Rights* (New York: Columbia University Press, 1990).

[7] Katrin Flikschuh, 'Freedom and constraint in Kant's metaphysical elements of justice', *History of Political Thought* 20 (1999), 250–71.

[8] Arthur Ripstein, *Force and Freedom: Kant's Legal and Political Philosophy* (Cambridge, MA: Harvard University Press, 2009).

the consent. We may argue, for example, that the danger or plain stupidity of consenting to dangerous treatment or profound violation of one's rights is evidence that such action cannot have been genuinely consented to by competent adults, that here consent is defective, just as in other cases it is defective because the consenting parties were not adequately rational, informed, free from duress and the like. However, this is a desperate line of argument: there is all too much evidence that people sometimes genuinely consent to action which may seem deeply unacceptable, even to action that profoundly injures, oppresses or degrades them.[9] Across the board insistence that any consent to such action must be flawed merely suggests an underlying refusal to consider the possibility that justification requires more than actual consent.

On the other hand there are plausible cases where actual consent does not seem necessary to justification. When laws are enforced, when parents control their children, when public authorities take emergency action, we have compliance rather than consent: yet the action taken may be wholly legitimate. No form of the Social Contract tradition even claims to show that all justifiable action receives actual consent. If we had to consent to every particular act of state for it to be legitimate, the central purpose of the Social Contract tradition – the justification of government – would be undermined. Clearly, actual consent is not always needed: it is no more necessary than it is sufficient for justification or just action.

Justification that appeals to consent in ethics and politics might, I suggest, more plausibly be thought of as having two stages, which are (generally) individually necessary and only jointly sufficient. First a certain type of action (relationship, institution, policy) must be shown acceptable; secondly, the parties involved in or affected by a particular instance of such an action (relationship, institution, policy) must (generally) consent to it. The only cases in which this second element of actual consent is not required is where the particular action (relationship, policy, institution) is of a type that has been shown exempt from such a requirement – for example because it is an instance of legitimate coercion, or legitimate exercise of authority.

---

[9] Phenomena such as adaptive and addictive preferences are deeply unsettling for attempts to base justification on actual consent. Some people adapt their preferences to the world and then go along with, accept, endorse, consent to being injured, exploited and oppressed; others are dominated by preferences they cannot adapt. See John Elster, *Sour Grapes* (Cambridge University Press, 1983) and *Alchemies of the Mind: Rationality and the Emotions* (Cambridge University Press, 1999); John Elster and O.-J. Skog (eds.), *Getting Hooked* (Cambridge University Press, 1999); Onora O'Neill, 'Justice, capabilities and vulnerabilities' in Martha Nussbaum and Jonathan Glover (eds.), *Women, Culture, and Dependency* (Oxford University Press, 1995), 140–52.

Daily life is full of examples of two-stage justifications. The myriad activities and transactions of domestic, commercial and professional life can be justified by showing that they are consensual, provided that such activities and transactions are of acceptable types, but not otherwise. Political life incorporates processes for allowing for actual consent and dissent: democratic consent given in elections, more rarely in referenda, most rarely in constitutional conventions, can justify governments, policies and states, provided that they are of acceptable types.[10]

Actual consent is not then unimportant either in political or in other forms of justification; but it needs to be supported by other arguments to show that the types of action (relationship, institution, policy) to which consent is given are acceptable. Moreover, even when actual consent is given to an action (relationship, institution, policy) that is of an acceptable sort, its justifying power reaches only a certain distance. Actual consent is a propositional attitude, so is given to a particular act or policy or institution as described by the agent. Since propositional attitudes are referentially opaque, actual consent will not automatically transfer from its initial object to the logical or causal implications of that initial object. This is why actual consent theories, although well designed to take note of consent given by those affected by action (relationships, policies, institutions) as perceived, are not well designed to show whether those affected also consent to related, even closely and necessarily related matters. Actual consent bears on aspects of the particular action (relationship, institution, policy) that an agent may take herself to encounter, and can offer a justification when these are of an acceptable type; it does so in a clear but necessarily narrow way. It cannot justify aspects of action (relationship, institution, policy) of acceptable types to which agents do not attend.

These considerations may suggest that any Social Contract theorist, and any contractualist, should rely as much as possible on appeals to hypothetical consent. Hypothetical consent theories are well designed to justify types of action (relationship, institution, policy); they do not demand demonstrations that anybody actually consents, so avoid the tiresome chore of demonstrating that consent has actually been given, and under which descriptions it has been given.

---

[10] These examples do not show that actual consent is a simple matter. On standard views, any actual consent that justifies must be informed consent. This small phrase covers a multitude of conditions: possession and use of adequate capacities to understand, to reason, and to exercise choice, absence of duress, ignorance and the like. Consent is a defeasible notion, which an indefinite number of conditions can render void, so without justifying power. See Neil C. Manson and Onora O'Neill, *Rethinking Informed Consent in Bioethics* (Cambridge University Press, 2007).

Although they are clearly designed to reach far, hypothetical consent theories do so at high cost. For two linked reasons a switch of focus to hypothetical consent fails to provide reasons for thinking that consent can justify. First, if hypothetical consent theories invoke conceptions of rationality (reasonableness, disinterestedness, etc.), their applicability to the human case will be in question unless they deploy empirically plausible conceptions of each notion. But many versions of hypothetical consent theory have invoked empirically false, highly idealised conceptions of rationality (reasonableness, disinterestedness, etc.). Second, if hypothetical consent theories do without idealising assumptions, and use only empirically accurate assumptions true of all choosers, they may not get very far. To repair the deficit of premises, hypothetical consent theories usually add more specific, empirical premises that refer to features and characteristics that are distinctively true of certain choosers, such as references to their citizenship or membership in certain states or communities. However, in doing this, hypothetical consent theories forfeit the possibility of justifying the features or characteristics they presuppose.

Hypothetical consent theories face an uncomfortable choice between idealised ('metaphysical') justifications and restricted ('political') justifications. 'Metaphysical' justification fails insofar as it relies on idealised claims that are false of many, even all, choosers; 'political' justification fails insofar as it relies on conceptions it needs to justify. For example, John Rawls's own later philosophy appealed to a 'political' justification that refers to peoples and citizens in its basic justificatory arguments, so presupposes rather than justifying boundaries, and (seemingly) at least minimal state powers.[11] Appeals to hypothetical consent, which assume and build on political notions such as these, cannot justify fundamental political arrangements.

Analogous dilemmas arise for contractualisms that appeal either to hypothetical preference orderings that meet idealised conceptions of coherence (connectedness, transitivity), or to the empirically established preference orderings true of specific choosers. If idealised accounts of preferences cannot be established, hypothetical consent theories may well slide towards actual consent theories and in so doing presuppose not only the structure of preferences orderings but the content of preferences – but as they do so, questions about the capacities of preferences to justify, and in particular about appeals to adaptive and addictive preferences, will become pressing.

---

[11] The terms 'metaphysical' and 'political' are used to distinguish different types of justification in Rawls's later work, first appearing in his 1985 'Justice as fairness: political not metaphysical', *Philosophy and Public Affairs* 14 (1985), 223–52; revised version in John Rawls, *Collected Papers*, ed. Samuel Freeman (Cambridge, MA: Harvard University Press, 1999), 388–414.

However, these limitations of hypothetical consent theories do not show that theories of justice are impossible. There is no particular reason for thinking that all reasoning that aims to show which *types* of action (relationship, institution, policy) are acceptable (so setting the context for justifying their particular instances by reference to actual consent) needs to build on a conception of hypothetical consent. The claim that actual consent is a second step, needed to complete a justificatory process (in all but a restricted set of cases, where coercion is shown legitimate), rather than a complete justification by itself, could be linked with a variety of conceptions of justification and of justice. However, if the basic moves of a theory of justice do not appeal to consent, we may no longer be considering any recognisable version of the Social Contract tradition. With these thoughts, back to Kant.

Kant's Social Contract: hypothetical consent

Kant states his views on the Social Contract most clearly in Part II of *Theory and Practice*. The section begins with the assertion that the Social Contract is completely distinctive and defines the 'unconditional and first duty in any external relation of people in general, who cannot help mutually affecting one another' (*TP* 8:289). He then drops all discussion of the Social Contract for several pages in order to set out the Universal Principle of Justice and to explain why it entails the three components of republican justice, namely freedom, dependence on law[12] and equality under law (*TP* 8: 290).

Only towards the end of the section does Kant resume discussion of the idea of the Social Contract. When he does so, he makes a negative and a positive claim: the Social Contract should not be thought of as an historical event; it should be thought of as an idea [*Idee*] of reason offering practical guidance.

Kant expresses the negative point as follows:

> But it is by no means necessary that this contract (called *contractus originarius* or *pactum sociale*), as a coalition of every particular and private will within a people into a common and public will (for the sake of merely rightful legislation) be presupposed as a *fact* (as a fact it is indeed not possible) – as

---

[12] Kant means quite specifically dependence *on law*, which he sees as protecting the independence. Common dependence on law is one of the guarantees of adequate independence, an independence Kant in fact extends only to some (active citizens). In *PP* he states that the Social Contract mandates common dependence or subordination to law. In *MM* he points out that 'civil independence... allows him to owe his existence and sustenance not to the arbitrary will of anyone else among the people, but purely to his own rights and powers as a member of the commonwealth', but once again distinguishes the case of the active and passive citizen (*MM* 6:139–40).

if it would first have to be proved from history that a people, into whose rights and obligations we have entered as descendants, once actually carried out such an act, and that it must have left some sure record or instrument of it, orally or in writing, if one is to hold oneself bound to an already existing civil constitution. (*TP* 8: 297)

Here Kant is on uncontroversial ground. His position amounts to selective rejection of the claim that actual (past) consent (by others) can justify state coercive powers.[13]

Kant's second, positive claim can be, and often has been, read as showing his adherence to some version of hypothetical consent theory. For he asserts that the idea of the Social Contract is an Idea of Reason. In *Theory and Practice* the point is summarised as follows: 'the idea [*Idee*] of a social contract would remain . . . not however as a fact . . . but only as a rational principle for appraising any public rightful constitution'.[14]

However, I believe it would be a misreading to take this passage as showing that, having rejected the view of the Social Contract as an historical event, Kant concludes that hypothetical consent is the source of political justification. Consider the most explicit passage on the Social Contract in *Theory and Practice*, and in particular its modalities, which Kant repeatedly italicises:

> The [Social Contract] is instead *only an idea* of reason (*eine bloße Idee der Vernunft*), which, however, has its undoubted practical reality, namely to bind every legislator to give his laws in such a way that they *could* have arisen from the united will of a whole people and to regard each subject, insofar as he wants to be a citizen, as if he has joined in voting for such a will. This is the touchstone of any public law's conformity with right. In other words, if a public law is so constituted that a whole people *could not possibly* give its consent to it (as, e.g., that a certain class of subjects should have the hereditary privilege of *ruling rank*), it is unjust; but if it is *only possible* that a people could agree to it, it is a duty to consider the law just, even if the people is at present in such a situation or frame of mind, that if consulted it would probably refuse its consent. (*TP* 8:297)

Kant does not say here that the *hypothetical* consent of (idealised) rational beings constitutes the touchstone for justifying constitutions and laws,

---

[13] It is selective because while he rejects the view that the Social Contract was an historical event, he does not consider whether actual consent to basic institutions might be currently but tacitly expressed.

[14] Kant repeats this criticism of actual consent approaches quite often: for example, 'these writers have assumed that the idea of an original contract (a basic postulate of reason) is something which must have taken place in reality, even where there is no document to show that any contract was actually submitted to the commonwealth' (*TP* 8: 302; see also *MM* 6:143 and 6:162; *WE* 8:39).

and thereby fixes the terms of the Social Contract. He suggests that it is *possible* agreement that is decisive. He appeals to *possible* universal consent, not to hypothetical consent. The criterion is apparently modal and not hypothetical.

On first consideration there are unappealing aspects to a modal conception of justification. One problem of any modal view is that it looks too weak either to identify determinate constitutional requirements, or to justify them. Surely all sorts of constitutions and legislation, including much that seems palpably unjust, *could* be universally consented to. A second problem is that it is far from obvious why an appeal to *possible* consent should count as an Idea of Reason.

Kant's Social Contract: republican institutions

However, on Kant's view the criterion of possible consent has crucial substantive implications, and can itself be justified. I shall turn to the implications first. Kant argues that the criterion of possible consent can vindicate a republican constitution which guarantees freedom within the law: constitutions that lack this structure *cannot*, he claims, be universally consented to; constitutions with this structure *can* be universally consented to.

A succinct formulation of the components of a republican constitution is given in *Perpetual Peace*:

> A constitution established, first on principles of the *freedom* of the member of a society ... second on principles of the *dependence* of all upon a single common legislation ... third, on the law of their equality – the sole constitution which issues from the idea of the original contract, on which all rightful legislation of a people must be based – is a *republican* constitution. (*PP* 8:350; cf. *MM* 6:340; *TP* 8:290)

Kant's arguments from the idea of the Social Contract to the three basic components of a legitimate republican constitution are no doubt overly compressed. Yet I do not think it is hard to discern how his thought runs. If the idea of a Social Contract is that of a constitution which *could* secure universal consent, then any constitution that exemplifies it requires the freedom of individuals, without which the possibility of genuine consent or dissent is undermined, at least for some, making universal consent impossible. Secondly, it requires *their common dependence on or subordination to law*: if anyone were above or outside the law, freedom could be systematically or gratuitously undercut, and once again the possibility of genuine consent or dissent would be undermined, at least for some, and universal consent consequently impossible.[15] Thirdly, it must endorse the *legal equality* of citizens, since the subordination of some individuals to others (rather than to the law) would once again undercut freedom, and with it the possibility of genuine consent or dissent, at least for some, and universal consent becomes impossible. In saying that these principles must be exemplified in any constitution that can be derived from the idea of the original contract Kant does not insist on constitutional uniformity: but he does claim that all just constitutions must meet these three quite demanding 'republican' conditions.[16]

There has, of course, been much criticism of Kant's limited conception of a republican constitution, and in particular of his lack of concern with democracy, his exclusion of those whom the world he knew made socially dependent (women, day labourers) from full citizenship and his tough views on the duty of obedience even to unjust rulers. I shall leave these interesting issues largely aside and comment on the fundamental reasoning which lies behind Kant's idea of the Social Contract and so behind the three elements of any republican constitution.

Kant's Social Contract: the Universal Principle of Justice

Kant's conception of the Social Contract undoubtedly has appealing features. These lie not so much in the particular constitutional demands for which he argues, as in his distinctive conception of the reasoning that lies behind his accounts of justice and of justification. These features of Kant's argument may enable him to avoid some of the difficulties of Social Contract theory and of contemporary contractualism that were discussed above (pp. 172–6).

---

[15] The term 'Idee' (Idea: capitalized in many translations) is a technical one for Kant, see below. In *Theory and Practice* he speaks of 'die Idee von einem ursprünglichen Vertrag, die immer in der Vernunft zum Grunde liegt' (*TP* 8:302); 'The social contract is *only an idea* of reason, which, however, has its undoubted practical reality, namely to bind every legislator to give his laws in such a way that they *could* have arisen from the united will of a whole people' (*TP* 8:297).

[16] Kant makes well-known and severe comments on the duty to obey and the wrongness of all rebellion even against a harsh ruler yet insists that his position is entirely different from Hobbes's (*TP* 8:303–5; 84–5). Hobbes had claimed that the sovereign has no obligations to the people, so can by definition do no injustice to a citizen. Kant insists that 'Whatever a people cannot impose upon itself cannot be imposed upon it by the legislator either' (*TP* 8:304; 85). He characterizes Hobbes's position as 'quite appalling' [*erschrecklich* – also translated as terrifying]. However, although Kant insists that the people have inalienable rights, these rights do not include a right to rebel against rulers who violate their rights, 'a coercive right against the one who has done him injustice'. In many (arguably not in all) his discussions of obedience Kant argues that the only legitimate action citizens may undertake in the face of injustice is to make representations: 'the freedom of the pen is the only safeguard of the rights of the people' (*TP* 8:304; cf. *WE*).

Kant reaches the view that his conception of the Social Contract is *'only an Idea* of Reason' (*TP* 8:297). The notion of an 'Idea of Reason' is a technical term which Kant explicates as early as the beginning of the *Transcendental Dialectic* of the *Critique of Pure Reason*, where he writes:

> A concept is either an **empirical** or a **pure** concept, and the pure concept, insofar as it has its origins solely in the understanding... is called *notio*. A concept made up of notions, which goes beyond the possibility of experience, is an **idea** [*Idee*] or concept of reason. (*CPR* A 320 / B 377)[17]

Already in this section of the *Critique of Pure Reason* Kant offered his version of the Social Contract as an example of an Idea of Reason:

> A constitution providing for the **greatest human freedom** according to laws that permit **the freedom of each to exist together with that of others...** is at least a necessary idea, which one must make the ground not merely of the primary plan of a state's constitution but of all laws too. (*CPR* A 316 / B 373)[18]

What lies behind the idea that this constitutional principle, unlike others, is an Idea of Reason? Put schematically Kant's justification of the Social Contract as an Idea of Reason relies on three linked claims. Proceeding from the most to the least abstract, these claims are:

A. The Categorical Imperative is the supreme principle of practical reason, so an Idea of Reason.
B. The Universal Principle of Justice states a version of the Categorical Imperative, restricted to the public domain.
C. The republican conception of the Social Contract is a special case of the Universal Principle of Justice, adjusted to certain historical conditions.

These three stages of justification may be traced as follows:

---

[17] See also a related passage that also articulates the modal basis of the Universal Principle of Justice: 'For, provided that it is not self contradictory that an entire people should agree to such a law, however bitter they might find it, the law is in conformity with right' (*TP* 8:299). The German is even sharper: 'Denn wenn es sich nur nicht wiederspricht, daß ein ganzes Volk zu einem solchen Gesetze zusammenstimme, es mag ihm auch so sauer ankommen, wie es wolle: so ist es dem Rechte gemäß.'
[18] Kant means quite specifically dependence on law. He sometimes speaks of dependence and at others of independence in this context. However, he has closely similar ideas in mind. Common dependence on law is one of the guarantees of adequate independence; independence Kant in fact extends only to some (active citizens). In *Perpetual Peace* he states that the Social Contract mandates common dependence or subordination to law. In the *Metaphysic of Morals* he makes the same point by referring to independence, 'civil independence... allows him to owe his existence and sustenance not to the arbitrary will of any one else among the people, but purely to his own rights and powers as a member of the commonwealth', but once again distinguishes the case of the active and passive citizen (*MM* 6:139–40).

*A1   From the Supreme Principle of Practical Reason to the
Categorical Imperative*

Despite the fact that critique of reason is evidently Kant's central task, the way in which he proceeds is often overlooked or slurred, and the frequently asserted status of the Categorical Imperative as a principle of reason – indeed the supreme principle of practical reason – is left quite obscure. I think this obscurity is remediable. Kant presents extensive and coherent accounts of his views on the vindication of reason in a number of works, and in particular in the Doctrine of Method of the *Critique of Pure Reason*. A bald summary is all that I offer here.[19] I think that it would run along the following lines: we should take seriously the thought that we may lack any adequate account of reason, in that we may be unable to vindicate any generally authoritative ways of disciplining and organising either thinking or doing. What we provisionally take to be the powers of human reason may, as Kant suggests vividly in the prefaces of the *Critique of Pure Reason*, betray us and leave us in darkness and confusion. Moreover, we cannot expect to find any transcendent vindication of reason, such as rationalists have sought. In the Doctrine of Method of the *Critique of Pure Reason* Kant argues that if any ways of proceeding, any theoretical or practical principles, are to have a general or unrestricted authority for organising our thinking and doing, they must be principles that can be followed by all for whom they are relevant: principles could hardly have authority for those unable to follow them. The fundamental requirement of reason is modal: any reasoned way of thinking or acting must be one that is (viewed as) possible for its intended audiences to follow.

This line of thought can be seen as vindicating at least a very abstract and minimal, doubly modal principle for anything to count as theoretical or practical reasoning. Anything that is to count as theoretical reasoning must at least be based on principles which are followable in thought by all whom it is to reach: intelligibility for the intended audience is an indispensable condition for any theoretical reasoning. Anything that is to count as practical reasoning must at least be based on principles that are followable in choosing or willing, that is adoptable by all whom the reasoning is to reach. Universalisability, alias the Categorical Imperative, is a doubly modal requirement, which insists that reasons for action *must* be ones that *can* be adopted by all for whom they are to provide reasons.

---

[19] See the chapters in Part I for more detail.

B1   From the Categorical Imperative to the Universal Principle of Justice
The Categorical Imperative is broader in scope than the Universal Principle
of Justice. Its most familiar version, and the one that makes its doubly
modal character most explicit, is the Formula of Universal Law: *act only
on that maxim through which you can at the same time will that it be a
universal law* (*G* 4:421). It covers maxims for all sorts of action, inward and
outward, personal and public. By contrast the Universal Principle of Justice
is restricted in two ways. First, it is concerned only with maxims for outward
action, that is with the aspects of action which could be enforced (hence
not, for example, with maxims for virtue or with moral worth). Second, it is
concerned only with maxims for *structuring* individuals' external freedom,
that is with maxims for shaping the public domain, hence not with maxims
for other outward aspects of individual conduct, such as the outward aspects
of duties to self or personal relations.

The Universal Principle of Justice formulates a restricted version of the
Categorical Imperative for the domain of 'the external use of freedom' –
that is to say the domain of justice: it requires the rejection of any basic
maxims for structuring the domain of *the external use of freedom* which
could not be consented to or adopted by all. So the Universal Principle of
Justice is a restricted version of the Categorical Imperative. This is wholly
explicit in the formulation from the *Rechtslehre*:

> Any action is *right* if it can coexist with everyone's freedom in accordance
> with a universal law, or if on its maxim the freedom of choice of each can
> coexist with everyone's freedom in accordance with a universal law. (*MM*
> 6:230)

Here there is no appeal to actual or to hypothetical consent: there is only a
doubly modal claim that justice *requires* rejection of principles that *cannot*
be adopted by all.

C1   Universal Principle of Justice to Social Contract
The Universal Principle of Justice remains very abstract; it might be satisfied
in many different ways. It does not even claim that state structures and
coercion are needed to secure a world in which people do not infringe one
another's freedom. Indeed, since state coercion obstructs external freedom
it may seem incompatible with the Universal Principle of Justice.

Kant argues that, contrary to initial assumptions, in *our world* only
coercive structures can secure the Universal Principle of Justice. We are
neither reliably altruistic, nor sufficiently scattered across the surface of
the earth to avoid interaction. Consequently without a system of enforced

laws we will inevitably limit and invade one another's external freedom. In our world justice requires coercion: we need a power that will 'hinder hindrances to freedom' and cannot achieve any more complete realisation of freedom for all.[20] The Universal Principle of Justice conjoined with coercive enforcement is the basis for Kant's version of the Social Contract, which is a less abstract idea than his Universal Principle of Justice, in that it takes account of specific historical circumstances of human life in which unsociable beings 'cannot help mutually affecting one another' (*TP* 8:209), so demands a constitution which deploys state power to enforce laws to which all are subordinate and which guarantee legal equality. *Theory and Practice* contains Kant's most significant discussion of the idea of the Social Contract, because these specific historical conditions are borne in mind throughout the essay. By contrast, in *The Doctrine of Right* Kant's initial focus is broader, and the specific historical conditions that make coercion essential are addressed only in a second move, after consideration of the more abstract Universal Principle of Justice (*MM* 6:230ff.).

There is good reason to distinguish the two principles. The Universal Principle of Justice, as stated in *The Doctrine of Right* and elsewhere, might or might not require coercive powers. For example, if certain communities of rational beings were never inclined to do one another injustice, or if human beings lived the isolated lives of Rousseau's earliest state of nature and could not interact or do one another injustice, they would not need coercive structures. But Kant thinks that this is not the human condition. We are evidently not perfect altruists, and unsociability runs through our sociability. And we unavoidably interact since we are now numerous yet still inhabit the closed space of the earth's surface. In the conditions in which we live, the Universal Principle of Justice can only be realised by way of the more specific idea of a Social Contract, which makes explicit that for us only constitutional structures of a republican type are objects of possible universal consent.

Is Kant a Social Contract theorist?

The strands of argument can now, I think, be pulled together. Kant's conception of the Social Contract is a special case of his Universal Principle

---

[20] 'if a certain use of freedom is itself a hindrance to freedom in accordance with universal laws (i.e. wrong), coercion that is opposed to this (as a *hindering of a hindrance of freedom*) is consistent with freedom in accordance with universal laws, that is, it is right. Hence there is connected with right by the principle of contradiction an authorization to coerce someone who infringes upon it' (*MM* 6:231).

of Justice: it spells out what this principle requires in actual human conditions. The Universal Principle of Justice is in turn a special case of the Categorical Imperative: it spells out the most basic maxims to which our lives must conform if the structures of the public domain are to meet the requirements of the Categorical Imperative. The Categorical Imperative is the supreme principle of practical reason, indeed an Idea of Reason, because its double modal requirement formalises the recognition that we are not in the business of offering reasons to others unless we offer considerations that (we take it) can be followed by all and taken as reasons. Kant's version of the Social Contract can count as an Idea of Reason because he derives it from his account of practical reason, rather than from any appeal to actual or to hypothetical consent.

Can the fact that Kant labels a derivative, but still very abstract Idea of reason 'the Social Contract' make him into a Social Contract theorist? Labels perhaps do not matter much, and it is probably not useful to make essentialist claims about what makes a theorist a Social Contract theorist. But I think that Kant has in fact moved away from the basic insights of other versions of the Social Contract tradition to a different type of justification, to which neither actual nor hypothetical consent is fundamental. His basic thought is that when we think that others cannot adopt, *a fortiori* cannot consent to, some principle we cannot offer them reasons for doing so.

This distinctive if minimalist approach to justice and to justification has the advantage that it avoids some of the central difficulties of justification that have arisen in the Social Contract tradition. Kant's thought is not that coercion is justified because its exercise, or the institutions that exercise it, or the principles behind these institutions, have been, are or would be consented to, but because certain types of republican coercive institutions *could* be consented to by all who live under them, whereas their rejection *could not* be consented to by all. Non-republican institutions are non-starters for universal consent. The rejection, removal and replacement of non-republican institutions is the foundation of justice, the basis for identifying acceptable types of action (policies, institutions) and for establishing the proper contexts for actual consent by those who will be actually affected by particular acts (policies, institutions).

Constitutions that cannot be objects of possible universal consent are all of them unjust on Kant's view. Societies that do not secure the rule of law (anarchic or despotic societies) undermine or jeopardise external freedom for some or for all, so do not secure even the possibility of universal consent. Societies that leave some persons above or outside the law (monarchs, dictators, states within states) undermine or jeopardise external freedom for some or for all, so do not secure even the possibility of universal consent. Societies that do not secure equality of status under law (feudalism, caste societies) undermine or jeopardise external freedom for some or for all, so do not secure even the possibility of universal consent. We may think that Kant's position would be improved by adding that further forms of social subordination which he accepted, but which also obstruct the possibility of consent, are unjust, and so that the rejection of patriarchy and the institution of full democracy are also required components of a just constitution. However, justifying these further claims may not be a simple matter.

If Kant is 'the most adequate of the Social Contract theorists' this may ironically be because he abandons the idea of the Social Contract as some sort of agreement or contract, actual or hypothetical, and thinks of it simply as formulating the necessary conditions for the possibility of universal consent to a political order for unsociable yet interacting rational beings.

However, although Kant insists that the people have inalienable rights, these rights do not include a right to rebel against rulers who violate their rights, 'a coercive right against the one who has done him injustice'. In many (arguably not in all) his discussions of obedience Kant argues that the only legitimate action of citizens in the face of injustice is to make representations: 'the freedom of the pen is the only safeguard of the rights of the people' (*TP* 8:304; cf. *WE*).

CHAPTER II

Historical trends and human futures[1]

Introduction

In the winter of 1784 Kant published two essays on politics, history and the future of mankind. These essays are *Idea for a Universal History with a Cosmopolitan Aim* (*IUH* 8:15–31) and *An Answer to the Question: What Is Enlightenment?* (*WE* 8:35–42). They are the earliest works in which Kant sets out some of the distinctive implications of the critical philosophy for politics, history and the future of mankind. Yet apart from some short, occasional works[2], Kant then turned aside from these themes for the better part of a decade. He resumed intensive work on the trend of history and the future of mankind in his late works of the 1790s. Arguably he found it necessary to go further towards completing a critique of reason, and in particular of practical reason, before returning to what he had come to see as the *practical* questions of history and politics.

The two essays of 1784 have often been read as occasional pieces that rehearse widely accepted Enlightenment views. *What Is Enlightenment?* has been read as a tepid defence of press freedom, marred by an embarrassing partial endorsement of enlightened despotism. *Idea for a Universal History* has been read as a conventional eighteenth-century account of the social dynamics by which conflict can lead to human progress. As I read them, both essays develop distinctive themes and arguments that are deeply rooted in Kant's critical philosophy and both are in various ways remote from conventional Enlightenment thought.

---

[1] 3.3 'Historical trends and human futures', *Studies in History and Philosophy of Science A*, 39, no. 4 (2008), 529–34.
[2] Immanuel Kant (1785), 'Reviews of Herder's Ideas for a Philosophy of History of Mankind', 8:43–66, and Immanuel Kant (1786), 'Conjectures on the Beginning of Human History', 8:107–23; also trans. H.B. Nisbet in Hans Reiss (ed.), *Kant: Political Writings*, 2nd edn (Cambridge University Press, 1991), 201–20, 221–34.

As I read *What Is Enlightenment?* the essay seeks to articulate central requirements for a critical conception of reason. In it Kant distinguishes 'public' and 'private' uses of reason in a distinctive way that hinges not on the size or composition of the actual audiences addressed, but on characteristics of the reasons that are offered. In Kant's view, 'private' reasoning is restricted, in that it assumes but does not vindicate putative authorities, such as the edicts of state or church, or the claims of happenstantial desires or opinions. It can therefore offer reasons only to those who accept the presumed authority, and any conclusions it reaches are conditional on that acceptance. This account of 'private' reasoning explains why Kant classifies the communication of those acting in an official capacity as 'private': they offer reasons only to others who accept the presumed 'authority'. As Kant sees it, private reasoning is a partial and incomplete form of reasoning, which cannot provide reasons to 'the world at large' however widely it is disseminated.

Kant contrasts such 'private' uses of reason with 'public' reasoning that is not premised on any unargued source of authority, so could in principle be communicated to 'the world at large', that is to any reasoning being. The central claim of the essay – that enlightenment is not (as others depict it) a matter of the growth and spread of knowledge, but one of the emergence of autonomy – is to be understood in this light. Kant views autonomy not as a matter of individual choice (that understanding of the term became prominent only in the second half of the twentieth century), but as a feature of principles that could be principles for all, that are both lawlike in *form* and universal in *scope*.[3] Autonomous principles (for action, and arguably also for thought) could be principles for all. *What Is Enlightenment?* may be a short essay, but it engages with the deepest themes of Kant's work.

Idea for a Universal History, on which I shall concentrate here, is only slightly longer, but it too engages with deep themes. It develops some of the implications of Kant's views on the limits of knowledge for the claims we can make about history, politics and the future of mankind. Rather than claiming that human progress is written into a divine plan, or can be read off historical trends, or that it can be inferred from what we know of human nature – all of them widely accepted views at the time – Kant argues that human progress must be seen as grounded in practical rather than theoretical considerations, in human freedom rather than in empirical evidence.

---

[3] See the chapters in Part II above.

The evidence of history

Idea for a Universal History begins by pointing to a seeming tension between human freedom and the possibility of knowing whether human destiny is one of progress, regress or endless oscillation. This tension calls into question the very possibility of discovering laws of social change that support an account of 'universal history'.

The problem is not that history reveals no regularities. Kant notes that although human action is freely chosen, we can find lawlike historical trends when we consider matters 'in the large' (*IUH* 8:17). He points out that although marriages, births and deaths (not all deaths!) reflect human choices, underlying demographic trends are often lawlike over considerable periods. So the fact that history is woven out of freely chosen human action does not *of itself* show that it is uncoordinated or random, or demonstrate that we can say nothing about progress or decline, about human destiny or purpose. However, the observable regularities are not enough to support *universal* claims about the human future. Kant concludes his introductory remarks by pointing out that

> Since human beings in their endeavours do not behave merely instinctively, like animals, and yet also not on the whole like rational citizens of the world in accordance with an agreed upon plan, no history of them in conformity to a plan (as e.g., of bees or of beavers) appears to be possible. (*IUH* 8:17)

There are two distinct reasons why historical trends cannot reveal the underlying character or trend of human history as a whole. In the first place, the evidence within any period is often variable. Secondly, even where it is not, the trends of a given period may not last indefinitely.[4] Consequently, the evidence available to us underdetermines universal claims. It points reliably neither to progress nor to decline, nor to indefinitely prolonged oscillation, so cannot answer the question *whether the human*

---

4 Kant's thought is as much mathematical as philosophical. In *IUH* 8:27 he puts the point as follows: 'for this cycle appears to require so long a time to be completed that the little part of it which humanity has traversed with respect to this aim allows one to determine the shape of its path and the relation of the parts to the whole only as uncertainly as the course taken by our sun together with the entire host of its satellites in the great system of fixed stars can be determined from all the observations of the heavens made hitherto; yet from the general ground of the systematic constitution of the cosmic order and from the little one has observed, one is able to determine reliably enough.' The point may be put more cheerfully in a limerick: A trend is a trend is a trend/ But we never know where it may bend. / It may suddenly swerve / Or cautiously curve / Or asymptote on to the end. (The limerick may be sung to the tune of 'I went to the animal fair'.)

race is progressing.[5] If we are to answer this question we must rely on other considerations, or use other methods.

This epistemological caution sets Kant apart from optimists who think that history reveals progress, from pessimists who claim that it reveals decline, and from those who think that it reveals neither progress nor decline, but only Sisyphean oscillation.[6] *Idea for a Universal History with a Cosmopolitan Aim* begins from the claim that the surface trends of history do not allow us to judge whether human destiny leads to progress, to decline or to oscillation.

Yet despite casting doubt on the prospects of finding historical evidence for the long-term course of history, Kant proposes to look for it 'in this nonsensical course of things human' ('*in diesem widersinnigen Gange menschlicher Dinge*', *IUH* 8:18) and hopes to find a guiding principle or thread (*Leitfaden*) to provide the 'Idea for a Universal History' (*IUH* 8:17, 18). As elsewhere in his writings, Kant shifts his approach when a question resists frontal attack.

Ideas of Reason and the teleology of nature

The most significant divergence between Kant and other Enlightenment thinkers who wrote on human progress therefore lies not in his specific claims about the dynamics of progress – on this he is insightful, but in many ways quite conventional – but in the types of arguments he offers in support of those views. Kant does not offer a metaphysical or theological argument to show that this is the best of all possible worlds, or that progress is inevitable. He also does not claim that history reveals or demonstrates progress. Nor does he argue that human history regresses, or that it oscillates. His most basic claim is negative: neither metaphysical proof, nor theological argument, nor adequate empirical evidence for any of these views is available.

---

[5] Kant formulates the problem of human perfectibility and historical progress in these words in various texts. See 'An Old Question Raised Again: Is the Human Race Constantly Progressing?' (*CF* 7:79–94), which forms part of *Conflict of the Faculties*, and in 'On the Common Saying: That may be correct in theory but it is of no use in practice'. For Kant's view that claims about the trend of human history are not demonstrable, see Elisabeth Ellis, *Kant's Politics: Provisional Theory for an Uncertain World* (Newhaven: Yale University Press, 2005).

[6] Those who thought of history as oscillating were known in Kant's time as 'Abderites' (because the road from Athens to Abdera goes up and down!). See C.M. Wieland, *Die Geschichte der Abderiten: Eine sehr wahrscheinliche Geschichte* (1780) (Frankfurt: Fischer Verlag, 1961). Moses Mendelssohn, to whose work Kant quite often responds, indeed argued that human history alternately progresses and declines. See Moses Mendelssohn, *Jerusalem, or, on Religious Power and Judaism* (1783), trans. Allan Arkush (Hanover: University Press of New England, 1983).

Rather Kant conceives of the underlying 'plan of human history' as an *Idea of Reason*. This fundamental point is signalled clearly in his choice of the title *Idea for a Universal History with a Cosmopolitan Aim*, and is the basic move behind his arguments to show that we have reason to assume that humankind is progressing, despite lack of metaphysical proof or encouraging empirical evidence.

Kant had developed his conception of Ideas of Reason at length in the *Transcendental Dialectic* of the *Critique of Pure Reason*. He provides a lucid definition at the beginning of Book II, where he distinguishes Ideas of Reason from the Ideal of Reason:

> **Ideas**, however, are still more remote from objective realities than **categories**; for no appearance can be found in which they may be represented *in concreto*. They contain a certain completeness that no possible empirical cognition ever achieves, and with them reason has a systematic unity only in the sense that the empirically possible unity seeks to approach it without ever completely reaching it. (*CPR* A 567–8 / B 595–6)

Ideas of Reason are necessary principles, which we must adopt if we are to undertake systematic reasoning. In the appendix to the *Transcendental Dialectic* Kant argues more specifically that the proper use of Ideas of Reason is as *regulative* principles or *maxims of reason*, which we must adopt in order to investigate the natural world or organise human societies (*CPR* A 643 / B 671ff.). As regulative rather than constitutive principles, Ideas of Reason are not demonstrably inscribed in the natural order or in human affairs. Rather they are practical principles adopted to regulate any search for scientific or other order in the natural world, and any practical attempt to introduce order into human affairs, for example by constitutional or political change.[7]

One Idea of Reason that we must assume or postulate is that of the purposive unity of nature. This purposive unity cannot be proven or disproved, but must be assumed as the ground of the formal unity and coherence needed to make sense of the pursuit of scientific knowledge or political reform (*CPR* A 677 / B 714ff., esp. A 699–702 / B 727–30). Unless we adopt this principle, we will not think of nature, or of parts of nature such as organs or organisms, as having the systematic unity required for the

---

[7] On the latter point compare Kant's unusual use of the concept of a Social Contract, which he also sees neither as historical fact nor as hypothetical agreement, but as an Idea of Reason. See 'Kant and the Social Contract tradition', Chapter 10 above, p. 180. In *Theory and Practice* he writes that '[The Social Contract] is only an idea of reason, which, however, has its undoubted practical reality, namely to bind every legislator to give his laws in such a way that they could have arisen from the united will of a whole people' (*TP* 8: 297).

project of seeking to bring events under natural laws and thereby to make sense of them.[8] Kant's claim is that the pursuit of science is impossible unless we assume nature's purposive unity.[9]

From the teleology of nature to human progress

Kant's views on the underlying Idea of human history as progressing are based on his view of the Idea of nature as purposive. But there is an evident gap between the thought that the purposive unity of nature is an Idea of Reason, and the thought that progress in human history – which Kant insists reflects free action – is an Idea of Reason. The argument of *Idea for a Universal History* is supposed to bridge that gap. In its first seven 'propositions', each developed in a short section, Kant claims that once we assume the purposive unity of nature we must also – despite the weakness and ambiguity of the historical evidence available to us – assume that human history progresses.

His argument begins with the claim that we must assume not only that nature in its parts and as a whole is purposive, but more specifically that all the purposes of nature will be realised at some point. Proposition 1 reads:

> *All natural predispositions of a creature are determined sometime to develop themselves completely and purposively.* (*IUH* 8:18)

This heady claim would be hard to justify; however, I shall leave its justification to one side because I think that the arguments of sections 8 and 9 of *Idea for a Universal History* suggest that it may be a redundant assumption (see below, p. 194).

If we must assume that nature is purposive and that its purposes will be realised at some point, Kant thinks that he has a basis for arguing that history progresses by means of the familiar dynamic of unsocial sociability. This dynamic of development moves human societies 'from the greatest crudity to the height of the greatest skilfulness' ('aus der Rohigkeit zur Kultur') (*IUH* 8:20), from 'thoroughgoing antagonism' to '*freedom under*

---

[8] See J. Steigerwald, 'Introduction: Kantian teleology and the biological sciences', *Studies in History and Philosophy of Science Part C: Studies in History and Philosophy of Biological and Biomedical Sciences* 38 (2006), 621–6, and 'Kant's concept of natural purpose and the reflecting power of judgement', *ibid.* 712–34; and Angela Breitenbach, *Die Analogie von Vernunft und Natur* (Berlin: De Gruyter, 2009).

[9] The Idea of the purposiveness of nature, as Kant views it, requires us to assume the purposiveness not only of parts of the natural world (including organs and organisms) but also of the whole. Although scientists may make mistakes in judging purposes, they cannot do science without assuming that nature and all its parts have some purpose. Cf. *CPR* A 688 / B 716.

external laws' (*IUH* 8:22). The same dynamic can propel international relations from recurrent wars, and 'the overstrained and never ceasing process of armament for them' (*IUH* 8:24) to a 'cosmopolitan condition of public state security' (*IUH* 8:26). The same dynamic process underlies the development of culture, of domestic justice and of cosmopolitan order.

Kant does not base his account of human progress on any specific claims about human motivation or historical trends (he could hardly do so given his reasons for asserting that we are ignorant of the trend!). His argument assumes only that human agents when faced with scarcity and difficulty seek to pursue some purposes or other, and so to overcome the obstacles they encounter, inevitably coming into conflict as they do so:

> It seems to have pleased nature to exercise its greatest frugality, and to have measured out its animal endowment so tightly, so precisely to the highest need of an initial existence. (*IUH* 8:19–20)

Nature's parsimony leaves human beings ill provided for, without knowledge or science, without guarantee of others' cooperation, indeed exposed to their depredations. We cannot avoid these realities by isolating ourselves. As Kant often remarked, the very fact that we live on the surface of a finite sphere means that, as population grows, contact is unavoidable, and with it numerous forms of conflict can arise.[10] Yet our unsociable sociability may prove a benefit by providing the context and the means for human efforts to make a difference.

Since nature provides no remedy for unsocial sociability, humans can only escape its dire consequences by their own efforts. Yet what humans freely do might simply exacerbate their problems. Unsocial sociability can fuel competitive 'ambition, tyranny and greed' (*IUH* 8:21);[11] it can drive each to seek status from others 'whom he cannot *stand*, but also cannot *leave alone*' (*IUH* 8:21). These compounding disasters create both the goad and the need to develop new capacities and new forms of social cooperation. The parsimony of nature proves a boon rather than a burden only if and as human beings freely use their powers to overcome the burdens of their natural condition. Kant concludes (making the best of dire realities!) with the words:

> Thanks be to nature, therefore, for the incompatibility, for the spiteful competitive vanity, for the insatiable desire to possess or even to dominate! For without them all the excellent natural predispositions in humanity would eternally slumber undeveloped. (*IUH* 8:21)

---

[10] See Katrin Flikschuh, *Kant's Political Philosophy* (Cambridge University Press, 2000).

[11] The German is pithier: human beings are 'getrieben durch Ehrsucht, Herrschsucht und Habsucht'.

Freedom to escape from unsocial sociability

Aspects of this conception of a transformative dynamic by which unsocial tendencies are progressively tamed and moralised are found in the work of many other writers of the European Enlightenment. Kant's account has some parallels with Hobbes's argument that the realities of 'a time of Warre, where every man is Enemy to every man'[12] provide reason for submission to a sovereign who can guarantee peace; with later arguments that private vices (paradigmatically greed) can foster public virtue; and with claims that the antagonisms of the market can be transformed by a 'hidden hand' to bring public benefit. If these, or similar piecemeal arguments, were all that Kant offered by way of an account of the underlying dynamic of history he would be one of many who argued that dissent and conflict can contribute to the emergence of order and justice.

However, Kant diverges from these predecessors in several respects.[13] In the first place he criticizes the absolutist political conclusions that some of them – notably Hobbes – drew, which he thinks too favourable to despotism. He argues that if unsocial sociability is the dynamic of history, then the preservation of a constrained context for that dynamic, rather than its supposed obliteration by subordination to an absolute sovereign, is essential for the continuing development of human powers and so for continuing progress towards a more just world. Human progress requires not an absolute sovereign, but a civil constitution that secures the greatest possible freedom under external laws, a constitution that institutionalises and limits rather than ends controversy and dispute (*IUH* 8:22).

Secondly, Kant diverges from others in arguing that domestic justice is incomplete without cosmopolitan justice (*IUH* 8:25–6). No fully just civil constitution can emerge in a world of many states, where each attempts to subordinate the others in unconstrained competitive struggles for power. On the contrary, the Westphalian world of many states (which is still with us) is marked by 'wars, [and through] the overstrained and never ceasing process of armament for them' (*IUH* 8:24). On Kant's view, a just system of states that puts an end to this ghastly stage of human history can emerge only when states are linked in 'a cosmopolitan condition of public state security' (*IUH* 8:26). In this anticipation of themes of his 1795 work *Towards Perpetual Peace*, Kant argues that until the context of

---

[12] Thomas Hobbes (1651), *Leviathan*, ed. Richard Tuck (Cambridge University Press, 1991), ch. 13.

[13] See Howard Williams, *Kant's Critique of Hobbes: Sovereignty and Cosmopolitanism* (Cardiff: University of Wales Press, 2003).

international justice (more accurately, *interstatal* justice) is not so much resolved as dissolved, there can be no more than provisional and local resolutions of *conflict*.[14]

Freedom and possible futures

Kant's account of unsocial sociability and its dynamic tendencies does not, indeed cannot, demonstrate substantive empirical claims about human history and progress. He does not go back on his view that we can offer neither metaphysical defence nor empirical vindication of the perfectibility of man or of human progress. He insists only that historical progress is an Idea of Reason that we *must* assume in acting, and that doing so may limit the potentially dire effects of unsocial sociability.

This conclusion is most clearly articulated in the final two sections of the essay. In stating the proposition of section 8, Kant makes it quite plain that progress in history, like teleology in nature, is *only* an Idea of Reason. It runs:

> **Eighth Proposition**
> *One can regard the history of the human species in the large as the completion of a hidden plan of nature to bring about an inwardly and, **to this end**, also externally perfect state constitution, as the only condition in which it can fully develop all its predispositions in humanity.* (IUH 8:27)

Here and throughout section 8, Kant insists that we can assume that nature provides us with everything we *need* to work towards the development of human capacities to reason, towards changing the world we inhabit, and towards transforming the human future – but with no more. He does not claim to *know* or to *prove* that human history progresses, or that we can *know* future history and human destiny *a priori*, but only that we can seek to change and improve our future.

If the argument from natural to historical teleology indeed assumed that all purposes will be realised at some time, then Kant might, it seems, have asserted not merely that we *can regard* but that we *must regard* the plan of nature as leading to human progress, and to the cosmopolitan political institutions that can reduce conflict between states. Yet in section 8 he treats it as an open question whether or not we *must* assume that the hidden plan of nature will lead to the full development of human capacities, to just

---

[14] See Elisabeth Ellis, *Kant's Politics: Provisional Theory for an Uncertain World* (Newhaven: Yale University Press, 2005).

CHAPTER 12

Cosmopolitanism then and now[1]

The last two decades have seen a truly stupendous amount of writing on cosmopolitan ideas, covering a huge variety of conceptions of international, cosmopolitan or global justice. This is hardly surprising in a globalising world. Nor is it surprising that those who now write about cosmopolitan ideas are quite often keen to invoke Kant's reputation and authority for positions they think important. However, contemporary cosmopolitan thought is extremely diverse, and many of the positions and arguments now discussed differ from Kant's views on international and cosmopolitan justice[2] and advocate positions that are remote from those that he advanced.[3]

I shall not say much about contemporary discussions of global, international or cosmopolitan justice, or about other cosmopolitan themes, let alone offer a complete taxonomy. They range from attempts to derive principles of justice from a global Original Position, arguments for other specific forms of distributive justice, and arguments for establishing more inclusive political authorities (from a stronger United Nations to a world

---

[1] A shorter version of this chapter was first published in Stefano Bacin, Alfredo Ferrarin, Claudio La Rocca and Margit Ruffing (eds.), *Kant und die Philosophie in weltbürgerlicher Absicht*, Akten des XI. Kant-Kongresses (Berlin: Walter de Gruyter, 2013), 357–68. The present version has been extended with some additional comments on Kant's political realism, that draw on my 'From transcendental idealism to political realism' in Nicholas Boyle, Liz Disley and John Walker (eds.), *The Impact of Idealism: The Legacy of Post Kantian German Thought*, Vol. II (Cambridge University Press, 2013), 12–25.

[2] Kant's writings on international and cosmopolitan themes are scattered, and unsurprisingly do not use the term 'global justice'. In this chapter I draw mainly on *The Metaphysic of Morals (MM)*, and in particular on its first part, *The Doctrine of Right*; on *Towards Perpetual Peace (PP)*; on *Idea for a Universal History from a Cosmopolitan Point of View (IUH)*, *Conjectural Beginning of Human History (CB)*, the *Conflict of the Faculties (CF)* and *Theory and Practice (TP)*. Unless otherwise indicated, quotations and citations use the Cambridge translations and refer to the Prussian Academy pagination.

[3] The same has happened to a number of other terms that are central to Kant's thought, including *autonomy* and *public reason*: those who now use these terms often claim Kantian ancestry, but have very different conceptions in mind. See the chapters in Part II above.

state), to positions that insist more narrowly on the equal standing or rights of all human beings, but see neither political plurality (multiple states) nor economic inequalities as invariably unjust.[4] Clearly Kant's position cannot lend its authority to all, nor perhaps to any, contemporary forms of cosmopolitanism. However, by setting out rather baldly some of Kant's central claims about cosmopolitan right and justice, and gesturing towards their links with wider themes in his work, it may be easier to see which parts of his legacy might be of interest for contemporary political thought.

Authorised coercion

Kant does not see principles of right or justice merely as specifying the proper configuration or distribution of rights or resources, or the proper structures for political and economic institutions. He does not focus on *patterns* or *distributions* of holdings or resources, or on conceptions of justice as fairness, or on specific equalities: none of these can be directly enforced. He sees *enforceability* as a central requirement for right and justice, which bears on *external* aspects of action.[5] *Internal* aspects of action, by contrast, cannot in principle be enforced, and Kant repeatedly insists that duties that cannot *in principle* be enforced are not duties of right, but (for example) duties to self, or duties of virtue.[6] Of course, duties of right also often cannot be enforced *in practice*, whether because institutions are lacking or ineffective or because some people breach or evade their demands. The aim of an account of duties of right is to identify standards that are required *and* could be enforced.

Kant's demand that duties of right be *enforceable* brackets concern with the principles people actually adopt as maxims, since the adoption of principles cannot be enforced. In other contexts, for example in discussions of good character, he thinks we must consider which maxims ought to be adopted, but duties of right are neutral about the maxims that agents actually adopt. An account of duties of right must therefore be silent about duties of virtue,[7] about duties to self ('ethical duties of

[4] For further discussion of contemporary cosmopolitanism see the chapters in Onora O'Neill, *Justice across Boundaries: Whose Obligations?* (Cambridge University Press, forthcoming).

[5] There is a good deal to be said about the translation of *Recht* and cognate terms (*Rechtspflichten, Rechtslehre, ein Recht*) either as *right* or as *justice*, which I shall not discuss here. The important point is that Kant presents an account of right that is often narrower than, but also likely to be indispensable to, various broader accounts of justice.

[6] For example see *MM* 6:230–1; 6:239; 6:383.

[7] This is a point Kant repeats many times, especially in his discussions of virtue. E.g. *MM* 6:388.

omission'),[8] and about unenforceable considerations of fairness or equity, since none of these is anchored in duties of right.[9] These considerations also show that Kant does not support any form of what Amartya Sen[10] has recently labelled *transcendental institutionalism*: he does not aim to specify standards for *ideally* just institutions, and empathises rather than ignores the importance of ensuring that duties of right can be realised among actual agents, with their determinate and limited capacities and resources.

Kant argues that if duties of right set enforceable standards *for everybody* they must both restrict and protect freedom of action in the same ways for all. Unrestricted freedom of action for everybody would inevitably fail to protect, and undermine possibilities for action for at least some others, so limit their freedom of action in unsystematic, nonlawlike ways. Consequently the 'Universal Principle of Justice' demands both the same freedom of choice and the same basic restrictions for all agents:

> Any action is *right* (*recht*) if it can coexist with everyone's freedom in accordance with a universal law, or if on its maxim the freedom of choice of each can coexist in accordance with a universal law. (*MM* 6:230)

This is an exacting criterion. It also shows why Kant holds that right must be enforceable. Duties of right are respected by *acting* in prescribed ways, rather than by securing some total outcome of action – e.g. a pattern or distribution of goods or activities that might emerge in an ideal society (perhaps an ethical commonwealth?) whose members spontaneously treat others well. Right sets a realistic standard for action in a world in which violations and restrictions of others' freedom are possible, tempting and can be all too frequent, but also can be prohibited and enforced. In such a world, enforcing right – and thereby central aspects of justice – can secure parity of external freedom for all by imposing a 'fully reciprocal and equal coercion brought under a universal law and consistent with it' (*MM* 6:233). As Kant sees it, 'Right Is Connected with an Authorization to use Coercion' (title of *MM* §D, 6:231) and 'should not be conceived as made up of two elements, namely an obligation in accordance with a law and an authorization . . . to coerce' (*MM* 6:231–2). Rather these two elements are indissolubly linked.

---

[8] Even those with abysmally bad characters can be made to, and may see reason to, conform to principles of right. Cf. Kant's famous remark at *PP* 8:366 that 'the problem of establishing a state . . . is soluble even by a nation of devils (if only they possess understanding)'.

[9] Kant offers as an example of equity the case of a contract where inflation leads to payment of lower value than originally intended, where only the stipulated payment can be enforced, but it might be fair or equitable for the other party to pay more, see *MM* 6:234–5.

[10] Amartya Sen, *The Idea of Justice* (Cambridge, MA: Harvard University Press, 2009).

Superficially one might think that anarchy, which enforces nothing, would offer a better model of a world in which external freedom for all is minimally restricted. But this is an illusion, since complete lack of authorised enforcement of requirements would in practice allow sporadic unauthorised and unjust coercion, so could secure only a 'lawless freedom' – in which 'freedom for the pike is death for the minnow' – rather than lawlike freedom. So duties of right must authorise coercive action in order to secure the same external freedom for all by subordinating them to common laws:

> coercion is a hindrance or resistance to freedom. Therefore, if a certain use of freedom is itself a hindrance to freedom in accordance with universal laws (i.e. wrong), coercion that is opposed to this (as hindering a hindrance to freedom) is consistent with freedom in accordance with universal laws, that is, it is right. Hence there is connected with right by the principle of contradiction an authorization to coerce someone who infringes it. (*MM* 6.231)

Kant concludes these arguments with the claim that 'Right and authorization to use coercion therefore mean one and the same thing' (*MM* 6.232).

This conclusion has decisive implications for Kant's accounts of domestic, international and cosmopolitan right, and more broadly for his accounts of justice in all domains. It leads him to a narrower and more realistic[11] account of what ought to be done than those proposed in many contemporary theories of justice, many of which advocate standards that are *not* directly enforceable. For example, those contemporary theories that identify justice in part with securing specific *distributions* or *patterns* (e.g. certain material equalities, specific limits to inequalities) cannot be directly enforced. The problem is multiple. Patterns, distributions, equalities and conceptions of fairness are hard to secure without total and effective central planning, which has not proved feasible in practice, requires countless restrictions on action, and may restrict freedoms in ways that would be hard to justify. And even if secured, patterns or distributions are unstable and constantly altered by trivial daily activity, such as routine market transactions, or small variations in effort, success or indeed luck, that are seemingly neither wrong nor unjust. Patterns and distributions can be maintained only by intrusive coercion that aims not only to limit irregular, lawless coercion, but specifically to control variations so that they fit a prescribed

---

[11] Kant's account of justice is not, of course, 'realistic' in the sense often used in international relations or in economic discussion, where realism is seen as a matter of pursuing only (supposedly) real interests (*raisons d'état* for states; self-interest for individuals). Kant is realistic in the broad sense of requiring that standards of justice be enforceable standards.

pattern.[12] This is not a general argument against redistributive taxation or against other policies that shape outcomes, but merely a comment on their limitations.

The problem of lack of enforceability is not, however, confined to patterned conceptions of justice or to conceptions of justice as fairness. Many other contemporary approaches to justice, including some with global or cosmopolitan ambitions that ostensibly bear on action (rather than on patterns or distributions), are also loosely, perhaps inadequately, linked to enforceability. For example, discussions of rights to goods or services, where the duties must fall on some rather than all others, are often vague about the allocation of the counterpart duties that would need enforcing, leaving it indeterminate *who* has to do *what* for *whom*. *A fortiori* they fail to show what may and must be enforced, or to link the standards of right proposed to authorised coercion.

For example, those who identify justice with securing the full range of human rights proclaimed in the charters and declarations promulgated since the 1940s (prominently the Universal Declaration of Human Rights and the European Convention on Human Rights and subsequently many others) soon concluded that human rights required institutionalisation if they were to be enforceable. They approached this task in part by way of two 1966 Covenants, which sought to assign the necessary counterpart obligations. Unfortunately – or fortunately? – these Covenants did not assign obligations to respect and realise the rights that had been proclaimed in the Declarations and Conventions to the states that ratified these international instruments. Rather they assigned *second order* obligations to assign these obligations to states. While most states party have been keen to *ratify* the Conventions, many have failed to assign, let alone enforce, many of the relevant obligations, lacking either the will or the power to do so, or both.[13] Consequently the rights proclaimed are often not enforceable.

From reciprocal coercion to a civil state

Back, then, to Kant. He sees 'Reciprocal and equal coercion brought under universal law' as a short formula for identifying principles that both can

---

[12] Cf. Robert Nozick's arguments against patterned conceptions of justice in *Anarchy, State and Utopia* (New York: Basic Books, 1974). He argues that the central planning needed to preserve prescribed distributions would be incompatible with some of the core rights and duties recognised in most theories of justice.

[13] See Onora O'Neill, 'The dark side of human rights', *International Affairs* 81, no. 2 (2005), 427–39, reprinted in *Justice across Boundaries: Whose Obligations?*

and may be enforced, and which must be enforced in a just society. He uses it to identify specific principles of right for the domains of private and of public law, including distinctive conceptions of property rights and of republican political justice. However, his approach to justice requires him to do more than offer a formula that defines *what* is to be enforced. If he is to maintain the link between right and enforceability he has also to determine *on whom* to enforce principles of justice by showing that obligations fall on specific agents or agencies with the necessary powers and capacities. Realism about justice comes at a price.

Kant's account of the proper allocation of duties to enforce justice begins by deploying classical arguments against private enforcement, and seeks to establish that there is both a need and a duty to enter a civil condition. In the parts of *The Doctrine of Right* that deal with public right, he offers extensive arguments against relying merely on coercion by individuals to enforce standards of right. Public justice, he insists, demands 'conditions under which alone everyone is able to *enjoy* his rights' (*MM* 6:306). For human beings, who inhabit the bounded terrain of the earth, so 'cannot avoid living side by side' (*MM* 6:307), the only way to enjoy rights with any security is to enter a civil condition, where enforcement is provided by a duly constituted public authority. Outside a civil condition there can be no assurance of others' restraint, and individuals would do no wrong if they coerced others whom they saw as threatening them.

The so-called 'Postulate of Public Right' is therefore conditional. It demands that 'when you cannot avoid living side by side with all others, you ought to leave the state of nature and proceed with them into a rightful condition (*in einen rechtlichen Zustand*)' (*MM* 6:307). Individuals are not, however, bound to right or justice *until* there is enforcement. Hence the only injustice those in a state of nature could commit would be if they refused to join willing others in entering a civil condition: such refusal would reveal that they willingly remained in a condition that is not rightful, and since it is not rightful they may be coerced to enter a civil condition: here no agreement is needed.

States and international justice

Kant views the requirement to help set up and to enter a civil condition as an enforceable requirement to help set up and enter a *state*. Yet he also holds that states cannot, either individually or severally, provide a full solution to the problem of allocating the enforcement of duties of right. Since there are many states, and conflicts between them are recurrent, assigning enforcement *wholly* to states offers only an incomplete realisation of authorisation to coerce. (Kant was more realistic than those who drafted the 1966 Covenants!) In particular, it cannot show where authorised enforcement should lie in conflicts *either* between states *or* between states and individuals who are not within their boundaries.

This allocation of authorisation to coerce to states is therefore no more than *provisional*, and in some ways unsatisfactory.[14] A Westphalian world, such as the one Kant knew – and many of its structures survive today – provides all too much evidence of the limitations of state enforcement. It has led, as he ominously points out, to a world in which wars end only in truces, followed by tense and escalating rearmament that presages renewed hostilities (cf. *IUH* 8:25; *CB* 8:121; *PP* 8:343ff.). So it is a serious question whether states can or should be the only or can be the best enforcing agencies. Seemingly justice may need further and better enforcing agencies. Yet there are reasons for hesitating about this thought. A mere *multiplication* of enforcing agencies would not resolve but exacerbate the problem, by creating competing agencies, thereby jeopardising rather than improving the enforcement of standards of right, or more broadly of justice.[15] Kant's solution to this fundamental problem is to offer carefully limited accounts of international and cosmopolitan justice, both of which he views as supplementing state action to enforce standards of justice.

The phrase *international justice*, Kant notes repeatedly,[16] is a misnomer. On his account, many requirements for justice beyond borders hold not between nations, but between states. Since states are by definition independent of one another, Kant insists in many passages that there is and can be no super-state that subordinates them. On the contrary 'The idea of the right of nations [international right] presupposes the *separation* of many neighbouring states, independent of one another' (*PP* 8:367). The relations between states mirror those between individuals in a state of nature, and conflict between them can erupt at any time. Nevertheless, Kant thinks that this plurality of states is 'better... than the fusion of them... into a universal monarchy (*in eine Universalmonarchie*)' (*PP* 8:367).

Given the risks that would be created by concentrating all power in a world state, enforcement of international right is achievable *only by*

---

14 See Elisabeth Ellis, *Kant's Politics: Provisional Justice for an Uncertain World* (Newhaven: Yale University Press, 2005).

15 Balkanisation risks return to a state of nature. Kant's awareness of the dangers of multiplying enforcers shows repeatedly in his arguments against the possibility of just rebellion or revolution, or a just counter-revolution. He casts a critical light on the Nozickean fantasy of (quasi-commercial) competition among enforcing agencies, from which one emerges dominant.

16 E.g. *MM* § 53, 6:343–4; *PP* 8:354, 356, 367.

agreement among states. States can form a 'free federation (or league) of states' that 'does not look to acquiring any power [like that of] a state, but merely to preserving and securing the *freedom* of [each] state itself and of other states in league with it' (*PP* 8:356; see also *MM* 6:350–1, *PP* 8:354–7). Such a league[17] of states ought not to be imposed by any state or superpower, but could emerge by a process of convergence and agreement, and could 'finally encompass all the nations of the earth' (*PP* 8:357). The enforcing power of this federation would derive entirely from that of its members, channelled by the agreements they had reached. Acting in concert, they could pursue a range of classical objectives of international justice: they could offer mutual guarantees of territorial integrity; repudiate any supposed unrestricted right to go to war; limit *ius ad bellum* to narrowly prescribed circumstances; set standards both for *ius in bello*, and (more unusually) for *ius post bellum* (which Kant sees as a matter of taking measures to avert future hostilities, such as peacemaking, peacekeeping and confidence-building measures, and efforts at reconciliation).

However, Kant does not argue that such a league should have a power – let alone a duty – to intervene in the internal affairs of member states to secure internal right or justice when it is lacking.[18] He does not endorse powers to undertake 'humanitarian interventions' in rogue or failing states, let alone in states that fall short of standards of republican justice in more limited ways. In particular, such a league should not have powers to go to war: 'The concept of the right of nations [international right] as that of the right *to go to* war is, strictly speaking, unintelligible' (*PP* 8:356). The Kantian league of states consequently has fewer and less intrusive powers than some ambitious contemporary conceptions of 'international' justice advocate.

Cosmopolitan right, cosmopolitan hope

Kant's accounts of international – more accurately *interstatal* – justice are, unsurprisingly, therefore more circumscribed than many current conceptions of justice beyond state borders, largely because many of the latter say

---

[17] There is some variation on whether the terms *Bund*, *Völkerbund* are best translated as *federation* or as *league*. Given the ongoing disagreements about what counts as a federation, and whether it can have coercive powers over its members that are not anchored in agreement, there is reason to stay away from the term.

[18] Cf. Pauline Kleingeld, 'Approaching perpetual peace: Kant's defence of a league of states and his ideal of a world federation', *European Journal of Philosophy* 12 (2004), 304–25 and *Kant and Cosmopolitanism: The Philosophical Ideal of World Citizenship* (Cambridge University Press, 2011).

less (and arguably too little) about the *feasibility, permissibility* or *necessity* of enforcement. This mainly reflects Kant's more realistic insistence that right must in principle be enforceable, coupled with his view that this cannot be achieved either by multiplying enforcement agencies (so threatening to recreate the problems of the state of nature) or by overriding state action.

A similar stringency marks his account of cosmopolitan justice. Kant sees cosmopolitan right, like international right, as arising from the fact that the inhabitants of a finite globe must live adjacent to one another, so must interact. In consequence conflict can arise not only between inhabitants of a single state, or between distinct states, but between individuals and states that they do not inhabit. Kant's seemingly meagre remedy for the last of these problems is a specific and limited form of *cosmopolitan right*, that requires states to accord everyone a right to visit the territories of states that they do not inhabit, which he sees specifically as 'a right *to try to* establish community with all and, to this end, to *visit* all regions of the earth' (*MM* 6:353).

This *right to hospitality* or *right of resort* (*Besuchsrecht*) may seem a particularly meagre, even pointless, conception of cosmopolitan justice. It is certainly distant from the rights with respect to states of which individuals are not members that are discussed (and often endorsed!) in contemporary accounts of international justice. It is not a right of asylum or refuge, or a right to migrate to other states, or to settle and take up abode in them, or to become a citizen (*MM* 6:355; *PP* 8:357–60). Still less is it a right to colonise regions already inhabited by others, a practice that Kant condemns as iniquitous (*PP* 8:353 and 8:358–60).

Equally, the right to hospitality is not merely a right to travel for trivial or touristical purposes. Kant characterises this modest right as one with vast potential. Although it is simply 'the right of a foreigner (or stranger) not to be treated with hostility because he has arrived on the land (territory) of another' (*PP* 8:358), this, he thinks, is what is needed in order to make it possible to 'work toward establishing perpetual peace and the kind of constitution that seems to us most conducive to it' (*MM* 6:354), which he characterises as 'the highest political good, perpetual peace' (*MM* 6:355). Without this modest right we could not take steps towards securing a more-than-provisional peace, or a more-than-provisional form of justice beyond borders, since we would have no secure right even to communicate with those whom we would need to persuade if a just order is to be extended beyond the boundaries of states, and right and justice either within or beyond states is to be made secure rather than provisional. Individuals' rights to hospitality in other states matter because they provide a necessary condition for the possibility of communication, reasoning and interaction between those who inhabit different states, hence a necessary condition for progress towards a more just world that is pursued by reasoned exchange and not via unjust forms of coercion. Here Kant's idealism (in the colloquial sense) is evident.

Cosmopolitan right, as Kant understands it, is enforceable. It is enforceable by states, which can ensure – or refuse to ensure – a safe passage and a hearing to visiting foreigners. But what is the point of enforcing this right, which seemingly does not add substantially to the duties or rights that link fellow citizens, and does not demand additional enforcing agencies? Kant argues that this meagre seeming right is of the greatest importance because it fosters the possibility of transformative change for the far future. By protecting this 'most innocuous freedom' (cf. *WE* 8:37)[19] states can ensure that citizens will encounter a wider range of reasoning, which may provide seeds for reasoned progress. Human progress from the uncertain, provisional forms of right and justice already secured by states, and the limited structures for international justice already established, may lead us some way further towards wider cosmopolitan peace and justice: although there is no guarantee that they will not leave us mired in the politics of social conflict and self-interest.[20]

But if unsocial sociability provides too little, we will need to create more auspicious conditions in which we can listen and learn, negotiate and pursue further agreement with others, whether compatriots or foreigners. The importance of these tasks for the future of mankind explains Kant's emphasis on this limited form of cosmopolitan justice, which aims to secure some necessary conditions for the possibility of moving towards perpetual peace. States can secure free passage and safety for foreigners, and thereby make it possible for their citizens to hear what foreigners are thinking. By respecting this limited right to hospitality, states may allow for their citizens to take steps towards perpetual peace, by allowing them to encounter reasons 'from far and near'.

---

[19] This traditional translation is clearer than some in current use. The idea is not wholly far fetched when we think about the transformative effects communication with 'outsiders' has sometimes achieved. Examples include Mahatma Gandhi; Tom Paine; many liberals, social democrats and communists; and the present wide availability of political ideas and literature that come 'from elsewhere'. Such openness contrasts with the state-controlled media and communication that remain widespread.

[20] See 'Historical trends and human futures', Chapter 11 above.

As Kant sees it, the action that can be taken where cosmopolitan right is established falls in part to 'philosophers' (in the broadest sense of the term) who can advise on '*the conditions under which public peace is possible [for] . . . states which are armed for war*' (*PP* 8:368). It is essential for states to '*allow* them ['philosophers'] *to speak* freely and publicly on the universal maxims of waging war and establishing peace' (*PP* 8:369). The minimal condition for human beings living in a plurality of adjacent states to progress towards peace is not its imposition by some global power, that either claims or indeed happens to favour right and justice. It is the limited 'right of hospitality', that permits those who seek to reason about public affairs to do so not only with fellow citizens but with foreigners, who are 'given a *hearing*' (*PP* 8:369) and allowed to speak publicly. These necessary conditions for the use of reason can provide necessary conditions for progress towards justice and the cessation of wars.

The evident cost of taking this reasoned road to right and justice is that their full achievement will be long delayed. Kant accepts this conclusion. He thinks progress is not guaranteed by securing its necessary conditions, and that justice and peace cannot be realised by violent and precipitate means, but only gradually and without violence or coercion, as favourable opportunities arise and are grasped (*PP* 8:377). The gradual consolidation of domestic justice within states, of international justice between states, and of cosmopolitan justice in support of reasoned progress are tasks not merely for the present but extending into the distant future.

Kant argues in numerous works that, although we can expect peace and justice to be long arriving, yet we have reason to think them possible. This is why it makes sense to strive to achieve them, even when things look dismal. The many setbacks that we can expect do not undermine the importance of working for a better future, or the hope that our remote descendants may succeed in instituting a cosmopolitan condition, provided that states accord them cosmopolitan right. But for now we have to view the wider aspects of that cosmopolitan future as matters of hope and striving. Towards the end of *Theory and Practice* Kant wrote:

> I shall therefore be allowed to assume that . . . the human race . . . is constantly advancing . . . toward what is better with respect to the moral end of its existence, and that this will indeed be *interrupted* from time to time but will never be *broken off*. I do not need to prove this presupposition . . . I rest my case on my innate duty, the duty of every member of the series of generations . . . so to influence posterity that it becomes always better. (*TP* 8:308–9)

Idealism with realism in politics[21]

To my mind, Kant's accounts of international and cosmopolitan right and justice raise interesting questions for us at the start of the twenty-first century. Does the road that he points to, with its distinctive combination of quite specific forms of political idealism and realism, still have any interest for us? Must progress towards global peace and justice be pursued solely by just means, or are there some quicker fixes? Should we prefer more ambitious and idealistic approaches to justice beyond borders, even if they take a more casual view of enforceability and of agents of enforcement? Is not the great glory of contemporary political philosophy its emphasis on patterns and ideals of just distribution, on wider conceptions of justice as fairness, that go beyond a stress on fair process and respect for rights, and strive for outcomes that are not directly enforceable? If so, is it not acceptable – perhaps essential – to limit individual right if it stands in the way of these broader conceptions of justice? Or will being casual about enforceability lead us into unrealistic demands that wrongly subordinate questions of right, and with them individuals' rights?

Are certain contemporary accounts of international and cosmopolitan justice perhaps unrealistically focused on supposedly idealised standards, but too casual about the possibility of their enforcement? Are they right to assume that we know what processes will implement standards or right without injustice? Do they say enough rights-violating short cuts to justice, or about the costs of proliferating enforcing agencies? Does it matter whether progress towards peace and justice is achieved without injustice? Why should not global right and justice be achieved by the power of some global hegemon? Should we dismiss Kant's qualms by asserting, as other more flinty realists often have, that we cannot make an omelette without breaking eggs, or justice without taking unjust means?

As I see it, contemporary discussions of justice, with their large emphasis on fairness, equalities and specific distributions of goods, face difficulties (that are not always acknowledged) in working out how those equalities and prescribed distributions are to be made compatible with individual rights. A Kantian account of right stresses enforceable duties to others, and so offers a firmer but more limited basis for action to preserve others' agency, including enforcing some duties to limit acute poverty and dependence where that can damage agency. But it does not regard achieving prescribed

---

[21] This section is based on the last part of my 'From transcendental idealism to political realism', in Nicholas Boyle, Liz Disley and John Walker (eds.), *The Impact of Idealism: The Legacy of Post Kantian German Thought*, Vol. II (Cambridge University Press, 2013), 12–25.

distributions of resources as a matter of right, since they are not directly enforceable.

Political Realism is a family of views that insists on the limitations (the inadequacy, the silliness, the riskiness) of assuming that political action can or should be directed at aims that elude enforcement. It takes many forms, but typically hinges on what is often depicted as a *realistic* view of the motivation of states or rulers or other agents, namely the pursuit of *self-interest* or *raisons d'état*, and regards moralism or idealism in politics as suspect, self-deluding, even dangerous. It has been influential in international relations.

Kant holds to a version of political realism, but also maintains that we have an 'innate duty . . . so to influence posterity that it becomes always better (the possibility of this must, accordingly, also be assumed) (*TP* 8:309). To some this position may seem to reject political realism and to espouse some version of political idealism. This reading has been favoured by many of Kant's admirers, who insist that he is a political idealist. And there is good evidence for thinking that he is an idealist in a certain sense when we consider his writings on perpetual peace, his anti-colonialism and his vision of a just political order. However, this view of Kant as a *political* idealist does not sit at all easily with large parts of his political philosophy.[22]

In many other passages it is apparent that Kant writes as a political realist, who cautions against the unthinking pursuit of moral aims in public affairs, if they are pursued without regard to what is prudent, feasible and enforceable. He takes a steely eyed and highly realistic view of the pursuit of self-interest by states. He not merely links justice to a right to coerce, but limits it to what is enforceable.[23] He is critical of a right to revolution, even in the face of injustice and oppression. He takes a circumscribed view of free speech, especially in institutional life.[24] He offers a more limited account both of international and of cosmopolitan justice than most political idealists find acceptable.

When one starts looking closely at Kant's account of justice there is an enormous amount at which many political idealists will balk. Consider for example his version of the social contract, which seems particularly weak:

---

[22] See Pauline Kleingeld, 'Approaching perpetual peace: Kant's defence of a league of states and his ideal of a world federation', *European Journal of Philosophy* 12 (2004), 304–25.

[23] Cf. in *The Doctrine of Right*, in *Metaphysic of Morals*: 'Right Is Connected with an Authorization to use Coercion' (title of *MM*, *PP* 8:388) and '[right] should not be conceived as made up of two elements, namely an obligation in accordance with a law and an authorization . . . to coerce' (*PP* 8:388–9).

[24] See in particular *What Is Enlightenment?*

> if a public law is so constituted that a whole people *could not possibly* give
> its consent to it (as, e.g., that a certain class of *subjects* should have the
> hereditary privilege of *ruling rank*), it is unjust; but if it is *only possible* that
> a people could agree to it, it is a duty to consider the law just, even if the
> people is at present in such a situation or frame of mind that, if consulted
> about it, it would probably refuse its consent. (*TP* 8:297)[25]

This is just one of many passages in Kant's writing on politics and history
that throws cold water on the idea that we can or should straightforwardly
pursue moral aims in politics, or that we may disregard or resist the demands
of states, even when they are unjust, or that states can or ought to set aside
self-interest, or that enforcement does not matter.

Is Kant then ultimately a realist *at least about politics*, because he takes
instrumental reasoning, prudence and the dangers of misplaced pursuit of
moral ideals in public life so seriously? There is a parallel but more narrowly
focused debate about Kant's claims about international and cosmopolitan
justice. Does he aspire to a league of free states (an idealist option) or to
a federal state of states – effectively a world state (a realist option)?[26] Is he
ultimately a political idealist, or is he a political realist below the surface?

The answer, I suspect, may depend on the time frame. Kant's conclusions
about what we may reasonably *hope* and *work for* are conclusions about the
indefinitely far future of mankind. They cannot be otherwise if the ample
evidence of recurrent dark times is not to undermine hope and working
for change. By contrast, his conclusions about what we can prudently
do here and now must be based on at least some evidence of means–ends
relationships, so will only be available for nearer times, for which we have at
least some grasp of what will work, what is prudent, what can be enforced.

By distinguishing the time frame of Kant's more idealist and his more
realist comments on politics, we can make at least some sense of his reasons
for thinking that the changes needed to bring about justice within states,
or peace between them, are not enactable at every time, and yet matter
immensely. He is idealist about the aims, but realist about the means, and
concludes that the journey forward may have to be slow since:

> [laws contain] permissions, not to make exceptions to the rule of right, but
> to *postpone* putting these laws into effect, without however losing sight of
> the end; he may not postpone to a nonexistent date . . . putting into effect
> the law . . . he is permitted only to delay doing so, lest implementing the law
> prematurely counteract its very purpose. (*PP* 8:347)

---

[25] *PP* 8:297.
[26] See Kleingeld, 'Approaching perpetual peace', 304–25, and P. Kleingeld, *Kant and Cosmopolitanism: The Philosophical Ideal of World Citizenship* (Cambridge University Press, 2011).

Moreover

> permissive laws of reason . . . allow a situation of public right afflicted with injustice to continue until everything has either of itself become ripe for a complete overthrow or has been made almost ripe by peaceful means. (*PP* 8:374n.)

Prudence in action; idealism in outlook; prudence for the near future; idealism and hope for the far future. This combination offers a way to combine realistic prudence with idealistic hopes. Both prudence and hope are orientations to action.[27] Kant's wider philosophy bars the way either to a metaphysical defence or to an empirical vindication of the perfectibility of man and of human progress. But we can make sense of his claim to combine hopes for the long future with prudence for the here and now: they are compatible practical commitments.

It is this combination of time frames that, Kant argues, must be understood if we are to take a view of history that is not merely a retelling of what has happened, but a harbinger of human destiny:

> How is it possible to have history *a priori*? The answer is: it is possible when the one who foretells events shapes and *creates* them. (*CF* 4:80,[28] trans. OO'N)

History of the far future, of the destiny rather than the past of mankind, is possible, but only in so far as it is taken as a practical rather than as a theoretical task, as a matter of adopting a specific commitment or attitude to the future, and of working towards that future, rather than of looking for proof or evidence to support a prediction. On this account, the achievement of peace and justice are tasks ahead, rather than historical predictions or inevitabilities. The last sentence of *Perpetual Peace* says it all:

> If it is a duty to realize the condition of public right, even if only in approximation by unending progress, and if there is also a well-founded hope of this, then the *perpetual peace* that follows upon what have till now falsely been called peace treaties (strictly speaking, truces) is no empty idea but a task that . . . comes steadily closer to its goal. (*PP* 8:386)

---

[27] See Katrin Flikschuh, 'Hope or prudence: practical faith in Kant's political thinking', *Yearbook of German Idealism* 7 (2009), 95–117.
[28] This is the separately published second part of the *Conflict of the Faculties*, titled 'The Conflict of the philosophical faculty with the faculty of law'.

PART IV

Authority in interpretation

CHAPTER 13

Kant on reason and religion I: reasoned hope[1,2]

Kant's philosophy of religion has perplexed even his warmest admirers. Nobody has pointed this out more amusingly than Heinrich Heine, who saw in Kant the Robespierre of the intellect. The orderly philosopher of Königsberg, whose daily constitutional was attended and sheltered by his servant Lampe, armed with a modest umbrella, was really a terrorist who destroyed the *ancien régime* of European religion and philosophy. The *Critique of Pure Reason* was the sword that killed deism in Germany. Yet Kant, Heine suggests, derailed this sublime and terrifying philosophy, that pointed towards the death of God, when a domestic difficulty arose. He relented and patched a God together because his servant, old Lampe, was disconsolate. Heine lampoons Kant:

> Immanuel Kant traced his merciless philosophy up to this point, he stormed heaven . . . there was no more allmercyfulness, no more fatherly goodness, no otherworldly rewards for this worldly restraint, the immortality of the soul was at its last gasp . . . and old Lampe stood there with his umbrella under his arm, a miserable onlooker with anxious sweat and tears running down his face. And so Immanuel Kant had mercy and showed that he wasn't just a great philosopher, but also a good person. He thought it over and

[1] 'Kant on reason and religion I: reasoned hope' in Grethe B. Peterson (ed.), *The Tanner Lectures on Human Values*, Vol. XVIII (Salt Lake City: University of Utah Press, 1997), 267–308. This is the first of two Tanner Lectures delivered at Harvard University in 1996. As a graduate student at Harvard in the 1960s I had read – even taught! – Kant's philosophy of religion and was fascinated and baffled. I was particularly puzzled by Kant's reasons for giving the title *Religion within the Limits of Reason Alone* to a work that seemed so remote from most writing on reason and religion. Both as Read-Tuckwell lecturer in the University of Bristol in 1986 and as Tanner lecturer at Harvard University I tried to work out how Kant's writing on religion connects reason, hope and interpretation. I am grateful to the Tanner Foundation and to colleagues at both universities for the opportunity and encouragement.
[2] The Cambridge translations of Kant's work had not appeared at the time this and the following chapter were published. References to Kant's writing are given parenthetically using the abbreviated titles listed in the Bibliographical Note, but referring to the older translations and editions in Part 2 of that note. When quoting from a translation that does not include the Prussian Academy page numbers I have added them *in front of* the pagination of the cited translation.

said, half kindly and half in irony: 'Old Lampe must have a God, or the poor fellow can't be happy – but man ought to be happy on earth – practical reason says so (at least according to me); so let practical reason also disclose the existence of God.' By this argument Kant distinguished theoretical from practical reason and, as with a magic wand, brought back to life the corpse of deism which theoretical reason had killed.[3] (trans. OO'N)

If Heine and other critics are right, Kant's retreat is ignominious. In the *First Critique* he asserts the death of God: 'No one indeed will be able to boast that he *knows* that there is a God and a future life' (*CPR* A 828–9 / B 856–7); in the *Second Critique* he argues for God and immortality. Can practical reason really produce a magic wand to revive the corpse of deism – let alone a more comfortable religion for old Lampe? Or does it provide no more than an old man's umbrella as defence against the terrifying weapons of theoretical reason? Heine is not the only critic who concludes that Kant's 'practical' arguments fail, that there is no real consolation to be had, and that we cannot escape the colossal wreck of rationalist metaphysics and theology, and the threat to religious faith.

The great gulf

If these critics are right, the defects of Kant's account of religion are symptoms of wider problems in his philosophy. The arguments for God and immortality that Kant advances in the *Critique of Practical Reason* are supposed to bridge a 'great gulf' (cf. *CJ* 5:175–6; also translated as 'an incalculable gulf') between Kant's accounts of the natural world and of human freedom. If no bridge can be built, Kant is committed to a spectacular but wholly implausible metaphysical position, which claims that human beings live in two unconnected worlds. They are part of a natural, phenomenal world that is temporally structured, causally ordered, and knowable by theoretical reason. Yet they are also free agents who are part of a noumenal or intelligible world that is inaccessible to theoretical reason and neither temporally structured nor causally ordered.

I shall take it that Kant and Heine are both right in thinking that the critical philosophy leads us towards the brink of a great gulf, which seemingly separates self from world, freedom from nature and acting from knowing. It is therefore entirely reasonable to ask what sort of bridge Kant tries to build across the great gulf, and whether it reinstates the God for

---

[3] Heinrich Heine, 'Zur Geschichte der Religion und Philosophie', *Gesammelte Werke*, 6 vols. (Berlin and Weimar: Aufbau Verlag, 1951), Vol. V, 110.

whom Lampe pined, or is as flimsy as Heine suspected, or whether there are other ways of looking at the matter.

In this chapter and the following one, I shall offer reasons for thinking that the critical philosophy indeed destroys and neither revives, nor aims to revive, either deism or more familiar forms of theism. Nevertheless, I shall argue, Kant offers good reasons for thinking that the great gulf can be bridged by an account of religion, and also for thinking that this account of religion can lie 'within the limits of reason alone'. The key to this alternative understanding of 'religion within the limit of reason alone' lies, I shall argue, in proper attention to Kant's distinctive account of reason and its authority.

I shall begin by sketching the 'great gulf' that is to be bridged, and by outlining Kant's conception of reason. I shall then turn to his view that the bridge that is to cross the great gulf is a bridge of hope, and finally will try to say something about what it would take for hopes to be reasonable. In the following chapter I shall build on this account of reasoned hope to understand why in his last writings on religion Kant constantly cites (and often misquotes!) and interprets the texts of Christian Scripture,[4] while still claiming to offer an account of 'religion within the limits of reason alone'.

The two standpoints

A common view of the predicament in which Kant believes we find ourselves, and of his solution to it, is that it is a predicament of his own making, and could have been avoided. There is no gulf between self and world, between nature and freedom, between knowledge and action, and so there is no need to work out how the gulf might be bridged. Put more prosaically, the proper task of philosophy is to provide an adequate account of human freedom and action that is not only compatible with but integrated into an adequate account of our knowledge of a causally ordered world. By avoiding Kant's problem we would also avoid any need for his desperate remedy.

I cannot within the framework of these two chapters trace the arguments that led Kant to the contrary view, but will outline the position that he reaches, and some of the reasons he offers for thinking that it is not internally incoherent. The point can be put in a compressed form by noting

---

4 For discussion of Kant's use of Scripture see Henri d'Aviau de Ternay, *Traces bibliques dans la loi morale chez Kant* (Paris: Beauchesne, 1986), and 'Kant und die Bibel: Spuren an den Grenzen' in Friedo Ricken und François Marty, *Kant über Religion* (Stuttgart: Kohlhammer, 1992).

that Kant offers not an ontological but an epistemological argument.[5] The predicament in which we find ourselves is not that of having to lead our lives in two distinct ontological orders, but that of having to adopt two seemingly mutually irreducible standpoints in leading our lives. The theoretical standpoint is naturalistic: from it we see the world and human life as subject to natural law and causal inquiry. The practical standpoint is that of human freedom: from it we see ourselves as agents who intervene in limited ways in that natural order. Only the theoretical standpoint can accommodate science; only the practical standpoint can accommodate morality.

We are unavoidably, deeply and thoroughly committed both to the naturalistic standpoint and to the standpoint of freedom. We can dispense with neither standpoint, since neither makes sense without the other. If we do not see ourselves as free we can give no account of activity, hence none of the activities of judging and understanding by which we establish the claims of knowledge; if we do not see ourselves as parts of a causally ordered world we can give no account of the effective implementation of human projects, including moral action, in the world. Our lives would be impossible without commitment to freedom *and* to causality in the robust senses in which Kant understands these terms: neither can stand alone. Yet we do not understand, let alone know, what makes them compatible. The strangeness of human life is that we find a hiatus at the core of our self-understanding, which cannot be comprehended within any single perspective. We have to adopt both standpoints: neither is dispensable and neither is subordinate or reducible to the other – yet their conjunction is a challenge and an affront to the very project of reasoning, which aims at coherence. This hiatus is the 'great gulf' that threatens Kant's philosophy.

A traditional reading of Kant – Heine's is one among many – is that Kant resolves this problem by reinstating some form of transcendent realism, within which the coordination of nature and freedom is secured by metaphysical means – as it were off stage. I believe that the strategies Kant mainly deploys to solve the problem are more modest. The first and the most fundamental aspect of his more modest approach is a surprisingly minimalist view of the powers and authority of human reason.

---

[5] For epistemological readings of Kant's account of the two standpoints see Henry Allison, *Kant's Theory of Freedom* (Cambridge University Press, 1990), and Onora O'Neill, 'Reason and autonomy in Grundlegung III' in *Constructions of Reason: Explorations of Kant's Practical Philosophy* (Cambridge University Press, 1989), 51–65.

Human reason

From the very beginning of the *Critique of Pure Reason* Kant insists on the limits of human knowledge: our knowledge cannot reach beyond human experience and our experience is confined to the natural world. The deficiency is not easily remediable, since it arises from the limits and failings of human reason, which 'is burdened by questions which, as prescribed by the very nature of reason itself, it is not able to ignore, but which as transcending all its powers, it is also not able to answer' (*CPR* A vii).

Even everyday methods of reasoning can lead into incoherent conceptions of the soul (the paralogisms), of cosmology (the antinomies) and of God (the critique of rational theology). Try as we will, we find ourselves torn between insatiable desires to know metaphysical truths and the frustrated realisation that attempts to do so repeatedly lead us into dialectical illusion. However, the problem of providing a proper account of the character and tasks of human reason is postponed for many hundreds of pages, until the discussion of philosophical method in the *Doctrine of Method*, which begins with a candid acknowledgement that the whole edifice of the critical philosophy remains insecure because we still lack any account of the methods to be used if these cognitive shipwrecks are to be avoided.

All that Kant proposes as remedy for this uncomfortable situation is that we *accept* that our grandest cognitive ambitions must be set aside and that we *adopt* a form of cognitive *discipline* to protect ourselves from error:

> The greatest and perhaps the sole use of all philosophy of pure reason is therefore only negative; since it serves not as an organon for the extension but as a discipline for the limitation of pure reason, and, instead of discovering truth, has only the modest merit of guarding against error. (*CPR* A 795 / B 823; cf. A 709 / B 737)

He admits that this is an uncomfortable conclusion to reach after long philosophical efforts:

> that reason, whose proper duty it is to prescribe a discipline for all other endeavours, should itself stand in need of such a discipline may indeed seem strange. (*CPR* A 710 / B 738)

At first consideration the proposal may seem worse than strange. If reason is or is to be subordinated to a *discipline*, then it seems that Kant must have given up the ambitions of philosophy, or perhaps have settled for some for anti-rational appeal to common sense or shared understandings or the like, which usurps the authority and title of reason. However, the *Transcendental Doctrine of Method* offers quite another picture, in which reason itself is construed as a certain sort of negative self-discipline. Kant's account of the discipline of reason has several aspects.

First, in calling reason a *discipline*, he is claiming that it is a *negative* constraint on the ways in which we think and act: there is no set of axioms of reason, whose content can fully steer processes of reasoning; there are merely constraints.[6]

Second, the discipline of reason is *nonderivative*. Reason does not derive from any more fundamental standards. On the contrary, it appeals to no other premises, and can be turned on *any* claim or belief or proposal for action. Neither church nor state, nor other powers, can claim exemption from the scrutiny of reason for their pronouncements and assumptions. The authority of reason would be nullified by subordinating it to the claims of one or another happenstantial power:

> Reason must in all its undertakings subject itself to criticism; should it limit that freedom of criticism by any prohibitions, it must harm itself, drawing upon itself damaging suspicions. Nothing is so important through its usefulness, nothing so sacred, that it may be exempted from this searching examination, which knows no respect for persons. (*CPR* A739 / B 767)

If reason has *any* authority, it must be *its own* rather than *derivative*.

Third, while reason does not have derivative authority, authority it must have. Authority is needed to distinguish between ways of organising thought and action that are to count as reasoned and those that are to be dismissed as unreasoned. Kant traces this authority to the requirement that reasoning be lawlike, in that it adopts only principles of universal form, and when directed to an unrestricted audience only principles of universal reach or scope. Reasons must be fit to be given or exchanged, shared or challenged, so at least capable of reaching their audiences. Ways of organising thought and action that are not lawlike in form and universal in scope will be unfollowable by at least some others, who will then rightly view them as arbitrary or incomprehensible.[7]

The minimal, modal requirement that reasons be followable by others, without being derivative from other standards, is Kant's entire account of

---

[6] Kant uses the term *discipline* for a form of *negative instruction,* 'by which the constant tendency to disobey certain rules is restrained' (*CPR* A 709–10 / B 737–8). See more generally chapter I of the *Transcendental Doctrine of Method*, titled *The Discipline of Pure Reason* (*CPR* A 707 / B 735ff.), especially the first few pages and the considerations that lie behind rejecting the geometric method that are rehearsed in section I of the chapter titled *The Discipline of Pure Reason in Its Dogmatic Employment*.

[7] See the chapters in Part I above.

authority of reason. Yet mere nonderivative lawlikeness combined with universal scope has considerable implications for the organisation of thought and action. In the domain of theory it demands that reasons for believing be followable by, so intelligible to, all; in the domain of action it demands that reasons for action be ones that all too could adopt.[8]

The three aspects of Kant's conception of reason are summarised in the thought that reason requires a 'wholly nonderivative and specifically negative lawgiving' ('da scheint eine ganz eigene und zwar negative Gesetzgebung erforderlich zu sein') (*CPR* A 711 / B 739, trans. OO'N). The same trio of requirements – that reason's discipline is negative, not derivative and lawlike – are linked in numerous Kantian formulations, and most notably in the best-known version of the Categorical Imperative, which demands action only on maxims which can at the same time be willed as universal laws. Here the supreme principle of practical reason is presented as a *negative* (formal) requirement that is *not derivative* because it appeals to no other spurious 'authorities' (that would be heteronomy) and demands adherence to *lawlike* maxims (i.e. to maxims of universal form that could be adopted by all to whom reasons are offered).

How far does this meagre conception of reason help us to understand Kant's claim to offer an account of religion 'within the limits of reason alone'? Evidently it cannot offer reasons for thinking that the impasses to which speculative reasoning leads are likely to be overcome. This meagre conception of reason will not yield proofs of human freedom, or immortality, or of God's existence. However, Kant notes that our reasons for being interested in the soul and in God are primarily practical (*CPR* A 800–4 / B 828–32) and raises the question whether 'reason may not be able to supply us from the standpoint of its practical interest what it altogether refuses to supply in respect of its speculative interest' (*CPR* A 805 / B 833; cf. A 796 / B 824).

Kant's fundamental questions

Kant's surprising move far on in his discussion of method, almost at the end of the *Critique of Pure Reason* (*CPR* A 805 / B 833), is to assert that

---

[8] This formulation covers both cases of partially reasoned *heteronomous* action, where principles are lawlike, but derivative from or conditional on specific aims or desires, so relevant only to all who meet a specified condition, and the fully reasoned case of *autonomous* action, whose principles are not only lawlike but universally accessible. Reasons for action whether partial or complete must be followable by those for whom they are to be reasons for action.

human reason is fundamentally interested not in two questions – one about knowledge, one about action – but in three questions:[9]

1. What can I know?
2. What ought I do?
3. What may I hope?

The grouping of questions was hardly new. For example, a summary of Christian commitment would comprise answers to each question: I can know God; I ought to love God and my neighbour as myself; I may hope for the life to come. The answers state the underlying principle of each of the traditional theological virtues, faith, hope and charity: faith centres on knowledge of God; hope centres on the life to come; charity centres on love for God and neighbour.[10]

Kant does far more than take over and resequence these three traditional questions. His answers to 'What can I know?' and 'What ought I do?' are developed without any reference to God and without use of religious discourse. But it is these answers that supposedly open up the great gulf that Heine, like many others, thinks will swallow up Kant's whole philosophy. Kant thought that he could avert this disaster by showing how a reasoned answer to the third question, 'What may I hope', could bridge the great gulf.

---

[9] Elsewhere Kant adds a fourth question, 'What is man?', e.g. *Logic*, trans. Robert Hartman and Wolfgang Schwarz (Indianapolis: Bobbs-Merrill, 1974), 29, and 'Jäsche Logic' in Immanuel Kant, *Lectures on Logic* (Cambridge University Press, 1992), 538. However, this fourth question is viewed as comprising the other three, which would need to be answered within any adequate answer to the fourth. Since the fourth question is to be answered by anthropology (in Kant's understanding of the term), this arrangement of the fundamental questions confirms the view – evident from the outset of the *Critique of Pure Reason* – that Kant's philosophy begins from an anthropocentric rather than a theocentric starting point.

[10] It is notable that Kant displaces hope from the middle place that it holds in the theological triad. That intermediate position has been thought by some to suggest that hope is less fundamental than faith and less perfect than charity (cf. Aquinas, *Summa Theologiae*, IaIIae.62.4); or even that it is only an aspect of imperfect, doubting faith, to be superseded in the future fuller faith of those who 'possess' God, as mundane hopes are superseded when a hoped-for goal is achieved. However, some recent theologians – influenced in part by Kant – lay more weight on hope. For example Karl Rahner writes 'hope does not express a modality of faith and love' and that 'hope is . . . the basic modality of the very attitude to the eternal', Karl Rahner, *A Rahner Reader*, ed. G.A. McCool (London: Darton, Longman and Todd, 1975), 231. Jürgen Moltmann too in some ways places hope ahead of faith and charity: 'Christian proclamation is not a tradition of wisdom and truth in doctrinal principles. Nor is it a tradition of ways and means of living according to the law. It *is* the announcing, revealing, publishing of an eschatological event', Jürgen Moltmann, *Theology of Hope: On the Ground and the Implications of a Christian Eschatology*, trans. James W. Leitch (London: Student Christian Movement, 1967), 299.

Faith and hope

It is easy to miss the central place that hope has in Kant's philosophy, and in particular in his philosophy of religion, because his discussion of religion focuses as much on faith as on hope. In the preface of the second edition of the *Critique of Pure Reason* he famously asserted that 'I have therefore found it necessary to deny knowledge to make room for faith' (*CPR* B xxx; cf. A 745 / B 773). In the *Doctrine of Method* and in the *Critique of Practical Reason* he identifies three postulates of God, freedom and immortality, of which two are readily construed as articles of faith.

These passages taken in isolation might suggest that Kant expects to show that traditional theological claims, although they are not supported by the rational proofs to which deists aspired, can yet be reached by some non-rational 'leap of faith'. Yet neither in the account of faith offered in the discussions of the Postulates of Pure Practical Reason in the *Critique of Practical Reason*, nor in *Religion within the Limits of Reason Alone*, does Kant take this line. He does not assert that if we are prepared to overlook the claims of reason, then we can embrace religious truths without needing reasons. Rather he proposes that although articles of faith cannot be known or proven, the grounds of faith lie within the limits of reason. He is, it seems, neither deist nor fideist.[11] What then is his account of faith?

Meinen, Wissen, Glauben

Late in the *Critique of Pure Reason* (*CPR* A 820 / B 848ff.), shortly after he poses the three questions that interest human reason, Kant distinguishes three forms of cognitive attitude. Mere *opining* (*Meinen*) is holding something true, being consciously aware that one has no sufficient objective grounds. Even opinion requires some grounds – or it would be no more than imagination – but the grounds of opinion are not even subjectively sufficient. *Knowing* (*Wissen*) is holding something to be true for reasons that are both subjectively and objectively sufficient. Between opinion and

---

[11] For a contrary view see Allen Wood, 'Kant's deism' in Philip J. Rossi and Michael Wreen (eds.), *Kant's Philosophy of Religion Reconsidered* (Bloomington: Indiana University Press, 1991), 1–21, and also in his earlier work, *Kant's Rational Theology* (Ithaca, NY: Cornell University Press, 1973). Wood sees Kant as a deist despite his insistence that we can make no religious knowledge claims, and even speaks of Kant's *Religion* as a rationalist interpretation of Christian doctrine. This expansive use of the terms *deist* and *rationalist* obscures the fact that Kant nowhere endorses the knowledge claims of natural religion, and so takes a position very distant from deism as usually understood. The same view of Kant's insistence that we do not *know* religious truths can be seen in the articles by Joseph Runzo and Nicholas Wolterstorff in the same volume.

knowledge Kant places *Glaube*, whose obvious translation would be *belief* or *faith*, and which he characterises as holding something for reasons that are objectively insufficient and not merely subjectively sufficient, but *subjectively unavoidable*.

Glaube is a form of cognitive propositional attitude that is neither mere opinion nor knowledge. What can it be to have faith in this sense? Kant draws on an image (*CPR* A 825 / B 853), familiar from the writings of both Blaise Pascal and Soren Kierkegaard, that strength of faith or belief can be understood in terms of a wager. *Glaube* is apparently to be understood as commitment, or trust. We know how strong our trust or commitment is when we realise how much we would stake on it. A measure of commitment is not, however, the same thing as a reason for making the commitment, and unless Kant can show reasons (even if not the objective reasons that can ground knowledge) for religious commitment he will not have shown that it is other than credulity. If religion is to be considered within the limits of reason alone, it must not merely be possible to make religious commitments: there must be reasons to do so. The reasons that Kant concludes that religious faith cannot be a matter of knowledge, and must be a matter of taking a hopeful view of human destiny.

Kant stakes a great deal on the claim that religious commitment is not any sort of knowledge. He claims that if the rationalist dream was fulfilled and we knew the truths of deism, religious belief would be coerced and morality impossible. In the *Second Critique* he asserts that it is *because* faith is not provable and human beings have to struggle with doubt and commitment that morality is possible:

> [If] God and eternity in their awful majesty would stand unceasingly before our eyes . . . Transgression of the law would indeed be shunned, and the commanded would be performed. But . . . because the spur to action would in this case always be present and external . . . most actions conforming to the law would be done from fear, few would be done from hope, none from duty. The moral worth of actions . . . would not exist at all. The conduct of man would be changed into mere mechanism. (*CPrR* 5:147)

It would be a religious and moral disaster if *per impossibile* God were the demonstrable God of the rationalist tradition: religion (as Pascal also understood) *requires* a hidden God. *Deus absconditus* coerces neither belief nor action. Far from it being a misfortune that 'no one indeed will be able to boast that he knows that there is a God and a future life' (*CPR* A 828–9 / B 856–7), this cognitive limitation is indispensable for uncoerced morality and leaves open the space in which the question 'What may I hope?' can be asked. In this respect, as in so many others, Kant is wholly at odds with his rationalist predecessors, who grounded optimism about human destiny in the conviction that no less-than-optimal destiny would have been created for us by the demonstrable creator of the best of all possible worlds. Enlightenment optimism, unlike hope, is indeed grounded in (supposed) knowledge.

If Kant had offered *only* an argument from ignorance and the limits of human knowledge, his claim to show what we have reason to adopt any form of faith or hope, let alone specific faiths or hopes, would be quite unsatisfactory. However, the argument from the limits of human knowledge is only one part of the picture. The other part of the picture consists of arguments for the indispensability and the irreducibility of the two standpoints. We cannot fail to act on the assumption of our own freedom, if only because the very activities of cognition require us to assume our own freedom; conversely, in acting we cannot fail to assume that we know a causally ordered world in which our action is to intervene. Hence we have to make sense not simply of the thought that our knowledge is limited, but of the further thought that we must accept some set of assumptions under which the answers we give to the first two questions that interest human reason are rendered mutually consistent. In short we must assume that there is some sort or degree of coordination of nature and freedom that ensures that our future is one in which we can act, and in which the aim of moral action is not absurd: it must be possible to insert the moral intention into the world (cf. *CPR* A 807–8 / B 836–7; *CJ* 5:176).

Of course, this is not to say that we *know* how or how far the natural and the moral orders are coordinated, let alone that their full integration is possible, or will come to pass. It is only to say that for practical purposes we must take it that some degree of their coordination is possible. In doing so we commit ourselves to the view that the future for which we act is not inevitably frustrating – in short we must entertain at least a minimal hope that the future on which we take our action to bear is a future on which it can bear. The core of any answer to the third question 'What may I hope?' is the thought that whatever I may hope must incorporate a hope that human destiny leaves some room for action and specifically for the moral intention to be realised by acting in the world. Rather than grounding hope in faith, Kant in fact construes the basics of faith as a form of hope.[12]

---

[12] Cf. *CJ* 5:469–71.

Several large questions arise at this point. I shall take up three of them. First, does the reality that hope can fail show that, contrary to Kant's view, we do not need to live in the light of (any sort of) hope? Second, does he show that *only* religious hopes as traditionally conceived will provide the right light? Third, does he show that religious hopes as traditionally understood, or any other specific hopes, can be reasoned hopes?

Hope and despair

We may begin with the most general difficulty: is Kant right to insist that human reason must ask a third question that points to the future, and whose answers point to hopes for that future? Isn't hoping a splendid but optional matter? What makes the question of the future an unavoidable interest of human reason, and not merely a topic of emotional or personal concern to each of us? The very idea that commitment to action and morality requires hope can seem implausible. Do not many reasonable people with strong moral commitments look to the future more with fear or foreboding, or even with indifference and despair, than in hope? Do not others hope unreasonably, building their lives around illusory or even self-deceiving aspirations or wishes? In short, isn't hope unnecessary?

The most plausible of Kant's moves is surely the claim that we must be committed to *some* view of the future if we are committed to action of any sort. If we were entirely noncommittal about the future, we could make no sense of any commitment to action. We see this clearly when we remember what it would be to think that there is no possible future: *complete* despair overwhelms all commitment and stifles action. In acting we look to the future; if we can bring about any change, it can only be change in the world, in the future. Those who think action that changes the future is impossible can aim for nothing: we cannot aim to achieve what we know to be unachievable. Conversely, if we act at all we reveal at least a minimal commitment to, a minimal hope for, some future in which some action takes place and may have some results. That we have some intimation of a future that is open to action in some respects is constitutive not only of the moral life, but of the life of action, and so on Kant's view also of cognition.[13]

---

[13] What happens in dark conditions when action is barely possible is instructive. Consider Nadja Mandelstam's *Hope against Hope: A Memoir*, trans. Max Hayward (London: Collins Harvill, 1971), or Bruno Bettleheim, *The Informed Heart: The Human Condition in Modern Mass Society* (London: Thames and Hudson, 1960), with its poignant discussion of those who gave up hope in the death camps and became walking dead. It may be sober truth rather than whistling in the dark when we tell one another that while there is life there is hope.

Kant does not, of course, claim that despair is impossible. His claim is conditional: commitment to action and morality, that is commitment to acting morally within a causally ordered world, demands that we hope that our commitments are to some extent realisable in that world. He aims to show not simply that lack of hope is psychologically hard, but that it is incoherent unless action and morality too are given up.

Modalities of hope

The second large question is whether a requirement for hope must be or must include religious hopes as traditionally conceived. On this Kant apparently gives several differing answers. The different views are in part a reflection of the different modalities of hope.

Kant formulates the third question in which human reason is unavoidably interested permissively. He asks not 'What *must* I hope?', but rather 'What *may* I hope?' Yet in many passages in various works he concentrates on what must rather than on what may be hoped. Of course, any adequate account of what we *may* hope will have to incorporate some account of anything that we *must* hope. There might, however, be many distinct answers to the question 'What may I hope?' that had in common only those aspects of hope that are required. It may, for example, be the case that various quite distinct hopes for human destiny each incorporate a convincing account of what we must hope.

Notoriously Kant puts forward a very strong account of what we must hope in the *Critique of Practical Reason*. He there argues not only that we must hope that the moral intention can be inserted into the world to some extent, but that we must hope that the moral and natural orders can be *fully* coordinated in an optimal way in which happiness and virtue, our natural and our moral ends, are eventually perfectly coordinated in each of us.

These demanding hopes are presented as following from certain Postulates of Practical Reason. On Kant's account a postulate is 'a *theoretical* proposition which is not as such [i.e. theoretically] demonstrable, but which is an inseparable corollary of an *a priori* unconditionally valid practical law' (*CPrR* 5:122). In the *Second Critique* Kant argues for the demanding claim that we must aim not only to introduce the moral intention into the world but to work towards the *summum bonum* or *complete* coordination of natural and moral good, of happiness and virtue, in each free agent, so must hope for a correspondingly strong and complete degree of coordination between the natural and the moral order, and so must postulate or hope for our own immortality and the existence of God:

> This infinite progress is possible, however, only under the presupposition of an infinitely enduring existence and personality of the same rational being; this is called the immortality of the soul. Thus the highest good is practically possible only on the supposition of the immortality of the soul. (*CPrR* 5:122)

Accordingly each of us 'may hope for a further uninterrupted continuance of this progress, however long his existence may last, even beyond this life' (*CPrR* 5:123). Hence, Kant holds, we must also postulate

> the existence . . . of a cause of the whole of nature, itself distinct from nature, which contains the ground of the exact coincidence of happiness with morality . . . the highest good is possible in the world only on the supposition of a supreme cause of nature which has a causality corresponding to the moral disposition. (*CPrR* 5:125)

If we aimed only for a lesser degree of happiness or of virtue, or for a lesser degree of their coordination, we might need to adopt only lesser postulates or hopes. However, the maximal aim would make little sense unless one hoped to have eternity to achieve it and a deity to make it possible. These strong and specific claims about what we must hope which Kant defends in the *Critique of Practical Reason* are plausible if, but only if, we find good reasons for the assumption that we must take it that a *complete* coordination of happiness and virtue in each of us is our destiny.

Yet might we not make sense of our dual commitment to knowledge of a causally ordered world and to action, including moral action, within that world on the basis of lesser assumptions? Why should action not posit or hope for the possibility of moral progress, but make no assumptions about the possibility of achieving natural and moral perfection, or the full coordination of happiness and virtue? Might it be enough to postulate that we can insert the moral intention into the world as and how we can, rather than with total efficacy? If so, might we not construe the task of moral progress as a this-worldly, shared and historical, perhaps incompletable task, rather than as one that demands an eternal after-life?

In some of his political and historical writings Kant takes a this-worldly view of reasoned hope, in which neither God nor immortality is taken to be an indispensable corollary of our commitment to his views of our dual commitment to the natural and the moral orders. In place of the religious interpretation of the Postulates of Pure Practical Reason of *Critique of Practical Reason*, he articulates the hopes we must have as hopes for an earthly future, for the possibility of progress in which nature and morality are coordinated not in another life but on this earth. If moral action is seen as an historical goal, reasoned hope may fasten not on God and immortality, but on history and progress.[14]

There are many passages in which Kant articulates a this-worldly counterpart to the Postulates of Pure Practical Reason. Here one instance may serve for many: in *Theory and Practice* he wrote:

> I may thus be permitted to assume that, since the human race is constantly progressing in cultural matters (in keeping with its natural purpose), it is also engaged in progressive improvement in relation to the moral end of its existence... I do not need to prove this assumption... I base my argument upon my inborn duty of influencing posterity in such a way that it will make constant progress... History may well give rise to endless doubts about my hopes... however uncertain I may be and may remain as to whether we can hope for anything better for mankind, this uncertainty cannot detract from the maxim I have adopted, or from the necessity of assuming for practical purposes that human progress is possible. (*TP* 8:309)

Many moves in this passage mirror those by which Kant argued in the *Critique of Practical Reason* to God and immortality: we are committed to moral aims whose feasibility we cannot prove theoretically; to make sense of this we need to postulate, assume or hope for a human future that allows room for human intervention in the world and so for progress (not in this case necessarily for progress to perfection); these hopes for the future of mankind cannot be renounced if we are committed to morality. Here and elsewhere Kant pictures human destiny in this-worldly terms.

Only if any answer to the question 'What may I hope?' must include hope for God and immortality will Kant's answer to his third question vindicate traditional theistic religious claims; even if reasoned hope were to vindicate some rather abstract religious claims, it might not vindicate all the familiar Christian tenets that would restore Lampe's happiness. Heine's comments on Kant's strategy for consoling Lampe can be read as doubts whether the supposed constraints that reason places on what we *may* hope are sufficient to show that we *must* have any sort of religious hope. Even if the abstract claims of deism and the tenets of traditional Christian faith propose answers to the question 'What may I hope?', Kant's arguments may not show that either forms part of *every* answer to the narrower question 'What must I hope?'

Could Kant have supplied an argument for the unique status of hopes for God and immortality, so showing that we not merely may but must

---

[14] Cf. Yirmiahu Yovel's discussion of the Postulates of Pure Practical Reason and the Regulative Ideal of History in his *Kant and the Philosophy of History* (Princeton University Press, 1980), 72, and the chapters in Part III above.

hold such hopes? Does he establish his claim that it is 'morally necessary to assume the existence of God', so proving that any answer to the question 'What *may* I hope?' must incorporate a theistic claim? If he does not, will he have shown only that we must make *some* assumption about the grounds of the possibility of coordination between the natural and moral orders, without offering reasons to think that we must hope for God and immortality, let alone for the specifics of Christian faith? Would he have left it open that our hopes need not have a specifically religious form, and even that they might be more coherent if they do *not* take a religious form?

What are we to make of this apparent shift in Kant's views? Was he constantly revising his account of human hopes and destiny, searching for the most convincing answer? Or does he take it that there are no reasons to think that our hopes must take a unique form? Does he think that we may hope either for God and immortality or for historical progress? Or is there evidence that either religious hope or historical hope is his final view of human destiny, and that he rejects other views? Or does he merely vacillate between alternative answers to his third question?

Hope and reason

The broad sense in which hopes for the future in which action and morality are possible may be reasoned is that they render Kant's theoretical and practical philosophies consistent. The theoretical and practical uses of reason lead us to positions which seem to be far apart – separated indeed by a great gulf. Hopes for a future in which action, including moral action, in the world is possible may provide at least a slender bridge across that great gulf. The bridge is slender in that nothing shows us whether or how the natural world and the moral order come to be coordinated. Kant does not provide any basis for boasting that we *know* that there is a God and a future life, or even that we *know* that history will allow for progress. His account of what we must hope is, after all, only an account of the required core of hope which we must 'postulate' or adopt to achieve consistency.

It may be only this required core of hope that we are given grounds to think of as *reasoned hope* (a successor to *docta spes*). This core of hope is cognitively simple and indeterminate. It is merely formal, or *negative*, unlike more determinate hopes for God and immortality or for specific modes of historical progress. It is *nonderivative* in the sense that it does not invoke or presuppose the authority of any particular metaphysical system or religious revelation, or of any church, or state, or other power. Moreover it is *lawlike* in the sense that these minimal hopes are hopes that everyone who is committed to knowledge and action has reason to share.

However, much of Kant's writing on hope goes beyond this picture and invokes more specific religious or historical hopes. But can these accounts of more specific hopes be understood as answering his broader question 'What may I hope?' In the next chapter I shall consider the views of hope that can be found in *Religion within the Limits of Reason Alone* and consider whether Kant succeeds in showing that these more resonant and less abstract hopes lie 'within the limits of reason'.

CHAPTER 14

Kant on reason and religion II:
reason and interpretation[1,2]

Kant pursued his inquiry into the links between reason and religion into his final years. His last major complete work is his extraordinary and in many ways disconcerting *Religion within the Limits of Reason Alone*. At first encounter there seems to be a great distance between this convoluted work, with its numerous discussions of Scripture and of Christian dogma, of ancient authors and of anthropology, of comparative religion and of church governance, its speculations on etymology and on ethical associations, and the abstract arguments that lie behind the Postulates of Practical Reason of the *Critique of Practical Reason*.

The publication of *Religion within the Limits of Reason Alone* got Kant into wearisome troubles with the anxious Prussian censors. At first consideration this is a surprising response to a work that seems more respectful of established faith than his numerous earlier writings on religion, which had brought him no trouble.[3] Christian concerns and Christian Scriptures are in evidence throughout the book. It consists of four long linked essays, the first published in 1792 and the others in 1793. Each takes up an ancient and resonant thematisation of good and evil. The first discusses the *common root* of good and evil in human freedom; the second the *conflict* between good and evil; the third the *victory* of good over evil; and the last the life

---

[1] 'Kant on reason and religion II: reason and interpretation', *The Tanner Lectures on Human Values*, Vol. XVIII, ed. Grethe B. Peterson (Salt Lake City: University of Utah Press, 1997), 267–308.

[2] The Cambridge translations of Kant's work had not appeared at the time this and the preceding chapter were published. References to Kant's writing are given parenthetically using the abbreviated titles listed in the Bibliographical Note, but referring to the older translations and editions in Part 2 of that note. When quoting from a translation that does not include the Prussian Academy page numbers I have added them *in front of* the pagination of the cited translation.

[3] The explanation is usually said to lie in the more conservative regime in Berlin, where Frederick William II had appointed as minister of justice J.C. Wöllner. He introduced a more restrictive censorship Edict in 1788, which permitted religious freedom provided that dissidents kept unorthodox opinions to themselves. Yet it is surely relevant that Kant confronted the censors with an entirely new and unsettling tone and approach in his late writing about religion. In the event, publication was permitted, but Kant was required to publish nothing further on religion.

lived in *service* of the good. This sequence follows a traditional Christian articulation of human origins and destiny: *original sin, temptation, conversion* and *ministry* are moments of the encounter of the pilgrim soul with good and evil. This Christian tenor is sustained by numerous discussions of Christian scripture.

Yet Kant's underlying line of thought appears to question rather than to endorse much of Christian faith and tradition. His task, he asserts, is that of the *philosophical theologian*, who approaches religion *within the limits of reason*. This task, he insists, is quite different from that of the *biblical theologian*, who defends ecclesiastical faith by appealing to church authority to guide his reading of Scripture, and whose defence of faith does not appeal to reason.[4] The discussions of Christian Scripture in *Religion within the Limits of Reason Alone*, however, are to be reasoned. Indeed, in the preface to the second edition Kant asserts that 'reason can be found not only to be compatible with Scripture but also at one with it' (*R* 6:13; 11). How can religion within the limits of reason conceivably be 'at one with' the Scripture of a particular religious tradition?

Much here will depend on one's understanding of Kant's conception of reason. I shall try here to show how the minimalist account of reason that Kant presents in the *Doctrine of Method* of the *Critique of Pure Reason* can be used to unravel his interpretations to Christian Scripture, and to make sense of his claim to approach religion 'within the limits of reason' alone by way of interpretation of the sacred texts of one tradition.

Relation to *Critique of Practical Reason*

Unsurprisingly, there is much continuity between Kant's earlier and his later writing on religion. Like the *Second Critique, Religion within the Limits of Reason Alone* argues to religious claims from moral claims. The book begins with the claim that 'morality thus leads ineluctably to religion' (*R* Preface, 6:6; 5) and ends with the thought that 'the right course is not to go from grace to virtue but rather to progress from virtue to pardoning grace' (*R* 6:202; 190). Morality once again appears as the parent rather than as the child of religion; charity once again does not build on but precedes

---

[4] The distinctions between philosophical and biblical theology are a major theme also of Kant's *Conflict of the Faculties*, published a year later. There (as also in *What Is Enlightenment?*) Kant cites obedience to the state as the ultimate reason why biblical theologians may not appeal to reason: 'the biblical theologian . . . draws his teaching not from reason but from the Bible . . . As soon as one of these faculties presumes to mix with its teachings something it treats as derived from reason, it offends against the authority of the government that issues orders through it' (*CF* 7:23).

faith. Once again we are presented with a reversal of tradition which old Lampe might not have found consoling.

Moreover, like the *Critique of Practical Reason*, *Religion within the Limits of Reason Alone* treats the question 'What may I hope?' as central. Here too Kant insists that hope forms the bridge that renders our dual commitment to knowledge and to moral action coherent. Our moral ambitions, indeed our moral intentions and our very plans of action, cannot be fully grounded in knowledge: we lack not only the relevant knowledge that the world is open to the possibility of moral or other intervention, but even the self-knowledge that would assure us that we are committed to moral action:

> Man cannot attain naturally to assurance concerning such a [moral] revolution... for the deeps of the heart (the subjective first grounds of his maxims) are inscrutable to him. Yet he must be able to *hope* through his *own* efforts to reach the road which leads thither... because he ought to become a good man. (*R* 6:51; 46)

Yet at many points *Religion within the Limits of Reason Alone* is less definite than the *Critique of Practical Reason* about the form that hope, even hopes for the highest good, must take. Often the text does not make it clear whether the hope that makes sense of our aspirations to morality is this-worldly, or other-worldly; sometimes it is not obvious whether the hope is religious or historical. Near the end of the work Kant claims that

> reason... says that whoever, with a disposition genuinely devoted to duty, does as much as lies in his power to satisfy his obligation... may hope that what is not in his power will be supplied by the supreme Wisdom *in some way or other*. (*R* 6:171; 159; cf. *R* 6:139; 130)

The same very abstract structure of hope is the appropriate corollary to intentions to seek the highest good:

> The idea of the highest good, inseparably bound up with the purely moral disposition, cannot be realized by man himself... yet he discovers within himself the duty to work for this end. Hence he finds himself impelled to believe in the cooperation or management of a moral Ruler of the world, by means of which this goal can be reached. And now there opens up before him the abyss of a mystery regarding what God may do... whether indeed *anything* in general, and if so, *what* in particular should be ascribed to God. (*R* 6:139; 130)

Whether we not merely *may* hope but have good reasons, indeed *ought*, to hope that supreme Wisdom will act in this life or the next, in history or in the hereafter, or in both, whether indeed anything in particular should be ascribed to God is often left quite obscure.

Scripture as a symbol of morality

There are also many ways in which the discussion of religion in *Religion within the Limits of Reason Alone* differs from and is far more specific than that in the *Critique of Practical Reason*. The most obvious puzzle is to understand how anything we would call *philosophical theology* can appeal to Scripture – or for that matter can be advanced by commenting on Roman and tribal religion, on superstition and clericalism. What part can discussion of the Fall of Man, or the Virgin Birth or the Second Coming have in an account of religion within the limits of reason? Surely a work on the religion of reason should invoke particular tales and traditions only as examples of lack of reason.

In the preface to the first edition Kant remarks (rather unhelpfully) that it would be a good idea to have a

> special course of lectures on the purely *philosophical* theory of religion (which avails itself of everything including the Bible), with such a book as this, perhaps, as the text (or any other if a better can be found). (*R* 6:10; 10)[5]

He is quite right that the text avails itself, if not quite of everything, still of too much; but this seemingly will make it harder rather than easier for us to read it as an account of religion within the limits of reason.

The reasons that Kant offers for thinking that his discussion of Scripture is appropriate to his task lie scattered in comments on narrative and interpretation at various stages of the book. The initial discussion of interpretation is interspersed with comments on the Adamic myths in Book I. Here Kant suggests that Scripture may be understood as a group of narratives which offer a temporal *model* or *symbol* of a rational (hence atemporal) structure. For example, his reading of the story of Adam's sin and of the expulsion from Eden sees it as symbolizing the subordination of moral principles to natural inclinations.

> Holy Scripture (the Christian portion) sets forth this intelligible moral relationship in the form of a narrative, in which two principles in man, as opposed to one another as heaven is to hell, are represented as persons outside him; who not only pit their strength against each other but also seek (the one as man's accuser and the other as his advocate) to establish their claims *legally* as before a supreme judge. (*R* 6:78; 73)[6]

---

[5] The censors reacted rather promptly to this thought, if in the wrong way. In 1795, a year after the second preface was published, they issued an order to the academic senate at Königsberg expressly forbidding *any* professor to lecture on *Religion within the Limits of Reason Alone*.

[6] The restriction of this claim to the Christian portion of Scripture is immediately disregarded; later in the book it is clear that a restriction to the Bible is also to be set aside.

The drama of temptation and salvation may be read as symbolising a conflict between the moral principle and the principle of subordinating morality to desire. Although, Kant writes, the 'natural inclinations, *considered in themselves*, are *good*' (*R* 6:58; 51; cf. *R* 6:33; 31),[7] the subordination of morality to inclination would be freely chosen evil. This is appropriately symbolised in the story of the Fall, where an originally innocent being comes to moral awareness, is reminded by a good spirit of the demands of morality, is tempted by a spirit who personifies the principle of evil, freely chooses to subordinate morality to desire, and yet leaves open the possibility of a return to the good (*R* 6:42; 37).

Since the details of the Adamic myths can be read as symbols of the interrelationship between freedom, knowledge and morality in our lives, we can understand the story as told of ourselves, but symbolically. Kant quotes a line from Horace, who admonishes us not to scoff even at ludicrous tales about the gods, reminding us that *mutato nomine de te fabula narratur* (*R* 6:42; 37).[8] A story does not have to literally true, or even (as Kant suggests by quoting a pagan author) taken from the Bible, in order to be read in the interests of morality. The myth of the Fall can be *rehabilitated* rather than *repudiated* if it is read as a narrative that symbolically represents our understanding of evil as freely chosen and yet rejectable:

> For man, therefore, who despite a corrupted heart possesses a good will, there remains hope of a return to the good from which he has strayed. (*R* 6:44; 39)

Nobody will be surprised that the Adamic myths *can* be read in this way, or more generally that Scripture *can* be given an interpretation that makes it an appropriate symbol of Kant's views of the relation between knowledge and morality, and so of hope; but it is surprising that Kant makes this move. Why should *Religion within the Limits of Reason Alone* discuss Scripture at all? In making sympathetic use of the myths and symbols of biblical traditions Kant is very distant from the spirit of reasoned religion as generally understood. Deism, for example, aspired to a quite limited salvage job on the most abstract propositions of Christian faith – and was content to jettison the rest, and to deride bits of it as superstition. Kant can be as scathing as any deist in his denunciation of popular superstition, which he

---

[7] This point is notoriously missed in reading Kant's ethics. Yet it is an unavoidable corollary both of his view that happiness, which is the satisfaction of natural inclinations, is a component of the *summum bonum* and of his theory of action, which demands that maxims be freely adopted.

[8] 'Under another name the tale is told of you.' Horace, *Satires* in *Q. Horati Flacci Opera*, ed. E.C. Wickham, rev. H.W. Garrod, Oxford Classical Texts (Oxford University Press, 1984), Book I, i, line 69, p. 135.

castigates as religious illusion (*R* 6:168ff.; 156ff.), and of clericalism, which he denounces as fetishism 'which borders very closely on paganism' (*R* 6:180; 168): yet he does not denounce or renounce Scripture. Rather he regards it as important to show that Scripture can or may be read in a certain way.

In the interests of morality

The second element of Kant's account of the role of interpretation of Scripture within religion within the limit of reason is summarised by the thought that sacred tests not merely *can* be read as symbols of morality, but that they *ought* to be read in this way: 'this narrative must at all times be taught and expounded in the interest of morality' (*R* 6: 132; 123).

It would be easy to think that what Kant means is simply that we ought to seek a morally edifying meaning in the stories of Scripture, that it is a matter, as we say, of bringing out the moral of the story. This is a common enough view of how Scripture can or even of how it ought to be interpreted 'in the interests of morality', which has provided the basis for countless sermons and homilies. However, it will not serve Kant's purposes, since the idea of 'bringing out the moral' presupposes that a text of Scripture has an intrinsic, if sometimes obscure, moral meaning (which other secular or pagan texts may lack) and that this meaning is to be brought out.

Kant, however, does not attribute either special standing or moral wisdom to Christian Scripture. The Bible is a book that has 'fallen into men's hands' (*R* 6:107; 98); traditional faith may be no more than something which 'chance . . . has tossed into our hands' (*R* 6:110; 100). There is no reason to suppose that such contingent cultural documents and traditions are morally admirable or even sound. Nevertheless Kant insists not only that we can, but that we ought to read them 'in the interests of morality'. Doing so is not a matter of looking for their true meaning. The relevant interpretation may, in the light of the text

> appear forced – it may often really be forced; and yet if the text can possibly support it, it must be preferred to a literal interpretation which either contains nothing at all [helpful] to morality or else actually works counter to moral incentives. (*R* 6:110; 101)

This conception of proper interpretation can get going on the sacred texts of any tradition. Christian texts are neither unique nor indispensable. This can be illustrated by the fact that the philosophers of classical antiquity managed to interpret the crudest of polytheistic stories in ways that approximate a moral doctrine intelligible to all (*R* 6:111; 101), and by equivalent moves in Judaism, Islam and Hinduism (*R* 6:111; 102).

The issue behind these interpretive moves is highlighted by posing the question:

> whether morality should be expounded according to the Bible or whether the Bible should not rather be expounded according to morality. (*R* 6:110n.; 101n.)

Kant's firm answer is that morality rather than Scripture comes first:

> since...the moral improvement of men constitutes the real end of all religion of reason, it will comprise the highest principle of all Scriptural exegesis. (*R* 6:112; 102)[9]

Reasoned interpretation and authority

These moves show why Kant speaks of his work as defending *moral religion*, but do not make it entirely clear why he should speak of himself as defending *religion within the limits of reason*. It is, of course, true that Kant sees morality as based on practical reason, but it does not follow that all interpretation of Scripture 'in the interest of morality' must itself lie within the limits of reason. Even if morality is based on reason, the readings of texts which support or express moral principles might, as Kant notes, be forced rather than reasoned.

However, interpretations that are forced by the standards of literal or fundamentalist interpretation may conform to Kant's minimalist account of reason. Kant depicts reason as a way of disciplining thinking and acting, which is *negative*, in that it lacks all specific content, *nonderivative*, in that it does not invoke authorities other than reason, and *lawlike*, in that it uses principles that all can adopt. If there are reasoned ways of interpreting, they will have to meet these three standards, and in doing so will also meet the criteria that are combined in the Categorical Imperative, so will constitute guidelines for moral as well as for reasoned interpretation.

The first two standards are readily apparent in Kant's account of the sorts of interpretation which would be appropriate for the philosophical theologian. The philosophical theologian lacks any substantive standards of interpretation, and may not invoke any authority other than that of

---

[9] In *The Conflict of the Faculties* Kant again identifies reason as 'the highest interpreter of Scripture' (*CF* 7:41).

reason to guide interpretation. Scriptural exegesis 'within the limits of reason' may not appeal to revelation, state or ecclesiastical authority, or historical scholarship, let alone authorial intentions (cf. *R* 6:44n.; 39n.; cf. 6:110ff.; 101ff.), on which traditions of biblical theology may build.[10] Equally, scriptural exegesis within the limits of reason does not appeal to the no less suspect 'authority' of individual religious experience, conscience or feeling – a mode of interpretation that Kant thinks leads to enthusiasm or fanaticism (*R* 6:113–14; 104–5; cf. *WOT* 8:145–6).

However, none of this explains why religion within the limits of reason should refer to Scripture, except for polemical purposes, let alone why it should seek interpretations that rehabilitate rather than repudiate. Does not the activity of interpreting particular texts suggest some covert, if very indeterminate, assumption that they have some authority? If so, should not their interpretation be firmly excluded from religion within the limits of reason?

Reasoned interpretation and popular religion

Kant's central comments on interpretation deal mainly with issues of authority and do not show why religion within the limits of reason should engage with Scripture. At most they show that *if* (for some still obscure reason) reasoned religion did interpret Scripture, it would do so without assuming substantive starting points and in particular without taking any other authority for granted. However, the third aspect of Kant's account of reason – that it is lawlike – can, I believe, explain why Kant thinks that an engagement with accepted traditions and texts is an indispensable part of reasoned religion.

Kant puts his reason for thinking that the philosophical theologian needs to engage with Scripture as follows:

> the authority of Scripture . . . as . . . *at present* the only instrument *in the most enlightened portion of the world* for the union of all men into one church, constitutes the ecclesiastical faith, which, as the popular faith, cannot be neglected, because no doctrine based on reason alone seems to the people qualified to serve as an unchangeable norm. (*R* 6:112; 103, my italics)

---

[10] Kant acknowledges that as things are the *philosophical theologians*, who interpret Scripture by reference to the principles of morality and hence of reason, are far outnumbered by *scriptural scholars* or *biblical theologians*, who are usually expositors of one or another historically specific ecclesiastical faith, and who rely on the presumed authority of tenets of a particular church or tradition to guide their *doctrinal* interpretation.

These reasons for interpreting Christian Scripture refer to a time and a place: they are reasons for eighteenth-century Europe. Somehow, at some juncture, the philosophical theologian has to reason in ways that engage with actual religious conceptions as they are held and cherished by the people. Otherwise an 'appeal to pure reason as the expositor' could have nothing to say to the many millions who held to the time-honoured religion which sustained old Lampe and countless others, or to adherents of the other religions.

Kant not only accepts but insists that reasoning must reach its audience, so accepts:

> It is also possible that the union of men into one religion cannot feasibly be brought about or made abiding without a holy book and an ecclesiastical faith based upon it. (*R* 6:132; 123)

Reasoned religion must be lawlike, not just in the sense that it can be followed by any rational being, but also in taking account of the fact that rational beings, as things are, are adherents of particular religious traditions. So reasoned religion too must engage with the sacred texts and traditions of popular religion; it must start on familiar ground and show how the familiar sayings of Scripture can be interpreted without appeal to groundless authorities: otherwise it will be accessible only to a few philosophical theologians.

It follows that the philosophical theologian *must* interpret whichever sacred texts are actually widely understood and respected. Without this move, religious teaching cannot fully meet the requirements of reason. Surprising as it may seem, religion within the limits of reason not merely *may* but *must* interpret accepted texts, and their ordinary reception. Only this focus and strategy of interpretation can secure a conception of religion that is guided by principles which are negative (formal), underivative, and also lawlike, so support religion within the limits of reason.

Lawlikeness is, however, a slender constraint. Kant is not appealing to any conception of *lawfulness*, which would invoke some further, separate authority to guide the interpretation of Scripture. That is the unreasoned strategy of biblical theologians, whose problem is that the separate authority to which they appeal stands in need of but does not receive justification. So it is to be expected that the interpretations which the philosophical theologian reaches, although they lie 'within the limits of reason', may not be unique or even highly determinate reasoned interpretations. Reason will not fully fix the reading of Scripture, any more than it fully fixes the content of permissible hope.

Reasoned interpretation and polymorphous hope

This account of Kant's conception of reasoned interpretation is corroborated by the fact that he repeatedly states simply that we *may* or that we *can* read a passage of Scripture in a certain way, rather than that we *must* do so. For example, in speaking of the incarnation he writes:

> just because we are not the authors of this idea [of moral perfection], and because it has established itself in man without our comprehending how human nature could have been capable of receiving it, it is more appropriate to say [*kann* man hier besser sagen] that this archetype has *come down* to us from heaven and has assumed our humanity . . . Such union with us *may* therefore be regarded [*kann* . . . angesehen werden] as a state of *humiliation* of the Son of God. (*R* 6:61; 54–5) [My italicisation of modal terms]

In speaking of the temptation of Christ he writes:

> So it is not surprising [literally: it *may not* be taken amiss: 'es *darf* also *nicht* befremden'] that an Apostle represents this *invisible* enemy, who is known only through his operations upon us and who destroys basic principles, as being outside us and, indeed, as an evil *spirit*. (*R* 6:59; 52) [my italicisation of modal terms]

And in speaking of the end of the world he writes:

> The appearance of the Antichrist, the millennium, and the news of the proximity of the end of the world – all these *can* take on, before reason, their right [*gute*] symbolic meaning. (*R* 6:136; 126) [my italicisation of modal terms]

The reasons why Kant takes this tentative approach should now be clear. He himself puts it this way:

> Nor can we charge such interpretations with dishonesty, provided we are not disposed to assert that the meaning which we ascribe to the symbols of the popular faith, even to the holy books, is exactly as intended by them, but rather allow this question to be left undecided and merely admit the possibility that their authors may be so understood. (*R* 6:111; 102)

When Kant speaks of his approach to religion as lying *within the limits of reason* he does not mean that he identifies a unique set to reasoned beliefs or hopes, but only that he identifies a range of beliefs, or hopes whose structure places them within the limits of reason. The sense in which reason 'can be found to be not only . . . compatible with Scripture but also at one with it' (*R* 6:13; 11) is therefore weaker than it may initially have seemed: reasoned faith and hope are polymorphous.

Hope without doctrine

If Kant's minimalist account of reason and of reasoned interpretation allows for a plurality of interpretations of the Scriptures on which popular faith rests, it is not surprising that he thinks that his account of faith and of hope will be undogmatic and undoctrinal, even when it engages with the texts and tenets of received religion. Reasoned religion is, after all, to answer the third question that interests human reason, the question of human destiny, which asks not 'What must I hope?' but more openly 'What may I hope?' In asking this question Kant leaves open not only various ways in which identifiably religious hopes for human destiny may be articulated, but also the possibility that hopes for human destiny be articulated in social, political and historical, this-worldly terms rather than in other-worldly terms.

The pure religious faith for which philosophical theology is to provide reasons lies *within the limits* of reason, but it is not the only articulation of hope that lies within those limits. Every articulation of hope and belief that lies within the limit of reason must incorporate the *canon* of reasoned faith, that is to say, an answer to the question 'What *must* we hope?' Each ecclesiastical faith also proposes one *organon* of religious faith, that is to say, a specific answer to the question 'What may I hope?' Another ecclesiastical faith might use quite another vocabulary to support a different specific account of what we may or perhaps must hope.[11]

In *Religion within the Limits of Reason Alone*, as one might expect, the accent is on religious articulations of the hopes we may have. And yet even here, in a work that constantly comments on Christian Scripture and that refers repeatedly to Christian and more broadly to religious articulations of hope, the traditional, other-worldly formulations of Christian hope are constantly put in question.

The first and evidently the most basic way in which Christian hope is put into question is by the shift of religious concern from the first to the third question of human reason, from a question about knowledge to a question about hope. Although Kant views the language of Scripture as an appropriate articulation of the hopes we may have, nothing that he claims restores a realist interpretation of God or immortality. Hope is not backed by knowledge. Human destiny remains a matter not of knowledge but of hope.

---

[11] See Friedo Ricken, 'Kanon und Organon im Streit der Fakultäten' in François Marty and Friedo Ricken (eds.), *Kant über Religion* (Stuttgart: Kohlhammer Verlag, 1992), 181–94.

The second way in which Christian hope, as traditionally understood, is put into question in *Religion within the Limits of Reason Alone* is by the fact that the essential core of Kant's answer to the question 'What may I hope?' establishes so little about what I must hope. All that Kant argues is that we must postulate, assume, hope for the possibility that our moral commitments are not futile: we must hope for the possibility of inserting the moral intention into the world. This bare structure of hope can be expressed in a range of vocabularies whose permissible articulations of hope will be accessible to different people, who may hope for varying conceptions of grace or of progress that might bridge the gap between moral intention and empirical outcomes.[12] Religious articulations of hope are not to be rejected, but other forms of hope are also permissible. We may hope for grace, for progress, or for both, and for each in many forms.

Ecclesiastical faith and the ethical commonwealth

Behind these varied hopes lies a common commitment to action, which does not vary. Both in his accounts of religious and in his accounts of historical hope, Kant depicts the action to which we are committed as social as well as individual, and as this-worldly.[13] In *Religion within the Limits of Reason Alone* he puts it in the following terms at the beginning of his account of the victory of good over evil:

> As far as we can see, therefore, the sovereignty of the good principle is attainable, so far as men can work towards it, only through the establishment and spread of a society in accordance with, and for the sake of, the laws of virtue, a society whose task and duty it is to rationally impress these laws in all their scope upon the entire human race. For only thus can we hope for a victory of the good over the evil principle. (*R* 6:94ff.; 86 and ff.)

---

[12] Consider Kant's central claims about service to God at the beginning of Book 4 of the *Religion*. He starts from the thought that 'religion is the recognition of all duties as divine commands', which on the surface appears to require that God exists. But in the note to the text he immediately rebuts this reading by claiming that 'no assertorial knowledge is required (even of God's existence)' and that 'the *minimum* of knowledge (it is possible that there may be a God) must suffice' (*R* 6:154 inc. note; 142 inc. note).

[13] Kant does not think that we have any special duties to God (*R* 154n.; 142n.). However, viewing our duties *as divine commands* takes us beyond individual duty. One important passage is the following: 'Now here we have a duty which is *sui generis*, not of men toward men, but of the human race towards itself. For the species of rational beings is objectively, in the idea of reason, destined for a social goal, namely, the promotion of the highest as a social good . . . the highest moral good cannot be achieved merely by the exertions of a single individual towards his own moral perfection, but requires rather a union of such individuals into a whole towards the same goal – into a system of well-disposed men' (*R* 6:97; 89).

The fully achieved version of such a society would be what Kant terms an *ethical commonwealth* ('ethisches gemein Wesen'). An ethical commonwealth is a 'union of men under merely moral [as opposed to juridical] laws'; it can exist in the midst of a political commonwealth; it may even include all the members of a political commonwealth (*R* 6:94–5; 86). However, in human hands this ethical ideal 'dwindles markedly' (*R* 6:100; 91), although it can be approximated, more or less well, by the visible church (*R* 6:100ff.; 91ff.).

Both in *Religion within the Limits of Reason Alone* and in *Conflict of the Faculties* Kant depicts the visible church as a *vehicle*, which will finally be superseded as a purer, more fully reasoned faith supplants ecclesiastical faith:

> in the end all religion will gradually be freed from all empirical determining grounds and from all statutes which rest on history and which through the agency of ecclesiastical faith provisionally unite all men for the requirements of the good; and thus at last the pure religion of reason will rule over all, 'so that God may be all in all' . . . The leading-string of holy tradition with its appendages of statutes and observances, which in its time did good service, becomes bit by bit dispensable, yea, finally when man enters upon his adolescence, it becomes a fetter. (*R* 6:121; 112)[14]

If all of the outward and visible elements of church life and liturgy could be shed, we would be left with the abstract demands of purely moral religion. What we are left with is not however a mere hope, for whose realisation we must wait, whether patiently or impatiently. We are left with the moral commitment that underlies hope. This commitment sets a task from which we may not sit back leaving it either to Providence or to others:

> man [must] proceed as though everything depended on him; only on this condition dare he hope that higher wisdom will grant the completion of his well-intentioned endeavours. (*R* 6:101; 92)[15]

The context of action may but need not be framed by the life of a church. Kant's account of reasoned religion allows at least a *transitional* role to ecclesiastical faith and to the visible church, but it is not clear whether it allows more. Can the empirical realities and institutional structures of a church (or of another social but secular 'vehicle') be wholly superseded? If

[14] Compare this account to the secular, political and historical account of the maturing of reason which Kant offers in *What Is Enlightenment?*, where he describes the gradual emergence of human beings from immaturity to rationality, from a private, other-directed use of their incomplete capacities to reason to a fully 'public', autonomous use of capacities to reason.

[15] See also 'The only thing that matters in religion is *deeds* (*Alles kommt in der Religion aufs Tun an*)' (*CF* 7:41–2).

so, what is to bind the members of the ethical commonwealth together? If there are shared duties 'of the human race', will their enactment not require shared public practices and institutions? If so will not our hopes, including our shared hopes, have to be connected to shared activities and institutional structures, whether religious or this-worldly? Even if we hope for God and immortality, it does not follow that a time will come at which joint action in this life can dispense with all specific institutions and practices: the religious may always need to take the structures of a visible church seriously on this earth.[16] Indeed

> by reason of a peculiar weakness in human nature, pure faith can never be relied on as much as it deserves, that is a church cannot be established on it alone. (*R* 6:103; 94)

Equally, if the future for which we may hope is conceived of solely in this-worldly terms, it seems clear that we still could not dispense with all social structures in building towards an ethical commonwealth. The history of would-be purely intentional communities is discouraging, despite the fact that they have in fact built on many shared social structures. It seems that the only point at which joint action without shared structures might be possible is in the afterlife – of which we know nothing.

So a third way in which at least some forms of Christian hope are put into question is by the fact that, in the end, in this world, religious and social and political hopes must be closely connected. All types of hope are expressed in action, indeed in collective action, that aims towards an ethical commonwealth; all are a matter of taking it that the moral intention can be expressed in the world. However, different genres of hope answer the question 'What may I hope?' using different vocabularies and images, which can be woven into differing this-worldly practices and institutions. The religion of reason, on Kant's account, shows us that many religious and historical articulations of hope are permissible, that some articulations are congruent and compatible with others, but does not show that one type of hope is required to the exclusion of all others.

---

[16] Kant himself seems to hesitate on the dispensability of institutional structures in this life. In some passages both in *Religion within the Limits of Reason Alone* and in *The Conflict of the Faculties* he relegates all institutional forms to the status of a *vehicle* by which a transition from ecclesiastical faith to pure religious faith, shorn of observances and liturgy, of tradition and history, can be achieved. At other times he suggests that the vehicle is indispensable, at least in this life. See Hans Michael Baumgartner, 'Das "Ethische gemeine Wesen" und die Kirche in Kant's "Religionsschrift"' in Marty and Ricken (eds.), *Kant über Religion*, 156–67, and Allen Wood, 'Rational theology, moral faith, and religion' in Paul Guyer (ed.), *The Cambridge Companion to Kant* (Cambridge University Press, 1992), 394–416, for thoughtful discussion of this problem.

The censors of Prussia are long dead, but they were, I think, right to be worried. Although the surface of *Religion within the Limits of Reason Alone* presents a view of reasoned religion that seemingly takes Christian faith and Scriptures seriously, Kant's philosophical theology does not endorse religion in any straightforward way. Slightly below the surface of the work is a view of reason and of reasoned interpretation which assigns no unique status to religious hopes, to Christian hope, to Christian Scriptures, to the Christian church, or to all that old Lampe held sacred. The only moves Kant makes towards the specificities of the faith that Lampe knew and loved are that he gives general reasons for taking existing popular religion seriously in reading texts and existing ecclesiastical faith seriously in moving towards an ethical commonwealth. The outcome allows that traditional faith and hopes *may* be retained, but Kant's own hope is that both popular and ecclesiastical faith will be interim measures, and serve as vehicles to a purer faith and more abstract hopes that need no institutions and lack all specificity. The guardians of established religion could hardly be expected to endorse – even if they did not need to censor – a vision of religion that demotes the particular inflection of faith and hope that was in their care to the status of one among many permissible variants.

Index

action
  Kant's account of, 2, 39, 40, 109–10, 122, 124,
    132, 209, 210, 238. *See also* autonomy;
    heteronomy; maxims; practical reason;
    principles
actual consent. *See* consent
algorithms, 14, 28, 36, 50
authority
  'alien', 27, 30–2, 33, 34, 112. *See also*
    heteronomy
  arguments from, 1, 60, 105
  ecclesiastical, 4, 55, 59, 61, 241. *See also*
    theologians, biblical
  normative force of, 65
  political, 4, 59, 60, 151, 213
autonomy, 2, 5, 6, 31–2, 51, 53, 63, 67, 103, 150,
    187, 199
  conceptions of, 125–9, 187, 223
  ethics and, 42, 43, 54, 55
  form of law and, 121–36
  heteronomy and. *See* heteronomy
  individual, 6, 54–5, 65, 104–6, 111–13, 136
  Kantian, 6, 54, 55, 66, 103–20, 130, 132, 138.
    See also Categorical Imperative
  public reason and, 64–7, 137–50
  rational, 106–9, 112, 113, 115, 120, 126–9, 130
  self-legislation and, 113–14, 121–36
  universal laws and, 53–5

Babel, tower of, 3, 22–3, 25, 29, 33, 64
biblical theologians. *See* theologians
boundaries, 6, 58, 91, 95, 99, 100, 140, 144, 175,
    205, 207. *See also* states
Brandt, Reinhardt, 171

Categorical Imperative, 19, 21, 28, 42–54,
    73–85, 119, 132, 138, 148, 169, 180–5,
    223, 240
  equivalence of formulae, 52, 53
  Formula of Autonomy, 51, 53, 137
  Formula of the End in Itself, 51–4, 77

Formula of the Kingdom of Ends, 51
Formula of the Law of Nature, 51
Formula of Universal Law, 42–50, 51–4, 77,
    81, 84, 133, 182
supreme principle of ethics, 126
supreme principle of practical reason, 21, 29,
    34, 36, 163, 164
universal principle of justice, 182
Chomsky, Noam, 90
citizens, 25, 26, 56, 58, 62, 73–6, 81, 96, 139–45,
    176, 179, 180, 208
  fellow, 47, 71, 208, 209
  legal equality of, 179
  Rawls and, 175
coercion, 25, 44, 48, 82, 183, 184, 208, 209
  authorised, 200–3
  reciprocal, 203–4
commitment. *See* hope
commonwealth. *See* ethical commonwealth
communitarianism, 26, 30, 57, 59, 61, 71, 75, 81
Conflict of the Faculties, The, 32, 60, 61, 129, 138,
    189, 195, 198, 199, 213, 235, 240, 246, 247
consent, 170–85
  actual, 170, 172–7, 184
  hypothetical, 172–8
constructivism, 24, 69, 100
  construction of ethics, 69–71, 72, 83
  construction of reason, 4, 24, 26, 75–83, 84.
    See also public reason
  contemporary, 6
  contracts and, 86–7
  Kantian, 3–5, 69–85
  Rawlsian, 69–85
Copernican turn, 15, 16, 35
cosmopolitanism, 199–213
  hope and. *See* hope
  justice, 200, 202, 206–9
Critique of Judgement, 29, 32
Critique of Practical Reason, 43, 78, 109, 123, 132,
    138, 218, 225–6, 229, 230, 231, 234, 236,
    237

249

PAIN - subjective - never believes
SELF - dx
_____

2 choices
    ① Did not know about the pain
    ② Knew about it, but did not
        explore its source - what was
        causing it
          - Δal dx

Choice to move to Oregon
    had a job waiting
    taken trips there

Trʸd someone who was still having pain
(inexplicable XC that pain all the time
since ____) ⇒ in the records?? in deposit
but not recorded in medical records
Hx (pain) (Surgery given b/c of pain)
no redness, no swelling, no ____ [the site
of the differential dx ??] for this
invented Stal dx -- where in the records
does it say infection was suspected & R/O.
K pain ⇒ surgery to relief — did XC
last visit - pain 16 ⇒ now tfr
_____

↑ Not info (hx/pain) w/ which, n on ____/w
treating pt (trtmnt — what trtmnt
    Jr (other) (diagnosis — what did you do
    relτsp)   Δal dx

all b/c she says she had pain all
the time

societies or to a cosmopolitan political future. Section 8 is, I think, best read as offering a practical argument for making a commitment to work for human progress. If we look at human and political progress as practical aims rather than as theoretical claims, we presuppose human freedom, but we do not need to assume that all purposes are realised at some time.

This reading is confirmed by the fact that Kant assumes not that progress is the only option for human history, but only that it is *one* option. In section 8 he also suggests that philosophy could take a 'chiliastic' or 'millennial' view, i.e. a view of history as progressing. He asks why we should not adopt a stance of despair about the future of mankind, or assume that it will be a meaningless sequence of ups and downs, and why we should have hope for the future of mankind.

Both in sections 8 and 9 of *Idea for a Universal History from a Cosmopolitan Point of View* and in other works, Kant emphasises the *practical* reasons for adopting the 'chiliastic hypothesis' rather than either of the alternatives that are compatible with the surface evidence of history. His underlying thought is that by adopting this Idea of Reason we contribute to its realisation. The sentence in which he makes his claim taken in its entirety reads:

> Philosophy too could take a millennial view, but only one to whose realisation the Idea [of progress] can contribute, if indirectly. (*IUH* 8:27, trans. OO'N)[15]

Adopting this Idea of Reason – in effect, the *Idea for a Universal History with a Cosmopolitan Aim* – is a *practical* matter. By adopting it, by making it a guiding principle of our lives, we can contribute to the realisation of that better future for mankind. In a second passage expressing this thought Kant argues that 'it belongs to human nature not to be indifferent' given that 'it seems that we could, through our own rational contrivance, bring about faster such a joyful point in time for our posterity' (*IUH* 8:27). These passages suggest that the basis for acting 'under the Idea of Progress' need not presuppose that all purposes will be realised at some time.

Kant developed this practical argument for adopting the Idea of human progress, with its cosmopolitan corollaries, at greater length in some of his later works. In the second part of *The Conflict of the Faculties* he addresses and answers the crucial question:

---

[15] The German reads 'die Philosphie könne auch ihren Chiliasmus haben; aber einen solchen, zu dessen Herbeiführung ihre Idee, obgleich nur von weitem, selbst beförderlich werden kann'.

> How is it possible to have history *a priori*? The answer is: it is possible
> when the one who foretells events shapes and *creates* them. (*CF* 4:80; trans.
> OO'N)[16]

History of the future, of the destiny rather than the past of mankind, is
possible if it is taken as a practical rather than as a theoretical task, as a
matter of adopting a specific commitment or attitude to the future, and
so of working towards that future, rather than of looking for proof or
evidence for a specific prediction. We cannot know the full laws of human
history, but we can make an active commitment to a specific future, thereby
making it more likely.

An even fuller statement of this practical approach to human progress
is given in the concluding section of Kant's 1793 work *Theory and Practice*,
in the course of an explicit criticism of Moses Mendelssohn's view that
the human race neither progresses nor declines.[17] While Kant's argument
against Mendelssohn may be slender in this passage – he has after all dealt
with it in earlier passages of *Idea for a Universal History* – his statement of
the practical reasons for assuming human progress is forthright:

> I shall therefore be allowed to assume that, since the human race is constantly
> advancing with respect to culture (as its natural end) it is also to be conceived
> as progressing toward what is better with respect to the moral end of its
> existence, and that this will indeed be *interrupted* from time to time but
> will never be *broken off*. I do not need to prove this presupposition; it is
> up to its adversary to prove [his] case. For I rest my case on my innate
> duty, the duty of every member of the series of generations – to which
> I (as a human being in general) belong and am yet not so good in the
> moral character required of me as I ought to be and hence could be – so to
> influence posterity that it becomes always better (the possibility of this must,
> accordingly, also be assumed), and to do it in such a way that this duty may
> be legitimately handed down from one member [in the series of] generations
> to another. It does not matter how many doubts may be raised against my
> hopes from history, which, if they were proved, could move me to desist
> from a task so apparently futile; as long as these doubts cannot be made
> quite certain I cannot exchange the duty . . . for the rule of prudence not
> to attempt the impracticable . . . as it is merely hypothetical . . . and however
> uncertain I may always be and remain as to whether something better is to
> be hoped for the human race, this cannot infringe upon the maxim . . . that
> it is practicable. (*TP* 8:308–9)

---

[16] The separately published second part, titled 'The Conflict of the philosophical faculty with the
faculty of law', reads: 'Wie ist aber eine Geschichte a priori möglich?' 'Antwort: wenn der Wahrsager
die Begebenheiten selber macht und veranstaltet, die er zum voraus verkündigt.'

[17] Mendelssohn, *Jerusalem, or, on Religious Power and Judaism*.

Although these considerations are compatible with an argument that commitment to the Idea of natural teleology entails commitment to the Idea of a Universal Cosmopolitan History, the argument for them is distinct. Seen in the wider context of Kant's later writings on religion, politics and history we can recognize this practical argument as developing Kant's doctrine of reasoned hope as the link between the claims of knowledge on the one hand and of freedom and morality on the other. In *Idea for a Universal History with a Cosmopolitan Aim* this practical view of our reasons for commitment to this Idea is set out in the final section, whose proposition reads:

Ninth Proposition
A philosophical attempt to work out universal world history according to a plan of nature that aims at the perfect civil union of the human species, must be regarded as possible and even as furthering the aim of nature.[18] (*IUH* 8:29)

Far from it being 'strange and apparently absurd' (*befremdlich und ungereimt*) (*IUH* 8:29) to view history according to an Idea of how things must develop, this Idea is of the greatest practical importance.

Evidence, intimations and signs

Many of the other matters Kant touches on in the final sections of *Idea for a Universal History* refine his reasons for thinking that we cannot *establish* human progress by looking for evidence or proof. History of the past – 'history proper' – is possible, but merely 'empirical composition' (*IUH* 8:30), and 'philosophical history' – an account of human destiny – cannot be extrapolated from the empirical evidence of historical trends. Kant's practical arguments for commitment to natural teleology, to human progress and its cosmopolitan context, are based on arguments from human freedom and duty, and while they are – indeed, must be – compatible with what we know about the historical record, they have to go beyond that evidence. They assume only that there is no evidence that progress is impossible.

And yet, startlingly, Kant occasionally suggests that *some* evidence is after all available, that we can find specific *intimations* or *signs* of progress. In section 8 of *Idea for a Universal History* he suggests that there is, after all, *a little* evidence of progress:

---

[18] The German reads 'Ein philosphischer Versuch, die allgemeine Weltgeschichte nach einem Plane der Natur, der auf die vollkommene bürgerliche Vereinigung in der Menschengattung abziele, zu bearbeiten, muß also möglich, und selbst diese Naturabsicht beförderlich angesehen werden.'

> It all depends on whether experience reveals something of such a course as
> nature's aim. I say: it reveals *a little*.[19] (*IUH* 8:27)

What are we to make of this seeming shift in Kant's claims? Why did
he claim that empirical evidence is beside the point when we look at
the long course of human history, but also that there is at least *a little*
empirical evidence of progress? Is this claim on a par with other passages
in which Kant asserts points that he cannot establish at a given juncture
in his argument?[20] Or are we to think that these 'signs' are neither proof
nor evidence, but merely intended to encourage hope for a cosmopolitan
future, and thereby action that may bring it closer?

   Nearly fifteen years later, in *Conflict of the Faculties* Kant pointed to
the public response of disinterested sympathy to the French Revolution
as yet another 'historical sign' of an enlightened age. This 'attitude of the
onlookers' ('Denkungsart der Zuschauer', in other translations 'mode of
thinking of the spectator'), he claims

> Demonstrates a character of the human race at large . . . a character . . . which
> not only permits people to hope for progress toward the better, but is already
> itself progress. (*CF* 7:85)

We can at least be clear that Kant's practical argument for the Idea for a
Universal History did not *require* him to find definitive signs of progress.
He argues for taking a stance towards human history and politics that can
be maintained in the face of the evidence of hard times and evil deeds,
provided only that there is no proof of the impossibility of progress. If we
'disinterested spectators' find signs and portents of better things to come,
this may be at least encouraging. And if we find none, it is not decisive.
And if we find only confusing 'signs', this will not show that human destiny
must be one of darkness and failure. Our commitment to a better future
for mankind is anchored in human freedom rather than in knowledge of
that future.

---

[19] The German reads: 'Es kommt nun darauf an, ob die Erfahrung etwas von einem solchen Gange
der Naturabsicht entdecke. Ich sage: etwas weniges.'

[20] At some points where Kant cannot prove a claim, or cannot prove it at a specific stage of his
argument, he introduces it with phrases such as 'ich sage' or 'ich behaupte'. See, for example, *G*
4:428 and 4:448. Would this have been appropriate in discussing 'signs' of better times to come?